It's A Great Life If You Don't Weaken!

IT'S A GREAT LIFE IF YOU DON'T WEAKEN!

How to Deal with the Ups and Downs in Life and the *Jerks* in Between

BRIAN HAMPTON

NEW YORK

LONDON • NASHVILLE • MELBOURNE • VANCOUVER

It's A Great Life If You Don't Weaken!

How to Deal with the Ups and Downs in Life and the JERKS In Between

Published in New York, New York, by Morgan James Publishing. Morgan James is a trademark of Morgan James, LLC. www.MorganJamesPublishing.com

Proudly distributed by Publishers Group West®

Morgan James BOGO™

A **FREE** ebook edition is available for you or a friend with the purchase of this print book.

CLEARLY SIGN YOUR NAME ABOVE

Instructions to claim your free ebook edition:
1. Visit MorganJamesBOGO.com
2. Sign your name CLEARLY in the space above
3. Complete the form and submit a photo of this entire page
4. You or your friend can download the ebook to your preferred device

ISBN 9781636983202 paperback
ISBN 9781636983219 ebook
Library of Congress Control Number: 2023945516

Cover & Interior Design by:
Christopher Kirk
www.GFSstudio.com

Morgan James is a proud partner of Habitat for Humanity Peninsula and Greater Williamsburg. Partners in building since 2006.

Get involved today! Visit: www.morgan-james-publishing.com/giving-back

To My Everything
My Wife, a Shining Star
My Forever Bride

CONTENTS

INTRODUCTION 1

PART 1
HOW TO HANDLE "WELLWISHERS" AND TORMENTORS

CHAPTER 1: THE HOW-TO HANDBOOK FOR HUMANS 5
    They Are Everywhere: How To Deal With The Jerks! 6
    Kick Me For Being A Louse 6
    How Some People Have To Be Told 7
    "Making Money, Having Fun" 7
    Doctors, Lawyers, And Dreaded Dentists 8
    Chapters For Every Chapter Of Your Life 9
    Do You Want A Better Job? 10
    How To Come Across As Brilliant 10
    Walk Me Like A Dog? 11
CHAPTER 2: "HOW ARE YOU?" THEY ASK, AND YOU SAY? 13
    Larry King: Just As Friendly As We All Remember .13
    Do They Really Want To Know? 14
    Feel Sorry For You Or Me? 14
    Feeling Fine? 14
    My Hemorrhoids Are Acting Up 15
    Top Notch, And You? 15
    Better Than Ever. 16
    Saying More Than Fine, Thank You 17
CHAPTER 3: "PULL IT BACK!" HOW SOME PEOPLE HAVE TO BE TOLD 19
    Leave The Ball In Their Court 19
    Get Them Off Your Back 20
    So, You Say You Are Offended! 20
    Elizabeth Warren Fumes 21
    This Time, Mike Bloomberg Fumes 21

Never Complain. Never Explain 22
You Don't Appreciate It?! 22
Quick Comeback Counter 22
Credit Robert De Niro 23
A Whole Career Was In The Balance 24
Remember These Words: Communicate And Cooperate. 25
He Was Getting Chewed Up At Work 25
He Tried To Be Modest, But It Cost Him His Job. 26
Don't Assume They Know You're Brilliant. 26
You Have To Do It 27
Don't Learn The Hard Way Like Me. 27
Office Politics: Swim With The Sharks 28
Our Policy: Always The Customer Service Fallback. 28
More Rejoinders For Your Hip Pocket 28
I'll Be Off The Line Now 29
CHAPTER 4: PUSH BACK! HOW TO SAVE YOURSELF FROM LAWYERS 31
Attack! Attack! Attack! 31
Scare The Wits Out Of You 32
Never Tell Your Lawyer This. 32
Like Propping Up A Jellyfish 32
Double Trouble: Insurance Lawyers 33
Forty Dollars To Leave A Ten-Second Message 34
Scare The Wits Out Of Your Lawyer. 34
Remember: Attack! Attack! Attack!. 35
They Did What To Us? 36
Magic Words To Your Lawyer. 36
Fire Your Lawyer: Quick And Easy 37
Make Your Lawyer Accountable To You 37
You Can Scare The Wits Out Of Them. 37

PART 2

HOW TO DEAL WITH DOCTORS, DENTISTS, DRIVERS, DOG WALKERS, AND DOING EXERCISE

CHAPTER 5: YOUR DOCTOR ADVISES, BUT YOU ARE IN CHARGE
OF YOUR HEALTH 41
Bad Diagnosis. Bad Doctors 41

Be Sure To Have Your Questions Ready 42

Beware Of The Medical Vortex 42

Get A Double Reading 43

Prostate Cancer: Do Your Own Research 43

Are You Worried? 44

My Doctor Put On His Doctor's Hat And Scared The Wits Out Of Me 44

I Say Again: Beware Of The Medical Vortex 45

We Are The Deciders, Not The Doctors 46

"She Will Never Make It Out Of This Hospital Alive" .46

Talking To Doctors 47

Do The Biopsy Again? 47

No Doctor Told Me About This Possibility 48

Ever Have Stomach Pains? 48

"That Milk Is Killing You" 49

Hospital Discharge Confusion 49

Mr. Happy Is All Purple! 49

More Pain And Aggravation 50

Your "Confidential" Medical Records 50

Back Pain From Demon Rum? 51

I Gave The Doctor The Needle 51

Pain Killer In Place Of Real Care 52

What To Do About Knee Pain 53

There Will Be Side Effects: Find Out In Advance 54

I'll Be Pooping In My Pants? 54

Simple, Short Exercise For Back Pain 55

The Good Doctor Asked About Me?! 55

No Known Cause Or Cure? 56

It Could Be My Brain! 57

I Hypnotized The Problem Away 58

Finally: A Diagnosis! 58

CHAPTER 6: OUCH! ENDURING DR. PAIN, THE DENTIST **59**

The Colonel's Only Fear: The Dentist 59

The Dreaded Dental Appointment 60

Are You Seeing Dr. Pain? 60

But The "Numbing" Part Hurts The Most! 61

Show Me The Money, Not The Needle! 61

Teeth Extraction: Being Forewarned Is Being Forearmed 62

Dreaded Dental Decision: Help To Pick The Right One.....................64

What's The Deal With "Sedation Dentistry?" 65

Why Our Overall Dental Health Is A Big Deal.........................66

Difference Between Toothbrush And Teethbrush 66

Biggest House Gives Out The Most Candy.........................67

CHAPTER 7: YOUR DOG LOVES YOU! THE VET LOVES YOUR MONEY............ 69

A Child Or A Dog Or Both? 70

I Know Who You Are: Come And Get Your Poop....................71

Present For A Secret Agent 71

How To Keep Your Vet Bill Low................................72

The Licensing Board Is Their Hot Button........................72

Protect Your Dog From Identity Theft 72

CHAPTER 8: Watch Out! Protect Yourself From Crazed Drivers...............75

The Dreaded Tailgater..75

Hot Coffee In The Crotch 76

Just A Wave Or The Evil Eye?.................................76

One "Line" You Do *Not* Want To Cross!.........................77

Put Your Hands On The Wheel 78

Back Off: I'm A Postal Worker 78

Dealing With Backseat Drivers 78

CHAPTER 9: EXERCISE: HOW TO GET THE MOST OUT OF THE LEAST............ 81

Getting The Sense Of Control And Empowerment....................81

"Hell Week" Now Banned 82

Do What Your Body Tells You To Do.........................82

Lowest Whale Dung At Bottom Of The Ocean 83

Let Your Body Take Over From Your Mind 83

No Need To Figure Out Perplexing Directions....................84

Pop, Pop, Pop Without The Chiropractor! 85

Weekly Goals Are The Best Yardstick 85

Presidents Take Time And So Can We! 86

Beware Of The Shark Tanks 86

Sometimes, There Are Jerks In The Pool 87

Does Swimming In The Vertical Position Work?....................87

Scout Around For Free Pools 88

Primordial Walk: "Cruel And Unusual Punishment"................88

Dancing For Fun And Fitness.................................89

Yoga: Some Like It Hot! 89

Improvising: Those Stairwells Were Made For Walking. .90
Mancave Cross Training 90
They Are Running Their Mouths, But You Are Getting Fit 91

PART 3
HOW TO POWER UP YOUR CAREER

CHAPTER 10: TIME TO GET ORGANIZED, BUT WHO HAS THE TIME? 95
Be Your Own Boss And You Won't Get Fired!. 95
The Insidious Weekly Goals 96
"No Real Happy Hour On Friday. You Are Fired." 97
Axman Recommends A Bonus!. 97
Clear Of Your Desk Before You Leave. 98
Keep Your Office A Mess And People Out?. 98
Take Time To Get Organized And You Are Gaining Time 99
You Now Know You Are Doing Exactly What You Should 100
One Page For One Week: A More Fulfilling Life. 100
CHAPTER 11: HOW TO INTERVIEW AND GET THE JOB .103
The Biggest Interview Mistake 103
It's Talking Too Much! 103
Keep The Answers Short. 104
Say What You Are, Never What You Aren't. 104
Decide How You Want To Come Across. 105
The Incredible Power Of Body Language 105
We Manipulated The Psychology Prof. 106
How To Be At Ease At The Start Of An Interview. 106
You Go First On The Money And You Lose 107
Be Ready For The Questions With Your Answers 107
CHAPTER 12: KEY TO WEALTH: YOUR OWN MASTERMIND GROUP 109
Knowing The What Is Good. Knowing The How Is Better 109
Seven Traits Of Successful People Revisited. 110
Classic Negotiation Dodge. 110
Now It's Time For Your Mastermind Group 111
People Are Happier On Friday!. 111
Number Of People That Make The Most Efficient Group? 112
Business Is The Heart Of The Mastermind 113
"Are You Talking About Me With Your Masterminds?". 113

CHAPTER 13: PUBLIC SPEAKING: PATH TO POWER AND INFLUENCE **115**

Can You Own The Room? 115

Your Mindset 116

Mental Preparation For Every Speech And Talk 116

Detailed Preparation. 117

Bad Form For Notes = Bad Speech 117

Consider Everything In The Walk-Through 118

The "Best" Speaker Froze—Me! 118

You Won't Get Lucky. You Have To Practice 119

Warning On Jokes: A No-Lose Way 119

Showtime 119

Secret Technique For Getting Relaxed. 120

Hecklers And Sharpshooters 120

Working The Crowd. 120

Close It Out 120

Introducing Presidential Surrogates. 121

CHAPTER 14: BE A POWER PLAYER WITH WORDS **123**

Three Got To Be President And Never Sent An Email. 123

Two Big Words And They Thought I Was A Genius!. 124

I Misspelled My Name During An IQ Test! 125

Only A Handful Of Words Needed For A "Big" Vocabulary. 125

The Dynamic Dozen: Top Words For Your Personal Power 126

CHAPTER 15: WHEN AND HOW TO REINVENT YOURSELF **129**

How Many Times Have You Moved? 129

Are You Ready To Employ The Ratchet? 130

Think. When Did You Last Invent Yourself? 130

Decide What You Are Willing To Settle For 131

There Is A Far Better Way To Make A Living! .132

Get In The Door And Get Liked! 132

Be Sure To Get This Clause In Your Contract 133

PART 4

HOW TO "SCHEME" THE SYSTEMS

CHAPTER 16: THERE IS ALWAYS A SYSTEM: MAKE IT WORK FOR YOU **137**

There Are "Systems" Everywhere. 137

How To Make The System Work For You 138

Imagine Giving A Speech In Prison 138
They Were "Getting Some" In Prison!.................................139
Organizations May Be Different: Techniques Are The Same 139
Is A Ruffian On Your Case? 140
What's The Game Where You Work? 141
Do You Know And Work Your Office Politics? 142
Why Hit Yourself On The Head With A Hammer?.......................143
How Not To Show Up And Stand Out! 143
You Can Hate It And Still Be Good 144
Pick Your Openings Or Be A Wiseacre Like Me 145
Magic Pull With The Federal Government 145
Eliminate Unnecessary Paperwork 146
Know The System And Pull Off Amazing Things 146
Learn Your System First. Work Your System Next.....................148
Front Door A No-Go? Go Back Door 148

CHAPTER 17: MAKE THE GOVERNMENT WORK FOR YOU **151**
Your Member Of Congress Works For You............................151
Getting Your Member Of Congress In Your Corner 152
Most People Have No Clue How This Works Best 152
Not Time-Consuming, And Very Effective 153
Take Bold Action And The Force Be With You.........................154
Your Federal Government At Work...................................154
"We Have A Problem Here" 155
I Resigned In Protest 155
Outrageous Truth To Power 156
You Can Employ The Awesome Power Of Public Opinion 157
Annoying Government In Your Neighborhood? 157
How Is Your County Organized? 158
A Way To Fight City Hall...158
After All, It Is "We The People" 159

CHAPTER 18: WANT TO TAKE OVER? HOW TO WIN AN ELECTION. **161**
They Don't Know What They Don't Know.............................161
I Rode The Campaign Train With Jack Kennedy 162
They Picked Me Up And Put Me On The Moving Train! 163
MLK And JFK...163
You Need A Simple, Compelling Message.............................164
You May Not Win With Money, But Without It, You Lose 164

The Cynics Don't Count: Those In The Arena Do. 165

CHAPTER 19: BEING THE HOUSE MANAGER: DO IT OR GET OUT OF IT!. 167

Don't Get Ripped Off On Appliance Repairs 167

A Slug On The Phone Means A Slug Company 168

Asking Questions Helps You In Four Ways. 168

Almost Jailed First Time As House Manager. 169

The House Manager Takes The Lead! 170

First Rule: Don't Do It!. 170

Plumbing: The Scourge Of The Hose Manager. 171

Accept The Responsibility But Not The Blame 171

Splish Splash, Don't Take A Financial Bath. 172

Oh No, More Plumbers 172

Adjusted Shower Head And Saved $2,000 173

One Hundred Dollars To Take A Breath. 173

Make A Record Of The Plumbing Process 174

Mother Of All Plumbing Disasters, Flooded Home:

                Manage The Chaos And Confusion .174

Disaster Strikes: What To Do First? 175

Delicate Dance Between Insurance And Restoration Companies. 175

Critical: Documenting All Phases Of The Process. 176

"Magic" Technique For Putting Repairs Into Overdrive 177

Plumbing Fiasco: "Raindrops" Falling On My Head. 178

Junkyard Dog Lawyer To Run TV Spots On Your Company! 178

It's A Warning And A Promise. Don't Get Mad. Get Even! 179

The Art Of The Tip 180

Cure For Sloppy Roommates 180

Sorry, They Have Come For Your Mattress. 181

PART 5

HOW TO DEAL WITH THE UPS & DOWNS AND GET HAPPY!

CHAPTER 20: LIVING WITH AND OVERCOMING DEPRESSION. 185

Your Three Billion Brain Cells 185

Fired, Divorced, Homeless, And In Prison 186

How Can We Even Keep Up With The Losers?. 187

Who's The Man Behind The Bushy Beard? 187

CHAPTER 21: TIME TO GET HAPPY!. 189

First, Let's Try To Reduce The Worry 189
The Perception Becomes The Reality. 189
Start Getting Happy Right Now! 190
Put Worry In Compartments And Put Them Away. .190
Think The Ball Into The Basket! 191
Proper Sleep Helps Build Our Resilience 191
Three Keys To Happiness 192

CHAPTER 22: HOW TO FIND THE TIME TO MAKE REAL FRIENDS 193
How Many Real Friends Do You Have? 193
It Takes Time To Make Real Friends. 194
Super Bowl "Friends" 194
A Skunk At The Top Of The Town 195
Beware Of False Flattery. 195
Your Friends And Family 196

CHAPTER 23: LOVE AND MARRIAGE ON AN OCEAN CRUISE 197
Finding Love In The Buffett Line 197
More Buffett Means Bigger Belly Flops. 198
Parrot In The Bedroom Says What?! 198
Secret Of A Happy Marriage Is What? 199
The Best Day Of His Marriage Was 199
Listen Up, Son-In-Law! 200

CHAPTER 24: GETTING HAPPY WITH YOUR FAVORITE FOODS 201
Eat Your Favorite Foods More Often And Get Happier! 201
Will You Irritate The Chef If You Ask For Medium-Well? 202
Eating Without The Calories And Falling Asleep 202
What, Me? A Wiseacre!. 203

CHAPTER 25: IS IT HAPPY HOUR YET? 205
She Drove Me To Drink And Thank You! 205
Knee Walking After Pub Crawling 206
They Don't Call Them The Blue Devils For Nothing. 206
What Never Fails? A Dry Martini! 207
The Great Man Had Brandy For Breakfast 207
The Best Place To Go On A "Bender". 208
Breakfast Of Champions 208

CHAPTER 26: THE LAW OF THE UNIVERSE 209
You're Not Late Until You Get There 209
Don't Compliment Your Car When You Are In The Car! 210

CHAPTER 27: WHAT IS THE MEANING OF LIFE? **211**

How Big Is The Universe? 211

Don't Count The Days. Make The Days Count 212

We Decided The Meaning Of Life And Then Sent Emails. 212

No Clue On The Meaning Of Life? Okay, Where Is The Soap? 213

She Was Short And Simple: Be Happy. Do Good! .214

We Can Bring Peace In Unexpected Circumstances .214

Wait! That's On Aisle Seven 215

ACKNOWLEDGMENTS **217**

ABOUT THE AUTHOR **219**

Introduction

The author of this book offers the reader a myriad of techniques for how to deal with life's distressing predicaments and challenging people, as well as advice for career management, personal development, and all the day to day things in between. The techniques and advice offered by the author are based on his own life experiences and do not necessarily reflect the views or opinions of the publisher or editor. The techniques and advice are offered on an "as is" basis without guarantee by author or publisher as to results or outcomes. The contents of the book are not intended to substitute the competent professional assistance of a medical, legal, or trade professional when appropriate.

PART 1

How to Handle "Wellwishers" and Tormentors

PART I

Chapter 1

How-To Handbook For Humans

Like an old elevator, life has lots of ups and downs and jerks in between.

When those old elevators jerked a bit on the way up or down, that was okay. But it's the human jerks who we all come into contact with too often who make life especially challenging.

The ever-popular self-help books are long on *what* to do about ourselves but strikingly silent on *how* to deal with all those distressing predicaments and people we encounter far too often.

Everything about us starts on the inside. We know that. What we think is who we are. We have to know and believe in ourselves, our strengths, and our limitations. It's not what happens to us, but how we think about it. We have to be self-aware. No one can make us feel embarrassed without our permission.

We know all the good things we should do. We should meditate. We should say affirmations. We should make a gratitude list and update it. We should have our own manifesto. We should follow motivational gurus. We should not procrastinate. We should listen to inspiring music. We should do this, and we should do that. We just have to get it together in our own heads.

And after we get a grip on ourselves?

We can be happier, richer, smarter, healthier, and sexier. We know we have lots of work to do on ourselves. While we might work on ourselves, life goes on. In the meantime, some people want to get ahead at our expense. They get a kick out of pushing us back, so maybe they can feel better. Your own friends can hurt you and desert you.

Of course, we should be happy. Our regret about the past causes us only despair, and our worry about the future causes only fear. We know all that, too. But where is the time for all this self-improvement? What to do, and in what order? Let's say we start to get it together on the inside, but how about the outside? Other than ourselves, everything and everyone else is on the outside.

They Are Everywhere: How To Deal With The Jerks!

On the way up or down, and up and down, there are plenty of jerks in between. How do we deal with them? How do we protect our own psyches?

Many people have read a dozen or more self-improvement books. I have read dozens and dozens. I cannot remember reading one that was not helpful, stimulating, inspiring. Many I have read more than once.

Most of these books are uplifting and helpful. Many are quite entertaining with personal and funny anecdotes. Most of these great books are written to help us be better people, but what about other people? What exactly did I remember after reading the books? How do I engage all the challenges outside my own head, in the big and often bad world?

IT'S A GREAT LIFE! has been designed to be versatile and handy, so you, dear reader, can refer to any chapter that relates to your whims and wishes of the time. Each chapter is self- contained, and the book can be your "Handbook For The Good Life" for years to come.

Let's start with small but significant slights. How often has somebody said something to you that was annoying, and maybe you didn't say what you would have liked to say? Did you carry it around, replaying it in your mind, restating what you should have said? Pretty often, most likely. Have you ever thought about, for far too long, the slights others inflicted on you? Are other people carrying them around? Of course not. They left the ball in your court, so you could fret over it.

Kick Me For Being A Louse

Some books suggest how to deal with difficult people. We need to know how to play hardball in a hardball world. But have we seen many, or really any, effective techniques for dealing with the knuckleheads who surround us?

I remember reading advice in a book on protecting yourself from difficult people. The author advises to always find some truth in what the other person is saying. That whatever anyone says about you, there is probably some truth in it.

Say what? The writer suggests that if you are told you are a lousy person, you should admit to some of it. "Maybe, possibly, sometimes, I am a louse." Better yet, we could put a sign on our back that says, "Kick Me."

Let's face it, some people have to be told, and sometimes in no uncertain terms. You are not going to get difficult people to like you by being very pleasant.

I have had a longtime fascination with human nature and how people communicate with each other. In a simple but overlooked mental strategy, in a contentious exchange, you make it about them, not you. It's among dozens of tactics I will share in this book.

How Some People Have To Be Told

I have refined and internalized many words and phrases that I can recall whenever the situation demands it. I am talking about rude customer service people or everyday folks who try to put you on the defensive. I have devised phrases that have proven remarkably effective, some in a few words. See Chapter 3, "Pull It Back! How Some People Have To Be Told."

Do you work in an office? Every office has office politics, some minor, some major. As you become more successful, some people cannot help themselves. They become envious and jealous. Maybe they simply want to get ahead by degrading you, benefiting from your demise or by diminishing you. Chapter 3 has techniques for dealing with that as well.

Are you anxious over confrontations that you know really would help you out if you handled them well? But how to do it? When to do it? How can you use techniques not only to protect yourself, but also enhance your position in the workplace in a relationship or even with your circle of friends? This book will help you.

Smaller, often more interesting and more regular dilemmas can be about what to say to people we meet on a regular day. In the checkout line at the drugstore, at the supermarket or the bank, someone says the inevitable, "How are you?" Do they really want to know? Of course, you know they don't. Do you play the game or maybe just amuse yourself? Chapter 2 has some witty and engaging answers.

First, we know we don't want to say, "Terrible." They might feel sorry for us, but who wants a stranger to feel sorry for us? We would feel only sorrier for ourselves.

The game is, they say, "Hello, how are you?"

Maybe you say, "Fine, how are you?"

Then they say, "Fine," and the charade is over.

How about you say, "Gosh, I have lower back pain, a migraine, and my hemorrhoids are really acting up."

You might not want to say that or anything so blunt and candid. But if you say anything out of the ordinary when you respond to "How are you?" they might look up and say, "Are you talking to me? Did I say something?"

"Making Money, Having Fun"

You get the idea. We either play the game or don't. Maybe you want to wake up the person a bit or maybe pick yourself up a bit, so you say, "Better than ever." That wakes them up. Or if the person is a bit annoying, you say, "Making money, having fun." They probably would wish they were you. How nice!

The Gallup poll says that the vast majority of people list good health as the best measure of "success." Though you could consider other yardsticks for success, everyone wants to be healthy, of course. But how?

The American Heart Association says we need 150 minutes of heart-pumping exercise and two sessions of muscle-strengthening exercise each week. How do we do this in our busy lives, especially when we don't want to?

There are many cross-training exercises one can do without leaving home. How to do them? As an old Army Infantry Officer, I have designed exercises for myself that I do every week, mostly without leaving the house. I don't like to exercise, but with what I call the Pretzel technique, I actually enjoy it. I will tell you how to do it in Chapter 9, "Exercise, Getting The Most Out Of The Least."

We want to stay healthy, of course. Everyone gets sick now and then. Some get injured. Too many have aches and pains and are forced to see doctors.

Doctors, Lawyers, And Dreaded Dentists

Doctors and other medical care providers are the heroes of our time. But how do some doctors get through the incredible rigors of medical school? Memorization, of course. Some doctors seem to lack analytical skills, which means they are not so good at what we most need from them—a diagnosis. There is a reason they call it "the practice of medicine."

How can you talk to a doctor to ensure you get the right diagnosis? How can you really be sure the radiologist properly read the test you had at the hospital? I found one easy but obscure solution, which is to insist you get a "double reading. I share details on that and other issues in Chapter 5, "Your Doctor Advises, But You Are In Charge . . ."

Because of athletic injuries and other mishaps, I have had the misfortune of seeing more doctors than I could possibly count. I've had operations and endless bouts with physical therapy and chiropractors than turned out to be necessary.

I first developed back pain when I was the captain of a college tennis team, a very long time ago. My back pain has appeared and reappeared over the decades and resulted in literally hundreds of medical visits and treatments. I will share with you two simple exercises I learned to alleviate back pain.

How can you limit the pain when you go to the dentist? How can you more or less ensure you don't get an unnecessary root canal because your dentist needs a new BMW SUV? See Chapter 6, "OUCH! Enduring Dr. Pain, The Dentist."

A bit like the iconic Frank Sinatra song, "That's Life," I have been up and down and all around. I have moved from more jobs and places to live than anyone else I have known. I have reinvented myself so many times that I could have many registered patents. I will share with you how I did it and how you can, too.

I have also had the misfortune of more misadventures hiring lawyers. But I have learned how to deal with lawyers, how to persuade them or even coerce them to do their job, and how to fire them efficiently. What I learned from four decades of dealing with lawyers is in Chapter 4, "Push Back! How To Save Yourself From The Lawyers."

Here is a preview: What do you do if you want to fire your lawyer and still be on good terms? You simply say, you want to "settle up." It's like magic!

Like most people, I have learned the hard way. I have learned by accident and by endless experiences. What I have learned the very long and hard way, I can impart to you, dear reader, in a few minutes in each chapter.

Chapters For Every Chapter Of Your Life

I have written a kind of how-to handbook for humans. I have enjoyed writing this book about as much as anything I have done in my long, rocky, and rich life. I enjoyed it so much because it was not only cathartic for me, but also very energizing to believe that I have much to offer. By sharing my experiences with others I can help them make a positive difference in their lives.

You may go through the book in order, or you may cherry-pick through the chapters that are relevant to you now. Regardless, the book is designed to offer you specific techniques for "how to deal with the ups and downs and jerks in between." The book should have a long shelf-life for you. You can go back and refer to any chapter at your leisure.

Just in case you forgot about all the jerks out there who could make your life miserable, get in your car and drive around. Can you believe it? More drivers are honking when they don't need to. They cut you off and don't let you through the intersection when you are in a long line or trying to make a left turn.

What to do? How to act? Please see Chapter 8, "Watch Out! . . ." This chapter is your guide for how to deal with crazed drivers on the streets and highways.

Maybe you are interested in making a lot of money. A comic once said, "Whoever said money can't buy happiness didn't know where to shop." I don't know about you, but I have enough money to last me the rest of my life—unless I need to buy something.

What does almost everyone with great wealth have in common? In his iconic book, *Think and Grow Rich,* Napoleon Hill related that all the multimillionaires he interviewed over twenty years had set up their own mastermind groups.

But Mr. Hill stopped short of providing the mechanics of how the whole thing works. Whom should you invite to your group? Where and when do you meet? How often? Meeting agendas? I have led three different mastermind groups in three different cities—one of the most empowering things I have ever done. I share the details with you in Chapter 12, "Key To Wealth: Your Own Mastermind Group."

You need to get organized, right? But who has the time? Organization saves time. Working for a time-management firm, I learned how they got people organized. I have been perfecting their techniques for a very long time now. See Chapter 10.

Do You Want A Better Job?

Do you want to get a better job? Chances are you will interview for a job or several jobs in the future. What is the biggest deal breaker in a job interview, beyond being late or unprepared? In all the Pathways To Success seminars I led over the years, no one has ever guessed the biggest mistake. I will share with you what I learned from conducting hundreds of interviews and being interviewed dozens of times. See Chapter 11 for an ingenious body language technique.

The biggest fear men have is speaking before a group—more than jumping out of an airplane. For women, public speaking is about their fourth-greatest fear. I have taught college-level classes on public speaking, and given well over 200 speeches, including introducing about seventy members of Congress to audiences nationwide. I will reveal what I learned in a few short pages in Chapter 13, "Public Speaking: Path To Power And Influence."

Speaking of public office, do you want to help someone win an election, maybe even yourself? I have been part of more than fifty federal campaigns, a candidate for Congress, a political consultant, and a successful campaign manager. Most candidates don't know what they don't know, so they do not learn. See Chapter 18 on "Want To Take Over?" for much more to know than you might imagine.

How to Come Across as Brilliant

Our most important skill remains our verbal ability—not the fingers or the phone or even the internet but our ability to talk. Take a look at the Dynamic Dozen in Chapter 14, the only twelve words you will ever need to know to impress your friends and colleagues and confuse your foes.

There is more to life than just getting ahead and not letting others get the best of us. I have taken a long look and had many interactions with loved ones and friends and have reached some serious conclusions about how to be happy. I have discovered the keys to love and marriage on an ocean cruise (Chapter 23).

I have asked many people what they think is the meaning of life. The answers might surprise you. See Chapter 27, "What Is The Meaning Of Life?"

Taking time to make friends is one of the most important things we can all do. I share some techniques. Have you ever been depressed? Are you now? In my life, I made a study of how different people responded to successes and failures. I can share with you how many did it in Chapter 20, "Living With And Overcoming Depression."

Walk Me Like a Dog?

Do you have a dog or a cat? Far too many veterinarians deal in cash cows, as in a license to make money with charges that are often off the charts, unneeded, and unconscionable. Learn some ways for how to protect yourself from these unnecessary charges and for redress if you do get ripped off.

And just for fun at the end of that chapter, I added all the screwball things people say that take a dog in vain. Why do people tag dogs with such disdainful things—dog tired? Working like a dog? Accusing someone of dogging it? A junkyard dog lawyer? Such talk gives dogs a bad name.

And then, a TV actress said on her Twitter feed (now called X) to another actress that she will "Walk you like a dog." Wow! Now you have gone too far. See Chapter 7, "Your Dog Loves You! The Vet Loves Your Money."

It's a great life if we don't weaken, if we get happy and are prepared for how to deal with all the ups and downs in life and, of course, all the jerks in between.

Chapter 2

"How Are You?" They Ask, And You Say?

What do you say to the most common greeting of all, "How are you?" You can have real fun with all the options at hand.

This may sound goofy, but it really isn't. And for some goofy reason, I keep track of most of the possible answers.

I largely stopped asking people that question and have substituted other stuff that can serve to strike up a real rapport with people, to enliven their days and brighten their lives. But first, do people ask because they really want to know how you are doing?

In his book, *How to Talk to Anyone, Anytime, Anywhere*, the late Larry King related a story about how people are often poor listeners. He had a friend, Jim, who had the pet peeve of people asking how you are but then not listening to the answer.

Jim knew a repeat offender, and he decided to test just how poor a listener he was. King shares how the man called Jim one morning and began the conversation as he always did, "Jim, how are ya?"

Jim said, "I have lung cancer."

The guy said, "Wonderful. Say Jim . . ."

Larry King: Just As Friendly As We All Remember

Incidentally, I am happy to say I had an encounter with Larry King once for an engaging conversation. In the early 1990s, I was living in Rosslyn, Virginia, in the eastern tip of Arlington, just a couple-minute drive from any of three bridges crossing the Potomac for quick access to Washington, DC.

I was in the Rosslyn CVS, and I saw Larry buying a bunch of magazines. He was working for CNN at the time, and I happened to know he lived in the Prospect House, a high-rise overlooking the US Marines' Iwo Jima Memorial with the best view of Washington I believe there is. Ten years later, my wife and I staged our engagement party on the top floor at The Top Of The Town.

I was working on a novel at the time called *Saigon Warriors PSYOP in Saigon: They Fought for the Hearts and Minds*. I had printed out a publication with the first chapter, featuring a photo of about a dozen of us who were part of an army unit there.

I had the wild idea I could get on his show and get publicity for it. I approached him, said I wanted to show him something, and that I'd be right back. I ran to my River Place apartment and back. He was still there, and we had a very genial conversation. He could not have been more friendly.

Do They Really Want To Know?

I tried to cheer him up—at least make some human contact—and I said, "How's it going?"

In a sort of glum response, he said, "All right."

I knew this exchange was kind of a charade, so I decided to sort of break through it. I said, "You know people ask this question all the time, and they really don't want to know."

He brightened up just a little bit and said, "No, they don't want to know."

How many different ways do you answer the question? Do you tell it like it is, or not?

Feel Sorry For You Or Me?

I got into a discussion with a colleague once about why I should tell people how I am doing if I am not doing well. Why would I share that with a lot of people? She said because maybe they do want to know.

I said, "Most don't want to know, but let's say I am feeling terrible. Why would I want to say that?"

She said, "Well, maybe then they would be sympathetic and say, 'Oh, that's too bad.'"

"You are making my point," I said. "I don't want people to feel sorry for me."

Rarely in life is there ever a reason to say something negative about yourself. Avoid it. There are exceptions, like for close friends and loved ones, but maybe you have read some of these self- help books. You give some of your essence away, call it power, when you complain.

So, when people ask how you are, you may not want to respond, "Except for my personal life, health and finances, I'm doing fine."

Feeling Fine?

Since this is such a serious topic (just semi-kidding with you here), I got into a discussion with my wife about this very subject.

"When you get asked at work, what do you say?"

She says fine!

Then I said, "What if you're not fine. What do you say then?"

She says fine!

"But don't you agree that most people who ask that, really don't want to know?"

"Maybe they don't, but at least they ask," she said.

A happy wife is a happy life. No need to have the last word. But consider this: You are going through the checkout line in the supermarket. These are hardworking people. Do you ever see a place behind them where they can sit down? Everyone is always in a hurry—just not any easy job, to say the least.

Nevertheless, maybe it's the training. They greet you, you really don't get eye contact, but they say, "How are you?" Let's say you decide to tell the truth and say something longer than just a perfunctory, "Oh, gee, I don't know. I have done better, and I have done worse . . ." or along those lines.

They are good, hardworking people, but nevertheless, they will probably look up as if to say, "What? Are you talking to me? Did I say something?"

Or try this sometime. I have had the nerve to do many wild and crazy things, but say something like this one, just to see the reaction, "How ya doing?

My Hemorrhoids Are Acting Up

You: "Gee, my hemorrhoids are really acting up. I have a migraine headache and my back is killing me. How are you doing?"

If you try something along these lines, please send word to me, and I will arrange to get you a prize somehow.

So, how are you feeling about all this? Are you fine? Okay?

But now that we have it out of the way, here is my take on the meaning of it all.

Let's say your office mates are sincere, and they ask, "How are you?"

A good standard answer is, "Very well, and yourself?"

Occasionally, when you ask people how they are doing, they will say, "I'm above ground." When people say that to me, I say, "So is George Washington." After that, I add, in case they do not seem to know, that he is in a crypt. They usually chuckle—or not.

Now, how about those people that you are sure don't want to know? How about them?

Top Notch, And You?

You could say something different like, "Top notch!" Or you could say, "All right, so far." Now, there is probably an honest answer that observes "The Law Of The Universe" (see that chapter), but you never know.

I used that in the locker room of the swim club once, and a wiseacre said, "What? Are you expecting something bad to happen?" Doesn't happen often, but the ball is back in your court . . . not where you want it to be.

"Hanging in there" is an old standby that usually won't get much blowback, and maybe a "That's all you can do," which is good by the standard for these things.

Okay, now we get into the finer techniques. You see a grocery clerk. Maybe you have seen him before or maybe you know he is always grumpy. In these cases, I resort to the following.

Better Than Ever!

The grocery clerk says, "How are you?"

I say, "Better than ever!" Real happy, real chipper. I don't do this often. It seems dishonest and not called for. But occasionally, it pops out of my mouth.

One time, I tried it on a very surly young guy in the checkout line, who responded in a loud voice, "I find that hard to believe."

One has to be ready, and that day I was. I said, "If you don't want to know, don't ask. You need to go to a school for believing."

I needed to pick up some dog food for our dog, Jasper, one day. I pulled up to the pet store and saw a drug store right next door. Always trying to save time (what do we do with this extra time?), I had a prescription that needed filled, so I decided to drop off the prescription, get the dog food, and come back for the meds.

There were three women behind the pharmacy counter. I put the prescription in front of one and asked her how long it would take to fill it. She told me three days. I laughed. Then, she asked me for my birthday—if I could remember it. I laughed again. She then complimented me on my good sense of humor, saying that most people do not get it when she pulls those antics.

I bought the dog food, put it in the car, and went back for the medication. I asked if it was ready and told no. I said, "I have been waiting three days!" All three behind the counter laughed.

I got the prescription and then addressed the first woman I had seen. I told her she seemed like a lover of fun. I explained how I had made a study of answering the age-old question and suggested she might respond, "Better than ever" or "The best day of my life."

She responded that her niece had had a serious illness for over a decade and whenever she was asked how she was doing, she said, "Better than ever." Then the pharmacist said that just six months ago, her niece had been completely cured. We agreed that the better than ever response is a very inspired way to go.

Then I related the time when I told the grocer that I was better than ever, and he responded that he doubted that. All of us had another good laugh.

But here is one of my favorites to entertain myself or to tick someone off who I am pretty sure needs to be ticked off—the jerks we meet during the ups and downs of our lives.

"How are you doing?"

Me or you: "Making money, having fun!"

This line always gets attention. Actually, most people laugh and say that they are not doing both of those. Then maybe I confess the same and we have a little chuckle together.

How about you? How are you doing right now?

At least now you have some additional rejoinders in your arsenal and you can pull out whatever pops into your head.

Saying More than Fine, Thank You

Still, if after you have gone through the sort of pro forma, "Hi, how are you?" I have found some rewarding moments in life when I struck up a fleeting conversation at the drugstore or the grocery store while they are bagging it up. I try to say something pleasant that brightens people up because when we do that to other people, we know that brightens our life a bit too.

Maybe they have an original name on their nametag. I compliment them for having creative parents. Maybe they look like they are into sports. I ask, "Are you a Nationals fan?" The light goes on. Somebody actually wants to have a short, but real, conversation.

I find these sorts of fleeting moments really invigorating. They make life more worth living.

So, there you go, "Making money, having fun!"

Chapter 3

"Pull It Back!" How Some People Have To Be Told

You know there are unkind people out there, and plenty of them.

The more successful you are, the more people will be out to get you, at work, within your circle of friends, on social media, and even in the traditional media. They are everywhere—everywhere!

Many people cannot help but be jealous and envious of others because of what they perceive is the zero-sum game. There is only so much good out there, and if you are getting yours, they can't be getting theirs.

It's a jungle out there, and far and away, one of the most important things we can do is protect ourselves from the predators. Just because you are not paranoid doesn't mean they aren't trying to get you. There is always somebody coming at us from every direction, in ways big and small.

You know how you go through life, day by day, week by week, and so on, and there are things that just stick in your craw? Something that somebody said to you that you don't like and your comeback or no comeback is still annoying you in the back of your brain?

If so, you are like everybody else. Some are better at letting go than others. Some remember every slight that was ever sent their way. So, we know during the ups and downs in life, there are also plenty of jerks in between (an old elevator joke).

Leave The Ball In Their Court

Some people need to be told for their psychological good balance. We meet them, it seems, every day. The idea is to have more or less the last word, so they (rather than you) get to chew on it going forward. Like with tennis, the overall objective is to leave the ball in their court and get them off your back.

Years ago, for a summer, I drove carriages at Mackinac Island. What a summer! It's an island on the Straits of Mackinac, between upper and lower Michigan. No vehicles are allowed on the island, except for emergency vehicles. During an entire summer I drove tourists (called "fugees" because they all bought fudge from fudge shops) around the island in a two-horse-drawn carriage.

Talk about the time of my life. A couple times, a passenger said to me, "Driver, is this island completely surrounded by water?"

Me: "Yes, except at the bottom." I was having a great summer, except there is always *somebody*, isn't there?

I was young and gibe and full of myself. I gave a good verbal tour of the island as I rode around with the carriage that held about twelve people. A trail boss downtown with Carriage Tours really didn't like me—and probably the same for a handful of the other college student drivers who were mixed in with the larger number of older drivers who didn't give much of a verbal tour at all.

Get Them Off Your Back!

I would bring the carriage downtown to unload passengers and pick up new ones. This guy was always on my case. This went on for far too long. Finally, he was at it again between passengers, and I had tolerated enough and simply said, "Get off my back."

An amazing thing happened (to this nineteen-year-old college student), He never gave me a hard time again. I was treated with a sort of deference after that. Why had I waited so long to call this guy out?

I was just beginning to learn that some people have to be told, as well as learning when to tell them, how to tell them, and that the words are not as important as how you come across.

Over my lifetime, I have learned again and again, in different ways, the vital importance of this human communications reality. It's true in your personal life, at work, and out in the marketplace of your life.

So, You Say You Are Offended!

"Some people have to be told" is so important to your mental health and stability that I have made this tenet a major part of my seminars called, Pathways To Success. So, now, let me share it all with you and see if you can relate and use lots of it in your everyday life.

Here is one I learned from an Army Full Colonel. I had invited a friend of mine to speak at my weekly Army Reserve meeting in Washington, D.C, with army field grade officers (Majors and Colonels), a sprinkling of members of Congress, working professionals, and you name it.

Colonel Frank had an ego as big as the planet. He was a combat Vietnam veteran and federal prosecutor. Talk about assertive people. He was off the charts. Well, I introduced Frank as my guest speaker, in his dress greens, with big eagles on his shoulders, and a chest full of ribbons.

Within no more than two minutes, he had managed to infuriate almost everyone with his crass humor. A captain (no less) stood up and pointed at the door and told him to leave. This was a surreal scene. Frank read this guy the riot act in words I cannot repeat in any company. Whereupon a female fellow Colonel stood up and said, "I'm offended!"

You have heard that one before, right? Frank gave the comeback that I have added to my arsenal ever since.

"I'm offended that you're offended." Simple and direct.

She sat down.

I attempted to restore order, telling Frank to mind his manners and go on with his presentation. His presentation essentially dealt with how he had saved hundreds of marines at the Battle of Khe Sanh and other various perils of legal military wisdom. He got polite applause at the end, however, no one joined us for drinks afterward.

Elizabeth Warren Fumes

I saw Senator Elizabeth Warren (D-MA) in action at a Senate oversight hearing once that was played and replayed on the evening TV news. Senator Warren is very smart. Among other things, she won the Oklahoma high school debate championship.

She was grilling some witness, and he was put off and pulled out the old, "I'm offended." The evening news carried her question, his "I'm offended" statement, and ended by showing her silent and fuming. She probably carried that around for a bit. If she had pulled out the, "I'm offended that you're offended!" she would have been featured last on the clip and would have carried the news cycle.

This Time, Mike Bloomberg Fumes

Former three-time New York City Mayor, Mike Bloomberg, lost the chance he had to be president within two minutes of his first debate experience. The Democratic nominees for president were squaring off for one of their many TV debates. Mayor Bloomberg was at the end of the row and Senator Warren was next to him. She got the first question and lit into him.

There had been news reports of sexual harassment at his multi-billion-dollar company. She related several of the media reports and asked him if he would release women who signed non-disclosure lawsuit settlement agreements (NDAs) and allow them to talk about what happened. He said no, equivocated, and stared straight ahead. Politics is a blood sport, and I knew immediately he was finished.

For starters, I knew he should have said yes right away, that he would release them and then sort it out later. This is what happened a couple days later, but it was too late. Here is what he should have said, "Of course, I will release them. But they are the ones who will decide if they want to speak out. When I was mayor of New York City for twelve years, I was a well-known champion for women. Within my company, I am a well-known champion for women. But I have a question for you, are you a champion for men?"

Never Complain, Never Explain

There are exceptions, of course, but there is an old saying, "Never complain, never explain." I will add that your friends don't need it and your enemies only consider it a sign of weakness. In politics, you are always losing if you are explaining.

There is never a reason to say what you are not. If need be, you say what you are. For example, one never says, "I'm not a crook." People will just remember the last part. You say, "I am an honest person."

You do not say, "I never cheated on my wife." You say, "I have always been faithful to my wife."

As a wag once said, "I never believe a rumor until I hear it denied." Besides, people might not have heard the rumor before you deny it.

Years ago, a very obscure Washington DC publication ran an article about what it said was a poll of hundreds of Capitol Hill staffers, to find who they thought was the dumbest member of Congress. The "winner" convened a news conference that got nationwide coverage.

At the conference, he denied he was the dumbest member.

You Don't Appreciate It?!

"I don't appreciate what you said." Who hasn't heard that one?

Save this one for when you need it, "That's good, because you were not meant to appreciate it!"

How many times have we heard this? "I am only trying to help."

And your response when appropriate, "You're offering the kind of help that I don't need!"

Maybe you have noticed something here. The key, usually, but not always, is to get the focus off you and on to them. In other words, it's you, not me, who is the problem here.

Like tennis, you leave the ball in their court; the point is not to refer back to yourself, as in *I*, it's you, *you*. That is a simple formula to remind yourself how to keep the jerks you meet during the ups and downs in life off-balance.

Quick Comeback Counter

Here is one for almost every occasion—simple, short, and very effective. Somebody is telling you this and they are telling you that. They talk like they have it all figured out. What is the real blunt, put-them-in-their-place thing to say?

"You're confused."

This is as good as it gets to tip the playing field in your favor. Here is the challenge: you can do it, but you have to pick your spots. Don't let people verbally walk on you. You will be carrying it around, not them. Give it back to them, then you can forget it and let them carry it around.

Here is another one to save for special cases: make a mental note and put it in your quiver of arrows to shoot when needed. I remember having a long business relationship with a man. I knew he had a strong personality and I had heard him really jump on the cases of a number of people in every walk of life.

I thought he knew the kind of person I was. I guess not, not even after ten years. So, one day, we are on the phone and, out of nowhere, he starts browbeating me, or trying to. Has this ever happened to you? I will bet that it has.

I guess I had the arrow in my quiver all along because after he took a breath, with lots of projection, I simply said, "Pull it back." There was silence. No response, and again, I said, "Pull it back."

He seemed to collect himself on the other end of the line and resumed his side of the conversation like none of it had happened. I never had such a problem with him again.

Credit Robert De Niro

Now that I think about it, I first got that line, "pull it back," from Robert De Niro, from one of his great movies. Maybe it was *Rodin*. I heard it and said to myself, "Boy, save that one up, Brian!"

But you have to do it. You just have to do it to protect your well-being when needed. Interestingly enough, you will find, if you have not already, that you only have to do this one time with any given person. Then they will file away in their memory bank that you are a strong person, and they will not forget.

I will save some of these one-liners for the end of the chapter. You can add to your arsenal: for the phone and for in-person with customer service people. You know, the ones who don't like their jobs and/or are having a bad day.

Here is a very early lesson I learned about protecting yourself in the workplace, and I really think that I had to reflect on it for many years until I realized the impact and power it could have for me.

Back to Vietnam at the height of the war in 1969. I was an infantry officer but was tasked by the Army to work in "intelligence" with the 4th Psychological Operations Group. The army, never too subtle, slatted me as Chief of Propaganda Development and gave me an actual name plate on the desk in Saigon that said that.

So, one day, there was an "interrogation" of a "bad guy" who had been captured, a North Vietnam regular. How did the interrogation work? There were about eight of us standing in a circle in the S-2 Intelligence shop with the NVA guy standing in the center. There was a translator there too.

A Whole Career Was In The Balance

The head of the S-2 ("Intelligence") shop, a captain, was doing the interrogation. We were going nowhere. Nothing was being learned. It was chaos—as folks in the military might say, a FUBAR situation (you can guess or check with a military type). The troops were becoming very restive. One after another actually started to call out the competence, intelligence, and probably the manhood of the captain conducting the interrogation.

As I reflect back, his entire persona before his peers, maybe even his army career, such as it might have been, was at stake. The captain, who would turn out to be one of my best friends for decades after we returned stateside, was very bright, with a PhD no less, but not really articulate. You know what I mean? Someone can be very bright, but the words don't really roll out all that evenly.

Suddenly, right out of the middle of it all, an amazing thing happened. It's something I will never forget.

My buddy got all silent, turned around in a full circle, eyeballing everyone and explained, "At ease! Maybe you didn't notice, but there is a war going on out here. People are dying and getting wounded. Lives are at stake here. Listen up! Now is the time when we need to pull together. We need to communicate and cooperate. The stakes are too high." He glared around the circle before saying, "Any questions?"

All the "intelligent" people were speechless.

Their eyes were as big as saucers, and they were speechless. No one offered a peep. A few nodded.

Then my buddy continued the interrogation again, just as incompetently as before. For all his smarts, he didn't know what he was doing. We, of course, learned nothing helpful.

Afterward, I said, "Hugh, what in Sam's Hill was that all about?"

"A little peer control," was all he said. No good with interrogations, but very, very shrewd about maintaining his credibility in the workplace.

Incidentally, we Saigon warriors obviously did not help to win any war, but we did help reduce the level of the killing. Through our Choi Hoi Program, over 60,000 of the other guys laid down their arms and otherwise went on with their lives.

Okay, now here is the deal. Please think about this amazing real-life story. What Hugh was saying had nothing at all to do with the matter at hand. It was just a way to regain control of the situation that could have haunted him for a long time.

Remember These Words: Communicate And Cooperate

Consider these words yourself. "What we are doing here is vitally important. What we need to do is communicate and cooperate."

Who can disagree with that? People can only nod their heads and think and say, "Yes, that is true." They cannot argue with that.

That is the ingeniousness of the tactic. You pick the words . . . they don't matter so much. When you need to, pull them out, try them on, and get them out. They will garner respect that will not be forgotten, and your work life will be much the easier for it.

He Was Getting Chewed Up At Work

I remembered this lesson from my experience there in a combat zone, and I pulled it out to aid a friend of mine one day. Here is another example of a kind of life-changing episode.

About five of us were having our Friday morning Mastermind meeting (see Chapter 12). One of the participants related that he was having the absolute biggest challenge of his entire life. He was working high up in the leadership of a nationwide association with its headquarters in Alexandria, Virginia. (More association headquarters sit there than anywhere else for some reason.)

This guy, Adam, was no spring chicken. He had been in the professional workplace for two or three decades. He related that office politics was eating him alive. He couldn't sleep. He could barely eat, and he was a nervous wreck. The top four or five of the leaders were eating his lunch on a daily basis. For some reason they were on him like a cheap suit.

I remembered my captain from Vietnam. I said, "Okay, Adam, here's what you do. Wait for the right time for the perfect opening, likely when they are wrong, or not—doesn't matter. Wait for a meeting of the five top brass, like when you are all around a conference table. It does not matter the words you use, but get their attention, look them right in the eyes, and serve up a high, hard fastball." I probably gave him the "communicate and cooperate" key words. Then I forgot about it.

A couple sessions later, during another Mastermind breakfast, Morris said to me and the rest, "Brian, you probably don't even remember, but I took your advice about calling out my peers. I waited for the right time, looked them right in the eyes with my most serious look, and leaned back and let 'em have it. And you know what? It's like the weight of the world is off me. They have treated me with nothing but respect since that time. It's a whole new ball game for me. Thanks, buddy."

I had another friend who had a similar type of work experience. He didn't do the key thing right, and he was out of a job. He worked for a national association in Silver Spring, Maryland. It was a non-profit organization with a kind of incestuous leadership (watch out for this—more later), with a wife and husband and a handful of other executive-type employees.

My friend George was new on board, a very talented guy and well-educated as well, but it did not help him keep his job. Here is what happened. Several months into his tenure, there was a leadership meeting where the co-heads of the organization asked everybody there who wanted to fill out a form applying for Combined Federal Campaign funding. Nobody wanted to do it.

George was new and wanted to earn his stripes, so he volunteered. I knew him, and he was an excellent writer. The others included a retired army general (not much of any writing is taught in the army, I can tell you) and research or medical types (few written skills taught there either). George, I am sure, did an outstanding job.

He Tried To Be Modest, But It Cost Him His Job

But these people were prickly, and they liked to get on people just for the sport of it. Later, they passed his ten-page-or-so application around the conference room table. The president asked everyone what kind of a job they thought George did. There were no comments. People just sort of shrugged.

The president asked George, "Well, what do you think? Did you write this well enough so we are going to have a chance for funding?"

George dropped the ball and made a very bad career decision right there and then. He decided to be modest. Bad idea! He told me he said that he was new there and he was just trying to learn the ropes. Maybe he thanked them for even giving him a paycheck every week, as far as I know.

After that, the smug president and most of the rest of them kept telling George, "Well, we know you are not a good writer. Too bad you can't do writing. Too bad, so sad." They would sit around and say, "George can't write" even though the fact was he really could. But it made not an iota of difference.

His credibility went down the drain with every passing day. Finally, with the inevitable end in sight, he resigned before he could be fired.

Don't Assume They Know You're Brilliant

The moral of this story is really obvious but also not so obvious. These people probably did not know good writing from bad. I knew George's past experience. I knew he was an excellent writer but that he did not stand up for himself.

It is not enough to be good. Some people won't figure it out on their own or won't want to. These people have to be told!

He should have said something simple and compelling and truthful. "You know what, I am an excellent writer. This application is extremely well done. Nobody else here wanted to do it. I think you probably knew that writing was not your strong suit, but it is mine, and I did an outstanding job."

For good measure, he could have added the communication and cooperation part.

You Have To Do It

I know I am making this sound easy. It really isn't. You have to develop the mentality and steep yourself. If you don't do the office politics, the office politics will undo you.

And I really had to learn this part the hard way . . . going through it again and again. Midwestern upbringing, I suppose. Don't be arrogant, but that's not it.

Early in my career I had a job as a political consultant. I was told to develop the campaign schedule for a candidate for a governor in Puerto Rico (he won by the way). I was to do this without going to Puerto Rico, mind you. I worked out a very good and logical campaign schedule for the candidate for a month. A real, long-time pro at the agency looked at the plan and said it wouldn't work. I knew it would.

When it did, I didn't say anything. This episode had no consequences for me that I knew of, but it stuck with me. I made the mistake of not standing up for my work, thus I didn't stand up for myself.

Don't Learn The Hard Way Like Me

Again, in another job working for the federal government, I was doing the work of about five people in our division. Sound familiar?

I was actually doing a lot of everyone else's job. My boss told me his new boss was coming by for a meet-and-greet.

I failed to prepare. I was doing the bulk of the work in the division, but when push came to shove at the division meeting, I was at a loss for words. I had not figured out the vital importance of not only doing the work but making sure those with a "need to know" would understand my performance and contributions.

Sounds very basic, doesn't it? It is. It took me quite some time to not be like George. I hope you will quickly pick it up and use this critical career protection mentality.

Are you doing great work and kind of leaving it on the conference room table? Are you sending around emails and just leaving it at that? Expecting people to figure out how good you really are? You cannot do that. You cannot assume that. People have to be told, and, if need be, be told *all* the reasons why your work is great. Even the sharpest will often not figure it out on their own.

I know this sounds counterintuitive, but I have seen it again and again and again. I have been bitten by this office snake too many times. It's not bragging if you are telling the truth.

People will form their opinion about you based on what they perceive your opinion of yourself to be.

Office Politics: Swim With The Sharks

Another sad reality is that in some high-stress work environments, one has to devote almost as much time to tending to office politics as doing the job. Don't take care of office politics, and you can do a great job and still be out of that job.

This is your job we are talking about—your career, your livelihood. You don't have to blow your horn all the time, but do not hesitate on a regular basis when the time is right. Don't be like George.

Okay, so now some of the better ones at the end of the chapter. The one-liners you can use on the jerks and weasels who may try to make you feel bad.

You know those people in the medical offices who seem to just love to make you fill out the same paperwork that you filled out the last time, even though nothing has changed?

Receptionist: "Here is the clipboard. Please fill out the pages." (Well, maybe you get a "please.")

You: "Nothing's changed. We are good to go. No need to fill out the paperwork again."

Nice receptionist, or not: "Well, that is our policy. You have to fill it out every time you come in."

Our Policy: Always The Customer Service Fallback

You, me: "Okay, that's fine. Let me tell you *my policy*—you know, the paying patient. I don't fill out forms when it's not required, when information hasn't changed."

Sometimes, I actually don't have to fill out the forms. Sometimes, a supervisor comes out. But always, I have a feeling of satisfaction because I explain my policy. You will find that it's new to them that you actually have a policy. Have some fun.

More Rejoinders For Your Hip Pocket

You have explained something to someone and they don't understand. Well, more likely, they pretend they don't understand. They are being difficult, *obdurate* (See Chapter on World Power, but you know what that means). So here you go. You put it back in their court, across court to their backhand, which they cannot return.

You: "Which part don't you understand?" Talk about putting them on the defensive. I pull that out of my verbal bag of tricks on occasion, and you can too. It's fun. People are flummoxed by this line.

The best response I ever heard, and you can hear it was pretty weak, was, "I don't understand any part of it." Too bad, so sad.

You know those really rude people in *customer service* on the phone? Lots of them are nice, but some aren't. They hate their job and want to pass it off on you.

You are telling them how the phone company or the home repair service has messed up and they keep interrupting you. They have bad listening skills and poor customer service. It happens all the time. Don't get mad, get even. Or, better yet, make it a game of satisfaction that you will win.

Here is what works for that. When it happens, when you are on the receiving end and they keep interrupting you, which, of course, they will, they want to score points, not provide customer satisfaction. Here you go . . .

"You are interrupting me . . ." You try again, and they do it again. "You interrupted me again. Let's do this. You talk, and I listen, then I talk, and you listen."

An amazing thing happens. They pause because they have never thought of such a thing. Occasionally, they will even do it, but usually not. So, for the really rude people you have a couple more aces in the hole.

I'll Be Off The Line Now

"You ought to get a job you like . . ." That puts them in the denial stance, which is always good.

"Oh, I do like my job!" they say.

The last resort, for the jerks among jerks is, "You know what? You missed your calling."

"Say what?"

"You should have been a revenue agent or a corrections officer, you know, like a prison guard."

Now, the worm has turned. They try to just get something in, and you politely say, "I will be off the line now." And hang up. The last thing you will hear is them trying to get in the last word before

Chapter 4

Push Back! How To Save Yourself From Lawyers

What is the difference between a lawyer and a skunk laying in the center of the road? Answer: There are skid marks in front of the skunk. How do you start a whole new civilization? Answer: First, you kill off all the lawyers. (Inspired by Shakespeare's line.) And so on.

Why are there so many lawyer jokes? Answer: Because there are so many lawyers. There are a multitude of superior lawyers to be found who can really help you. Then there are the others. Have you had any problems with lawyers in your life? If you have not, you have lived a charmed life. Either way, I can help you be prepared to take effective action and cleanse your life.

Attack! Attack! Attack!

The mantra of the infantry in which I served was to lay down an overwhelming field of fire. In other words: Attack! Attack! Attack! Same as when you are taking on the government.

What we are talking about is both having your lawyer attack the other side, pushing your own lawyer to find out how they are pushing back for you, and learning to play hardball to protect yourself. We will talk about the lawyers who may at some time oppose you, but let's start with your own lawyer.

There are many similar law firms out there. Dewey, Cheatem & How is one of the most prevalent of the lot.

You may have had this experience already: You hire a lawyer to help you and you become more upset with them than with the other people you hired the lawyer to help you with. Let me share some hard-earned techniques. I will start with the easy and then work out.

Scare The Wits Out Of You

Most lawyers can't seem to help themselves. They put their lawyer's hat on and try to scare the wits out of you by telling you all the awful things that could happen to you. Sound familiar? The worst-case scenario for them is the best-case scenario for them because of, well, higher fees.

Much of this may seem counterintuitive, and it is. There are plenty of things your lawyer will often fail to tell you, such as the law that is relevant to your case. How can that be? It happens every time because the lawyers want to keep you, the client (seemingly, the boss) in the dark on many matters to maintain their control over you.

You want to test out this reality? Study up on the state statutes and case law in your state on matters relevant to your case. Then, when your lawyer puts on that lawyer's hat again and wants to scare the crap out of you, to keep you in line and keep the fees coming in, what happens?

They will argue with you that you don't know what you are talking about. You know why that is? It is because they are the lawyer (and suffered through the drudgery of law school) and you don't know jack.

So, save your breath. In most cases, you are better off not letting them know what you know. Their regular refrain will be that they have your best interests at heart. Listen with a skeptical mind and know that what is to be done is ultimately for you to decide. You have to live with it, not them.

Never Tell Your Lawyer This

You have hired a lawyer or their firm to represent you in what becomes negotiations. You will find that your biggest job (and headache) is to push back on your own lawyers, so they will push back against the bad guys, whoever they are. Want to know what one of the worst things you can do with your own lawyer when you are in protracted negotiations? Give them your fallback position.

Nine out of ten times, they will fall all the way back to that from the beginning. We are talking litigators, "professional" negotiators. Because it's easier to fight you than it is to fight the opponents.

So, let's say you are caught up in a lawsuit of some kind. Do not sit back and wait for the bills and assume your lawyer is doing a good job. This is one of those things that seems so obvious, that one is really tempted to forget about it—to grill your lawyer on how they have pushed back.

Like Propping Up A Jellyfish

Unfortunately, I have had to confront lawyers on occasion by asking them exactly how they have pushed back. Seems a simple, direct, and worthy question, right? I did it once to a firm that was racking up huge bills on the company I worked for, and the lawyers for the firm were positively infuriated. Yes, why would I be asking such a thing? Why, indeed.

With another lawyer, I confronted him with this same simple question, and he responded that he did not make the case for me because he "did not want to argue." You heard it right: a lawyer who didn't want to argue!

Not excusable, but part of the problem was that he was negotiating with another lawyer—professional courtesy, you know. Beware, you may have a lawyer that you have to prop up like a jellyfish.

Double Trouble: Insurance Lawyers

There are lawyers and then there are insurance lawyers. You could find yourself squared off against insurance lawyers in one or two general categories: 1) when you know they are against you or 2) when they are supposed to be for you.

The first category is when an insurance company appoints a lawyer to protect their client from liabilities from you. You may have filed against an individual who rear-ended you. Their insurance company appoints a lawyer to defend against your claim. You could file a medical malpractice case or something much more mundane.

The other broad category where you have far more leverage is when the insurance appoints a lawyer and you are theoretically the client. Maybe you are affiliated with a company that has director's insurance, where if there is a legal complaint, the insurance company will retain a lawyer for you. In these cases, you are the client, not the insurance company.

But guess what? These lawyers may ostensibly work for you, but they really work for the insurance companies. Why? Because the lawyers have sweetheart deals with the insurance companies. The lawyers have gotten business from the insurance companies before you and will again after you.

So, you think the lawyer might come up with a settlement where the insurance companies have to pay some appreciable amount of money? You know the answer to that. No way! The lawyers will squeeze you and not their gravy train.

In a subset of this category, your insurance company uses their in-house lawyers to fight you off. Maybe you disputed the non-payment of a big medical claim or your homeowners' insurance refuses to pay. most of these cases fall in the second category, meaning, when you paid for the insurance, the best leverage for you is to take on the insurance company.

What is the simplest, fastest, cheapest, and most effective recourse? Regulator? Lawyer? Court? Letter? Yes, a letter, but a very ingenious letter.

You find out the full name of the state commissioner of insurance. You find out the full street address of your state insurance commission, and you use the street address, not any post office box.

Then you draft up a one-page letter to the commissioner. You put in a reference line, such as "Re: Investigation of ABC Insurance Company." In the letter, you state your policy number and about how long you have had the policy. Then, in non-inflammatory words, you describe the misdeeds of the insurance, just the facts.

Then you ask for an investigation of the insurance company because you believe it may be committing a pattern of abuse throughout the state. You close at the bottom of the letter with a stated copy of the letter to the CEO of the insurance company by name and the name of your agent's superior and title, which can easily be found online

The final person to get a copy is your agent, by name.

You do not send the letter to the Commissioner. You scan it and email it to your agent! In the email, you say this is a draft you are prepared to send if they don't get straight with you. You don't send it to the commissioner because there is no fallback position. The promise and warning of sending it is all it takes.

I have employed this exact strategy when the stakes were in the six-figure range, and it worked like magic!

Forty Dollars To Leave A Ten-Second Message

You have to love these guys. You have heard of these little counters that lawyers have, right? They usually bill in segments of ten per hour, that is six minutes for every segment. I have been shown a few of these lawyers' bills—a wonderful sight. I have been charged $800 for my own lawyer to devote two hours to writing up our retainer agreement, forty dollars each for leaving a voicemail message for me, and another forty dollars for listening to my voicemail message for him!

So, there we have it. Eighty dollars to leave a ten-second voicemail and to review a return call voicemail. Enough said.

If you have an excellent lawyer, hang on to them with all your might. Pay on time and count your blessings. If not . . .

Scare The Wits Out Of Your Lawyer

Technique number one: Having a real serious problem with your lawyer? You know what scares them most of all? Filing a complaint with the Legal Board of Ethics of your State Bar Association. No kidding. This is like you have waved a magic wand.

You can quickly look it up online. Your state bar may have, for example, nine member-lawyers on their ethics board, and you can typically find those names and the process for filing a formal complaint.

The point is, you don't want to file a complaint. What you really need to know is just the fundamentals of how it works and, really, just to know it is a powerful option for you.

As a kind of last resort, for when your lawyer is really screwing you, your best option is to tell them verbally that if your issues with them cannot be solved, you will swear out a complaint. In many states, even a complaint is made public in some regards. Have the exact name of the state board in hand, their address, and the chair, which might come in handy for credibility and real impact.

Want to be a little less nuclear? You say, "You know, Dewey, I told a friend of mine about the situation with you, and they told me that I should consider filing a complaint to the Board of Ethics of the Florida State Bar Association.

I had a couple experiences along these lines that I will share with you. I had signed a retainer agreement with a lawyer to sue a company on my behalf. The case was seemingly a slam dunk. He took the case on a one-third contingency basis, pure and simple. He really bungled the case and lost it.

This is the real world. So, a month later, he comes back and sends me a bill for fifty or so hours, based on his hourly fee. "Wait a minute, Dewey," (of Dewey Cheatem & How) I said. "We had a contingency agreement. You would get one-third of the amount of the judgment against the defendant. You lost. I don't owe you anything." He told me that I had to pay, or he would sue me.

I was incredulous. I consulted another lawyer, lawyer number two. He told me to tell him I would file a complaint with the State Bar Association. Bingo! I never heard again from lawyer number one.

I retained lawyer number two on another matter, another contingency matter. Lawyer number two dropped the case midway through and then sent me a bill for many hours of fees. I couldn't believe it. Déjà vu all over again. I told him what he had taught me. Yep, "I will complain to the bar." He disappeared. It was all stranger than fiction, except in legal circles.

Remember: Attack! Attack! Attack!

Maybe you are or will be involved in a lawsuit or a legal dispute, simple or contentious, like a divorce proceeding. When one is down in the weeds, it is very easy to forget the weeds for the forest, or the big strategy picture.

The key to many legal proceedings is to start on the offense and stay on the offense. Keep the other side off-balance by doing something to them before they do something else to you.

Get them into a reactive pose. You do not want to be the one reacting and always playing catch-up. Like artillery during battle, if those rounds are not going out from you to them, they have time to send them in to you.

More specifically, you want your lawyer sending out all those rounds: discovery demands, depositions, motions for this and that, and whatever. I will give just one arcane but apt example.

You are part of a lawsuit. Maybe you are the plaintiff and you are asserting that the defendant owes you money. Before you go to court, you can instruct your lawyer to file for a provisional remedy, meaning the motion to the court may ask that certain monies of the defendant be frozen because there is a belief that in the event of a favorable verdict, the money will not long be there.

They Did What To Us?

Your motion hits the other party like a ton of bricks. They think, What in the world is this? There are many cases where the party on the receiving end never gets word of a motion accepted by the court because proper service of the complaint was bungled. Lawyers did not get it, did not know about it, and therefore, did not respond in time, and so on.

The point in dealing with lawyers is that it is a game. Legal disputes are essentially games too. Sure, the facts or law may matter, but usually, it is who can play the game best.

Another technique you should use is "making a record." That is legal jargon for having your own record of exactly what transpired during your legal process at any key time. So, you may need to do something simple, like placing down your phone at a key dispute meeting and recording your conversation with your lawyer or your lawyer talking to other lawyers while you are on the phone.

About half of the states in the Union are one party consent states, meaning only one party, that would be you, has to be informed that the conversation is being recorded. This technique is invaluable because you do *not* tell them you are recording them. And of course, they could be recording at their end without telling you as well. With simple software, the audio can be converted to a transcript, which could be the best thing you ever did in the entire proceeding.

Magic Words To Your Lawyer

Tell him you want to settle up. I was sitting in the steam room of the Providence Recreation Center outside Falls Church, Virginia, one evening. As it happened, there were a bunch of guys sitting around, seating it out. There was a discussion between a couple guys about legal dilemmas. One decent-seeming guy said he was a lawyer and talked a bit about his profession.

I had nothing to lose. I was beside myself. I could not figure how to get out of the clutches of a lawyer who was running up my tab. I had hired the guy to sue an organization for a wrongful action. They counter-sued. They had more money than me. My lawyer was pulling me deeper and deeper into this. The good lawyer in the steam room told me what to do.

I went back and told my lawyer that I wanted to settle up. Bingo! The light went on. He was going to be paid, and we could both get out of it and move on.

Fire Your Lawyer: Quick And Easy

Heaven forbid, if you want to fire your lawyer and actually hire another one, what do you do? Well, in the first place, you never give documents to a lawyer for which you have not made copies.

It is malpractice if they refuse to give them back to you at any time, but if you try to get those documents back, they may resist or delay. Maybe you have not fully paid your bill yet. The lawyer is required to return all documents when you request them.

Whether you have gotten the documents back or not, after you have found a more suitable attorney, you merely sign a contract with her or him and the new lawyer sends a certified letter to the old attorney with a new Power of Attorney form that you have signed that designates the new lawyer as the one of record. Bingo! The bad lawyer is fired and, based on legal ethics, cannot comment on the case to anyone.

Make Your Lawyer Accountable To You

Some of the best use of read-notify software is probably checking to make sure your lawyer is opening and reading your emails and at what times. The recipients cannot tell you are using it on them. The lawyers like to play cloak and diggers, hide and go seek. You can get this software for peanuts and track exactly when and/or if your lawyer is actually reading your emails and all the good details as well.

The answer to lawyers? Try very hard to stay out of trouble, of course. Some things are almost unavoidable during the ups and downs of life. And all too often, we are attracting those jerks in between.

If you do have to take on a lawyer, hear them out, let them rest their case, and don't be worried by anything they tell you. They will always suggest the worst-case scenario.

Most of all, keep your own counsel. You are the client. You are the boss. Maybe you did not go to law school, but know you can play the game with the best of them.

You Can Scare The Wits Out Of Them

Sometimes it seems like there are so many jerks out there wanting to torment you, with lawyers standing at the head of the line. When the stakes are really high, don't be shy about coming off a bit crazy to put those big jerks totally off-balance.

One of the most legendary championship boxing matches of all time was the heavyweight thriller between Mohammed Ali (then known as Cassius Clay) and Sonny Liston in 1964. The line was 8 to 1 that the champ, Liston, would win. *Sports Illustrated* named it the fourth-greatest sports event of the twentieth century.

The day before the fight, during the weigh-in, Ali was acting crazy, yelling and hollering and carrying on. Later, Ali's famous trainer, Angelo Dundee, asked him, "What in the world was that all about?"

Ali said, "Liston is afraid of no man, but he is afraid of a crazy man."

Liston did not answer the bell in the seventh round.

The point is, if needed, your lawyer needs to be told, and to understand, that if you get inflamed, they will rue the day.

PART 2

How to Deal with Doctors,
Dentists, Drivers, Dog Walkers,
and Doing Exercise

Chapter 5

Your Doctor Advises, But You Are In Charge of Your Health

Everybody gets sick. Virtually all of you will have to visit a doctor. Has a doctor ever scared you by what they told you? Does a bear poop in the woods?

Too many people are intimidated by doctors. Doing what the doctor says may be a good idea, or it might be a bad idea. The doctor gives advice and administers care, but the patient is in charge of their health and too often needs to figure out what should be done independently through other opinions and research. And importantly, along the way, the patient has to know how to talk to the doctor, to take a strong stand for their own health.

Like lawyers, (See Chapter 4, "Push Back! How To Save Yourself From Lawyers") doctors can't help themselves. They are just sometimes scarier in a monotone, while lawyers are more animated. What can we do to get the best out of doctors?

Here are few things for you to keep in mind while working to keep your life great. Number one, the Hippocratic Oath. "First, do no harm." Wow, that is a pretty low bar.

Next, "Doctor, heal thyself." If they can't take care of themselves, how are they going to take care of us?

Bad Diagnosis. Bad Doctors

The thing that doctors are probably the worst at is what they should be the best at: the diagnosis. Far, far too often, doctors get the diagnosis wrong and often when they get it right, they don't seem to know what to do.

First and foremost, do your research *before* you go to the doctor. Know as much as you can and be ready to ask a bunch of questions regardless. You most likely know that doctors don't like to answer many questions. They are the doctors.

Doctors don't take courses in communications in medical school. They memorize a whole lot of stuff, so they get really good at passing medical school by test-taking.

Be Sure To Have Your Questions Ready

Here is our first clue. If your doctor does not seem to like to answer questions, there is a reason. It could be because they don't know the answers, they don't like to be questioned, and/or they are not good doctors. Here are just a few questions to ask your doctor during most visits:

- What is my diagnosis?
- How long will the symptoms last? Will they get worse?
- How many patients with my condition have you treated?
- What are my treatment options?
- What are the side effects of such treatments?
- What would happen if I delayed treatment?
- If a test is suggested, how accurate is it?
- When will I have the results of the test?
- Will I need more tests?
- How concerned should I be?
- What can I do with my lifestyle to improve my health?

Here are a couple examples that you may already know that relate to why it is important to do your research before you go to the doctor.

Are you a woman or do you know a woman who is concerned about breast cancer? The anxiety about breast cancer seems to touch everyone. I have done long research for loved ones before they went in for an examination. This is what I've found:

First, the more recent exhaustive studies have indicated that having mammograms have caused as much or more anxiety in people versus those who have not had the tests. When in doubt, the studies show that the test should be taken, but some women who are not of a certain age or beyond a certain age should consider trying to avoid them.

Perhaps, you have heard all about the false positives and the false negatives and the biopsies and mastectomies that were undertaken in mistake. But here is what you don't hear so often . . .

Beware Of The Medical Vortex

The people making these mistakes are not so much the advising doctors but the radiologists who read the tests. Now, here is where your knowledge becomes really invaluable. Has the radiologist done 1,000 readings or 20,000 readings? Based on the level of their experience, do they know what they are looking at? Is a rookie going to put you or a loved one into the medical vortex, from which you will have far more problems than you ever imagined?

And the tricky part? For any sort of exams requiring radiology tests, try to find out who the radiologist is, who will be doing the readings and how much experience they have. When you start asking questions along these lines, you will quickly find out that the hospital or clinic personnel really can't be bothered to provide that kind of information.

"The radiologists are all very experienced." "We don't know who is going to do the reading, because they rotate." And so on. It's like you shouldn't be bothered about such things. But you absolutely should. It is your body and your health.

Get A Double Reading

Reasonably, you could insist on having a radiologist with years of experience do the reading. Try if you will, this is often like trying to train a donkey to fly.

So here is your fallback position: demand a double reading. This means they employ two radiologists. Now, I have been through this for other types of tests. The good people in radiology usually say, "What? I have never heard of such of a thing." But if you insist, you can get the second reading, but the system will fight you every step of the way.

First, when you check into radiology, make sure to fill out the form that says that you want a copy of the results, meaning not only the film but the write-up. With modern hospitals, you can see these write-ups through your medical portal, if you can figure out how to get in there. But often, you fill out the form and they never send you the film. It's your body and your property and you have a right to have it. After all, you may want to have it read elsewhere.

So, you have to call the Film Library to get them to do what they were supposed to do in the first place. Better yet, when you check into radiology, tell them you are going to go around to the film library to pick up your copy of the X-ray, or CT scan, or MRI before you leave.

If and when you get the double reading, even if the second radiologist calls you on the phone (which happened for me once), it's like you just won the medical lottery. You have an excellent medical team.

Prostate Cancer: Do Your Own Research

Now on to you men and your friends and family and to the (also) dreaded prostate cancer.

Years ago, before the internet was really prevalent (originated by DRPA, Defense Research Projects Association around 1946), I felt the need to get checked for prostate cancer. I was highly motivated to not get scared out of my wits by a doctor, so I went to a library and read medical journals on the subject over three days. What I found really surprised me.

First, among the roughly twenty articles, I found an article in a highly regarded medical journal. This medical journal reported the results of a ten-year medical study that tracked 1,000 men (all originally in their 60s or 70s) who had been diagnosed with prostate cancer. Some got treatment and some didn't. I was stunned to read that only 3 percent were found to have died of prostate cancer after ten years.

Then I found that the majority of men die with prostate cancer. Then I found that for a very long time, Europeans had been puzzled why such a large number of American men undergo some type of prostate surgery, which often leaves the man impotent and incontinent.

Why, indeed. Serious cases need serious action. But the watchful waiting, or more conservative early approach, seems to be warranted in almost all cases. Be careful. Be aware. Ask questions.

We read about all these men who have died of prostate cancer (and one is too many for this dreadful disease) but we rarely read about those who opted out of the more drastic medical intervention.

Too many people say, "I am going to do what the doctor(s) tell me." Don't be one of those people who do that at all costs. Do not let the doctor scare you. Be informed. Do the research and be in charge of your own body.

Are You Worried?

I ask you again: Are you worrying needlessly about some medical or perceived medical condition? Are you worried if you do something and worried if you don't? The chances are you started to worry even more after you saw the doctor.

You have heard the line, "I am not a doctor, and I don't play one on TV," and while I obviously will not give specific medical advice, I can pass on some insights for dealing with the doctors who just might be causing you all the pain—as in anguish. I have learned the hard way through experience and likely some of my insights will help you know how to decide and feel better along the way.

Again, remember that doctors are used to doing the talking and not the listening. They are used to telling us and not to us asking them anything. If you don't ask the doctor the right question, you may never find out what you need to know. So again, have as many questions prepared in advance and remember not to put any doctor on a pedestal. Talk to him or her like a peer. You will get more respect and better results.

My Doctor Put On His Doctor's Hat And Scared The Wits Out Of Me

"You have something on your tongue. It may be cancer, so I am going to give you a referral to an eye, nose, and throat (ENT) doctor."

Later, I went to the doctor's office that was attached to a hospital. I was sitting there and in walked the now late Justice John Scalia of the Supreme Court. I recognized him immediately. These must be really great doctors, I thought.

The receptionist did not recognize him, however, and asked him his name. "Justice Scalia" he said. She got on the phone and in a nanosecond, the Justice was spirited into the inner doctor's office.

I waited my turn. If you only have to wait a half-hour to be seen, you can consider yourself lucky, of course. Finally, I was escorted to the examination room. The nurse practitioner came in and asked a bunch of questions. I then waited only a short period of time, and the good doctor came in. He asked me a couple questions and had me stick out my tongue.

"Could be cancer," he said. "I can do a biopsy and find out."

I should have been prepared for this, but I was not. I was hoping he would look at it and say it was something else. "You mean you have to cut out part of my tongue to find out?"

"Yes," he said, "that is the only way to find out. I have to cut out part of your tongue." He had this sort of gleam in his eyes when he said the word *cut*.

I said I wanted to think about it. And he said, "Most people want to know if it is cancer or not."

I Say Again: Beware Of The Medical Vortex

Of course, I wanted to know, but an instinct told me not to go down that road, at least not yet. I had already experienced the medical vortex where even the best and smartest of us can get sucked into a series of tests and procedures that seem to go on in perpetuity.

Two weeks later, I was in the chair of my then current dentist (Doctor Pain, I grew to call him, see Chapter 6), and this day he did me a big favor.

"Looks like you have an ulcer on your tongue. Get some of this Colgate Peroxyl. It's a mouth sore rinse."

I did, and after three days of rinsing, the ulcer was completely gone!

I had a follow-up appointment with the ENT guy and decided to go. First, he examined my tongue and there was nothing untoward to be seen. I told him I had rinsed with Peroxyl, and it went away.

"Never heard of it," he said dismissively.

Never heard of it? You're a doctor! I thought.

Four years of undergrad, about four years of medical school, and another three or four in your specialty of ears, noses, and throats, and you never heard of this?

While I was there, I decided, Why not? I will get another opinion on another matter just for a sort of test of him. I told him that I had a growth at the base of my throat. What did he suggest?

He said, "Well, we can do a test, or I can just cut it out." This guy was truly scary. Again, he said *cut* with that gleam in his eyes. I was out of there.

We Are The Deciders, Not The Doctors

Many doctors seem to feel it is their right to decide what you should do about your own health. Some people say, "Well, I am going to do what the doctor tells me." No, please . . . there is a third way. You get informed as precisely and quickly as possible, and then you decide what you are going to do about your own health.

The most egregious and unnerving example of a doctor as the high and mighty occurred with me many years ago. I would like to forget it, but I probably never will. A close friend was supposed to come by and see me. She was a dependable person, but she did not show up. I could not reach her on the phone. She seemly was in good health, but I had this very uneasy intuition.

I drove to her house and parked in front just in time to see some EMS personnel take a stretcher into her house. I followed them upstairs. There she was, stretched out on the floor. It did not look good. I rode in the ambulance to the hospital. In the underground entrance to the emergency ward area, a doctor was there and examined my friend for maybe three minutes. Then she was taken away.

"She Will Never Make It Out Of This Hospital Alive"

I remained there with the doctor. I was looking down, feeling downcast. He said to me, I remember it word for word still today, "She will never make it out of this hospital alive."

I looked at him, dumbfounded, speechless.

He repeated, "She will never leave this hospital alive."

I collected myself from the double shock and said, "I heard you the first time." Somewhere inside of me felt the cruelty of it all, and I managed, "You know what? I am glad I am not you."

"Why is that?" he said. "Because I believe that God is looking down on you now and is mighty mad that you are acting like Him."

During a several-day vigil at the hospital, as her life hung in the balance, I became the family and friend's spokesman to the lead hospital doctor. I was not appointed. I was the only one asking questions, and after a bit, they let me ask all the questions. I had many written down in a notebook.

The ER slug was right though: because of a severe aneurysm, she did not make it . . . but only after a couple of heroic-style operations by a brain surgeon that could not bring her back. The ER doctor projected whatever nightmare he had been through in his life. He had to be told.

Talking To Doctors

A couple days after my friend's memorial service, a mutual friend told me she had, "Never heard another person talk to a doctor like you did." She said I showed my true colors. I had not given it a second thought. Somewhere on the road of life, I picked up how to talk to doctors like people and not like they are the High and Mighty.

Years ago, I had an upper back X-ray and it revealed a growth around my thyroid. That X-ray sent me into a medical vortex. I was plenty scared for a long time. I got two opinions. I elected to have a biopsy done by an endocrinologist, someone I had happened to see about my testosterone level.

At the second visit, he did the biopsy and it most certainly did hurt, though the anticipation for days before was far worse.

I went back for a third visit for the lab results. And get this, maybe you have had an experience along these lines. He said he took fourteen samples, sent them to the pathologist, and there was no sign of cancer. They were all negative.

"You mean, I don't have cancer?" I said with a gathering semi-joy and relief.

"Yes," he said. "I can categorically say that you don't have cancer of the throat."

"Wow!" I said, "Say that again, so I can write it down for my wife."

Then amazingly, or not, he started to equivocate, "Well, I got fourteen samples, but it was really inconclusive, so I recommend we do it again."

Do The Biopsy Again?

"Do it again? If you got fourteen samples before and nothing was found, what is likely to happen next time?" I was more than a little incredulous.

"Well, you want to be sure," he said.

Goodbye, doctor, and good luck.

Later, I did some reading about such lumps around the thyroid area, some of which I had already done before. Some wonderful person had written an article about such X-rays (maybe it was a CT scan?), and it said if you found this shadow by accident, unless you have a constant sore throat or regular trouble swallowing, not to worry about it.

I started worrying less. I felt much better because I had none of those systems. (Don't want to jinx it though, so see Chapter 26 on the "Law Of The Universe.") Later, I did more reading (This googling is a Godsend for medical issues isn't it? Unless you become obsessed with too much, of course).

I read about goiters. That is when a thyroid gets extra secretion or something like that, and it forms around the thyroid, something that millions of people have and is virtually harmless. Regular ionized salt is thought to be helpful in such situations.

No Doctor Told Me About This Possibility

Nobody told me about goiters. One doctor, two doctors, three doctors, four . . . nobody said, "You might have a goiter." Why, oh, why not? Too obvious? Didn't care? Didn't know? Instead, I'm the doctor, and you're the patient, so you can only worry about it.

Here is what is so important to remember: you may not be told the what by the doctor, though it could be very obvious. In fact, count on this: there will probably be a backstory, so use your guile and resourcefulness and find out for yourself.

Do you have a doctor in your life? Who doesn't? Do you have more than one? Are you happy with him or her? Here's the thing about doctors: they are often the worst at what they should be best at, which is diagnoses. What exactly is my problem? So, when you know the problem exactly, you find the solution more easily.

Until recent years, doctors were never given courses in nutrition in medical school, and probably many do not learn it now. Unlike lawyers, who learn to think independently in law school, doctors do what they need to do to get through medical school, by and large. They memorize as I previously mentioned.

Think once, twice, and three times before you accept what your doctor says at face value. Find out for yourself to be sure. You can do it. Again, you are in charge of your health, the doctor isn't.

Ever Have Stomach Pains?

Ever have recurring pain in your stomach? If you have or ever will have, it could be any number of things. I once had intense and intermittent lower stomach pain. Ah, I am going to get right to the problem: a specialist! I went to see a gastroenterologist. I was on time and in pain. I filled out the five pages of obligatory forms and waited and waited and waited. Sound familiar?

I was ushered into an examination room for relief, I hoped. In walked a medical practitioner with the usual twenty questions, who checked my weight and height and blood pressure. The usual.

Finally, in walked the doctor. Even by doctor's standards, he was very officious. Another thirty questions ensued, including how long my mother and father had lived, all their medical history, what I ate for breakfast, lunch, and dinner, among other things. I told him I drank a lot of milk, even the healthiest kind—almond.

He checked my eyes, he checked my ears, and he checked my throat. Wait, had I mistakenly gone to an ENT doctor? But, wait again. Suddenly, he acted like he'd had an epiphany, and with great gusto, he exclaimed, "You have irritable bowel syndrome!"

"That Milk Is Killing You"

"What?" I said, "Our dog is supposed to have that."

"Yes," he said. He gave me a list of ten foods I should not eat, and he exalted again, "You have to cut out the milk. It is killing you." An exact quote. He was one happy guy, telling me all this.

Wait a minute, I thought. The good doctor never even examined my stomach, where I could feel it here and there. At that moment, I knew it was a misdiagnosis. I told him, "No, I don't believe I have that." I started to leave the room and walk out into the hallway.

"You have IBS!" he yelled at my back, and it reverberated up and down the hallway.

I turned around and said, "You're confused." (See Chapter 3, "How Some People Have To Be Told," the rejoinder to be used when brevity is important.) Three days later, I got the correct diagnosis of a hernia after an urgent care doctor did a simple physical examination.

I called the gastroenterologist's office back and told the receptionist to tell the doctor (four years of medical school?) I had a hernia, and he should have figured that out.

Hospital Discharge Confusion

Maybe you have had an operation or a procedure at a hospital before. Remember those discharge instructions that told you everything about what to expect? Did you know these write-ups are often understated, out-of-date, or just plain wrong? So, here's another one.

I finally got the proper diagnosis for the hernia, got the pre-tests, and had the surgery. No surprise, my wife and I waited five hours beyond the appointed time for the operation, from the chief of surgery, no less. I made the mistake of scheduling it in the afternoon because I did not like the idea of being at the hospital at 5 a.m. They do that a lot. These surgeons are overbooked, so I say, split the difference. Try to get a mid to late-morning appointment.

I walked out of there (actually was wheeled out because, insurance), and the discharge instructions said there could be a little red spot around my navel. They usually use the scope for hernias these days, a naval and lower stomach entry area. Anyway, it said I might have a little discomfort for several days.

Mr. Happy Is All Purple!

Five days later, I got ready to get into the shower, after giving it a break for about a day and a half. I was mortified. From my navel down to my groin area is all dark black and purple. And my testicles were purple and Mr. Happy was not at all happy; he was nearly all purple as well!

I called the good doctor's office and requested an immediate follow-up. "What is the need for the quick follow-up?" says Judy, the nice receptionist.

"My stomach and groin area are all purple."

"What?"

So, I got in to see the doctor, and without prelude, I threw down my pants and said, "What's going on here?"

"Purple testicles and a purple penis," says the sharp surgeon. "That happens," he says.

"That happens? The discharge instructions don't even hint at something like this."

"Well," says the chief of surgery, "those instructions should probably be updated."

"Well, as the chief of surgery," I told him, "I would think you would be just the one to do it."

More Pain And Aggravation

It's never over until it's over with some of these doctors. About a month after all this, I start experiencing excruciating pain in the lower groin, way down in the groin area if you know what I mean. There were shooting pains that I had to lie down on my office floor, so bad I nearly ran off the road going home. The pains came and went until I was forced to call Judy again—or whoever it was that time.

I described the shooting pains. "Oh, that happens for two months," the nice woman in the doctor's office says.

"What?"

I got back to see this guy again, who is not happy to see me, and I am not happy to see him. So, he examined me and said I didn't have a hernia any longer. Whatever it is, it's not his fault. Goodbye and good luck. He told me to go see a general practitioner.

Your "Confidential" Medical Records

Speaking of doctors and hospitals, do you know how confidential your medical records are? You guessed it. Not confidential at all. You make an appointment to see another doctor, and they say, "I see you were treated at the ER" for some such thing. How did they know that? Well, it turns out that all our records are part of some Epic System of medical data files. You make the appointments, and the doctor gets to see them, whether you want them to or not.

We can, however, request all our medical records, including hard copies, and they must be available within thirty days, according to federal law. We patients can see all the notes that doctors make on our cases, even when in the hospital—if we can work through those tricky hospital portals with the protected passcodes.

Some people have to be told. Doctors need to be told by people more than any other profession. It is good karma to do it, and please remember, you, not the doctor, are in charge of your health.

Oh, my aching back! Like almost the majority of people over forty, I have had recurring back pain over the years. What it took me decades to learn, literally, I can pass most of it on in the next couple of minutes to you.

So, I went to the spine and pain office. They offer non-surgical solutions to pain. Yes, there are such places. Just look around. But even these folks should be under strict supervision! I'd had dozens and dozens of medical appointments for my back. I was giving a new doctor a chance because he was actually an Army Major in the Medical Corp., getting part of his residential training, I suppose.

Back Pain From Demon Rum?

Ever hopeful, I described my back pain. He said, with a great deal of assurance, it is either one of two things. Either I was drinking too much or I had diabetes. I knew it was neither of those. I had my first serious back pain episode in college. I was captain of the tennis team, and out of the blue, I could not get out of bed one day. So, I knew it was not Demon Rum (back then I had just discovered it). Further, I had been checked for diabetes and didn't have that either.

But let's give this guy a chance. I was there for acupuncture, his supposed specialty. I lay on my back, trying to engage in conversation with the medical provider before some needle is going to go in. It should help you relax, depending on the topic, of course.

As I lay on my stomach, he started to put each of these fifty or so little needles in my back. Each one hurt. "Do you ever count these needles when they go in so you can count the number when they go out?"

"Ha, ha, ha. No, that never happens, no need. I have been doing this a long time; don't worry about it."

The good doctor knows best, right? You have already figured out the ending of this one, right? He got done, and I put on my t-shirt, and my outer shirt, went home, had dinner with my wife, watched TV, read in bed, and went to sleep.

I Gave The Doctor The Needle

I woke up in the middle of the night. I had to go to the bathroom. When I did, I noticed a pain in my upper back that would not go away. I woke up my wife, took off my t-shirt, and she found a little needle with a tiny little flag stuck in my upper back. I went back to that doctor's office, but for the good Major/doctor, I just put the needle in an envelope with a "kind" note for the doctor and left it at the front desk for him.

Some of these doctors have to be told. It's a good thing and good karma. After that, the first time I went to that office to see someone else, they said, "So you are the famous Mr. Hampton?"

I said, "No, more like infamous."

Do you have serious neck pain, often called cervical spine pain? I had it for years and years. I had an old girlfriend in Michigan before I moved to Washington DC. It was one of those off and on, great and terrible relationships. Back then, I had neck pain all the time, day and night.

Before I moved to Washington, she said that after I got away from her, the neck pain would probably go away. And for many months, the pain was actually gone! After a while of living in Washington, though, it became a pain in the neck again. No surprise.

I was living in an old church in Georgetown at the time, built by Presbyterians in the late 1700s, in the 1500 block of North 33rd Street, NW. We were planning one of our large parties. (Chris Matthews, remember him from when he was the Hardball host? He was a Capitol Hill cop at the time who never stopped talking, so we put him in the basement.) I had to be at my best that night. What to do?

I had another gal pal at the time who suggested she could take me to some clinic in Washington that did acupuncture. But how could I get in that day?

"Not to worry," she said. It turned out she spoke Chinese, and when we got there, she spoke Chinese to them. Electric acupuncture—little needles hooked up to some machine.

Within a couple of hours, the pain went totally away. Amazing! And it did not really come back for a couple of decades. So, acupuncture might just work for you, but you may want to take it with a grain of salt if they say you have to go back six or eight times to see if it works. Probably not.

When the neck pain came back with a vengeance a couple of decades later, the acupuncture gave no relief, so I went to see an orthopedic surgeon. I had the examination, I had the tests, and then I was called back to get the results. His office said I had some sort of narrowed discs or bulging discs or this or that or something else, and I would have to go find a solution elsewhere. I said I wanted to talk to the doctor, but he was not available. Call and repeat, call and repeat. He would not return my calls.

He worked out of two offices, so I called his other office to find out when he would be there. I went in the late afternoon and waited until he came out. He was not happy to see me. I told him I was in extreme pain and needed help. I told him that I believed that some sort of injections in my neck would help.

Pain Killer In Place Of Real Care

"No," he said, "you cannot do injections in the neck." He wrote me a prescription on the spot for some sort of pain killer and all but ran out of the office.

I never filled it.

Has a doctor told you what can get done and what can't? Chances are overwhelming that they have. Don't take it at face value. Find out for yourself. It is your body and you are in charge of it!

Later, I found my way to another no-surgery solution for pain, and they said, "Sure, we can give you an epidural in your neck. It's a combination of steroids and an anti-inflammatory that can break the cycle of pain, quiet down the inflammation, and enhance the healing."

In two days, the neck pain was totally gone.

Have you been to see a surgeon lately? I hope not, but have you ever met a surgeon who didn't recommend cutting? If you did, you likely got a good one.

Here is my long and really unnerving experience that can maybe save you much pain and despair. You most likely know this already, or maybe intuitively, but it is worth repeating: if you need to get cut into, try at all costs to avoid the open incisions. For years, orthopedic surgeons have done arthroscopic surgeries on knees.

What To Do About Knee Pain

I have had more than my share of these scope jobs for pain, swelling, heat, and maybe a torn meniscus. One can be out of there the same day and back in action in a few days, but don't think you should be running on it anytime soon. I was told I could, and that was a big mistake.

Even some lung cancer surgeries can be done by arthroscopy these days. The method offers far less of a shock to the system and a far better recovery time.

Of course, the idea of telling you all these episodes I have had with doctors is to share with you so that you can be on the lookout so it does not happen to you. I am going to share a cautionary story. It's most likely not going to happen to you, but it might be appropriate to say, "Forewarned is to be forearmed."

After years of tennis and jogging and three scopes on my left knee, I still had incredible pain and swelling in that knee. A surgeon convinced me to have a synovectomy, which is a procedure to remove inflammation. In my case this meant a big, open incision to rebuild the knee. I had the surgery, and the pain was so intense that people who came to visit me in the hospital had to leave. They could not stand to see me in such pain. The doctor could not be located to tell the hospital staff to do something.

There is no reason why anyone in a hospital should have to experience long and unremitting pain, so tell them in advance that you will not accept it. My sister had unbearable pain after a hip replacement and was left out in a hallway afterward, pleading for relief. Some people have to be told and, in this case, told in advance.

I got out and started the rehab and worked at it and worked at it and worked at it. I was at the rehab place for one day, and the guy next to me said, "You are not making much progress with that crooked knee."

It was dawning on me. No kidding! I had about a twenty-four-degree contracture in my left knee.

So, don't let something like this happen to you. Anticipate every single thing that can go wrong with any doctor's advice, including with getting treatment, especially surgery. You have heard the saying, "the operation was a success, but the patient died." Hospitals are a hotbed of infections.

There Will Be Side Effects: Find Out In Advance

After my knee fiasco, there began an almost endless saga of doctors and medications and treatments and more surgeries. I belatedly did some research on synovectomy. It said that a common side effect is a contracture. Why didn't anyone tell me that? Why didn't I ask? Why didn't I find out? You can never assume with a doctor.

So, I had him put me under to try to push things back in place to give me more range of motion. No dice. Still later, I found that such a manipulation under anesthesia on a knee has to be done within a week of the operation. Mine had been ten days after. I am okay now, but don't try to play catch-up with your doctors like I have had to do.

Thereupon foreshadowed dozens, well over a hundred, medical appointments, all to deal with this contracture. I had two operations to fix the fix, the last done by one of the very best, at the Vail Clinic. The top athletes in the country have been there.

My knee problem led to seemingly endless back problems. If you have one, prepare for the other.

But that is finally all behind me after a couple decades of coping, so I want to pass these things onto you.

Have you ever gone to physical therapy? If so, you likely know you *never* go to this kind of an office, one where they do the long evaluation and say in one session what they will do for you. Doesn't happen. But you know, you can learn these therapies in short order, and much of the therapy you can do at home, without the elaborate machines.

I'll Be Pooping In My Pants?

At one point after a referral from a doctor's office, I went in for physical therapy. Then I went back and back and back for more appointments until the nice young lady finally said she couldn't keep seeing me for the rest of my life. Really? She couldn't help me? She told me I could anticipate losing control of my bowels and bladder, that it was inevitable, and there was nothing I could do.

That did not sound so good. I wasn't ready for that and it never happened! But I had to figure it out on my own, so off to the chiropractor. I had dozens of adjustments over the course of at least a year. My flexibility seemed to get back after a treatment, and I seemed to maybe get better, but I sure loved to hear those popping vertebrae in my spine.

I had my last appointment because this, too, was not helping. I was going to tell them that this was it, the last session. The receptionist told me the chiropractor wanted to do a re-examination. That means everyone knows that nothing is working, but don't give up on us yet.

A decent guy did the re-examination and said, "I am going to show you how to do some exercises that I think could help."

Only then did it occur to me. Why didn't he suggest these before? I thought the adjustments would do the job, so the exercises did not occur to me.

He had me get down on the floor on a thin mat to do five or six exercises. The back really started to hurt, almost immediately. He gave me some pictures and some directions for the exercises. I took them home, but the exercises, even on a thick rug, really hurt and there was no relief from the pain.

Simple, Short Exercise For Back Pain

About two months later, I was reading a book on the mind, body, workouts, and nutrition. I saw two single paragraphs on what to do for back pain. Core strengthening exercises in two paragraphs, with two simple exercises.

Crunches: Lie on a bed (not any mat or the floor!). Let flat on your back, lock your hands behind your head, bring your knees to a forty-five-degree angle, raise up forty-five degrees, and go back down fifteen times. Rest and repeat five times.

Lie on the bed on your stomach, put your forward weight on your forearms and lift up your back in the air a foot or so. Put it down and do fifteen times. Rest and repeat the set five times.

Presto. My back pain went away. I now do them about every night, and it takes about ten minutes. Did the orthopedic surgeons tell me this? No. Did the spine and pain people tell me this? No. Did the physical therapist tell me this? Most assuredly not. Did the chiropractor tell me this? Kind of, after about fifty visits and when my health insurance would not pay anymore.

So, your doctor may want to tell you, but you may have to tell them, thanks for your opinion, and that is what it is . . . and I will consider it and decide what to do myself; thank you very much.

The Good Doctor Asked About Me?!

Several months after I stopped seeing the chiropractor, I got a handwritten note from one of the very nice receptionists in the office: "Dear Brian, Dr. So and So asked me about you the other day and asked if you were okay. I said I did not know. We would like to hear from you."

That note was followed by another one, with pretty much the same content, after another month. I called the office. "Suzie, how nice of you to send me these thoughtful notes. Am I the only one who gets them?" I teased.

"Tell me about it," said Suzie. "I spend about one day a month writing out over a hundred of these."

I can imagine what you are thinking. Why go through all this medical stuff?

Why, indeed? The idea is that I can pass on to you what I have learned from my experiences, to perhaps spare much pain and heartache, should you have one of these ailments now or in the future.

I woke up with a start. There was this incredibly loud noise, like a lawn mower, but much louder, and it went on and on and on. It was a team of leaf blowers who seemed to be right under my window. On and on and on. It was like 7 a.m. on a Saturday.

Do you know that some people in some neighborhoods have sued against the operation of such leaf blowers because they said it caused them to go deaf? The really loud ones (probably about all of them) are gasoline-powered. The quiet ones operate by batteries. Anyone use those? Of course not.

They went away, and I went back to sleep. When I started to get out of bed, everything was reeling and out of focus. I was weak and dizzy. These systems went on for days and days. Every time I got up, I could barely see or focus. Every time I lay back down, it happened over and over again.

I did not put two and two together about the leaf blowers until later. After a couple weeks of being more and more miserable and really very shaken, I went to the hospital's emergency department.

As you may know, this is not a place you want to be. Two hours to get checked in and get an examination room. Another three hours of visiting medical specialists and various tests, including an MRI on my head in one of those scary closed-in chambers. Why do even the "open" ones have to be closed?

These are good people in the emergency room. They work hard and late under stressful conditions. I had to wait for the specialist to come in. He said the MRI of my brain showed nothing. Ha-ha-ha. Actually, it was a relief.

But wait, the other good news was that there was an actual diagnosis! Vertigo, like in the long-ago Alfred Hitchcock movie where Jimmy Stewart has trouble with heights. This vertigo sounds like it doesn't amount to much, but it really does.

No Known Cause Or Cure?

So great, a diagnosis! But after about thirty minutes of questions and the good young doctor (resident? . . . the kind that work sixty hours a week) finally admitted that nobody knows what causes vertigo and nobody really knows what the cure is. But I could go see an ENT doctor. Just great.

So, when your doctor tells you to go see a specialist, that is not the time to say thanks a lot. That is the time to ask more questions. What is the purpose of seeing the specialist? What questions should be asked of them? As in, if there is no known cause or cure, what do you expect I will find? Be ready with questions for the doctors. The good ones won't mind, and if they do mind, you do not have a good one. This is a test you can perform on the doctor.

"Doctor shopping" is considered a term for finding a doctor who will prescribe what you want. But it is more important to shop and find a good doctor. The time it takes is really worth the effort.

So off to another ENT specialist about the vertigo. The obligatory forty-five-minute wait, with all the mostly pointless questions of the process. Does your doctor's office keep asking you to fill out the same forms on insurance even though none of your insurance has changed? When asked about it, they said, "Because it is our policy." Remember the chapter on "How Some People Have To Be Told" for the comeback on this one.

It Could Be My Brain!

Oh my gosh, off to see another specialist, another really seemingly decent guy. After all the examinations, his conclusion or diagnosis?

"You have vertigo," he says.

I knew that. "What is the cause? What can I do?"

"Well," he says, "it could be your eyes, your ears, or your brain."

"We have eliminated the brain, so what do I do?"

"Come back for some tests," he says.

Tests? I thought he did the tests.

"No, there is a special team of auditory specialists . . ." or some such thing. I was to check in at the front desk for an appointment. But wait, the auditory or whatever team can only see me from 8 a.m. to 10 a.m. on a Tuesday.

"Wait," I say, "I am the patient. How about arranging a time that is convenient for me? Anyway. What can I expect after all these tests?"

"After you have the tests, you can come back for a series of treatments, if what you have is treatable."

Bingo! Has something like this or something close happened to you? This office is not patient-friendly. Use your wits and try something else. Avoid the medical vortex.

Later, I talked to a family member who is a physician's assistant. She said you should try the Epley maneuver, a short series of exercises you can find online. I had not found this online with Google before, but with this in mind, I found a simple chart, a couple short exercises on the bed that I did a couple times a day. And *presto,* the vertigo drifted away.

Good to have the last word. Because I was not given this simple advice, I called back and waited on hold until I could talk to the doctor. Again, in this case, he was a really a decent guy, but he was just no help.

I Hypnotized The Problem Away

When he came on the line, I said, "Doctor, guess what? I hypnotized myself and through audio suggestion, I made the vertigo go away."

"That is great," he said. Though, he had never heard about such a thing, except in maybe Far Eastern medicine. He believed me and thanked me for the insight! And the next time the leaf blowers were under my window, I put ear plugs in—the kind you get from the airlines, just in case.

We have to love these doctors. Can't live without them and it's hard living with them in your life, too. But we can do our health homework and tell it to the doctor every time it is needed. It's our body and our life. Cheers to good health!

And a postscript, a friend said, "What are doctors good for anyway? They can write you the prescriptions that you can't get yourselves."

But wait, there is some good news you may know about. Many states are allowing physicians assistants (PAs, with usually two or three years of medical training) and in some states, nurse practitioners, to write prescriptions. Most of these PAs work in hospitals and in clinics with other regular MDs, but others have established their own practices.

Find out if your state legislature has approved such a practice. Guess who opposes PAs from being able to prescribe in many states? You guessed it: many state medical associations.

And postscript number two on doctors. If you have a real beef with a doctor and some unconceivable bill, either warn the doctor's office or send a letter of complaint to the state board that oversees medical professionals in your state.

Finally: A Diagnosis!

Years ago, my older sister, who is a clinical psychologist (PhD), was experiencing a recurring problem. She just did not have any appetite. This went on and on for a while, and then she saw a doctor.

The office and the doctor ran a series of tests and made her answer a series of questions. One cannot make this up. With a big run up and building up to the conclusion, the doctor was finally ready to offer his professional opinion. My sister waited in suspense, between hope and anxiety.

"You have no appetite!" the doctor said. That was it.

I am not sure what my sister told the Good Doctor, but knowing her, it was mighty good!

Chapter 6

Ouch! Enduring Dr. Pain, The Dentist

The patient is sitting in the dental chair. The good dentist is hard at work, filling a routine single cavity. One of his many assistants comes in and says, "Doctor, there is a call you have to take."

The dentist leaves the room and gets on the line. The caller is from the Mercedes Benz dealership. He gives the dentist a quote on the new Mercedes SUV he has in mind to buy.

The dentist gets back to the patient. "Gosh, it looks like you are going to need a root canal."

AARP says we can brush away many health risks. Wow! I like the general idea: a sharper brain, stronger heart, lower cancer risk, healthier kidneys, a fatter wallet, and a better sex life—all by brushing and flossing. There is one other thing they do not tell us in the dental offices, but first, let's talk about getting prepared to even face those dentists.

Do you know how to have the least amount of pain to your mouth and wallet when you have to go to the dental chair? This is the trial and error that nobody wants to have, so I believe I can help on one of these challenges we all face.

The Colonel's Only Fear: The Dentist

Many years ago, the Deputy Commander Officer of the 4th Psychological Operations Group in Saigon told me of his greatest fear. (Find it also in my future book, *Saigon Warriors PSYOP in Vietnam: They Ran the War for Hearts & Minds.)*

His name was LTC Bart Beers. One day, he said to me, "Brian, I am not afraid of anything, but I am afraid of going to the dentist."

One night, there was a roaring party in Saigon. It was "late," almost an hour past the 9 p.m. curfew for being off the streets.

A friend came up and said, "Brian, Colonel Beers is getting upset. He is talking about closing the party down because of the curfew. You better talk to him."

I ushered him over to the center of the room and told him that everyone would like to hear a few words from him.

"At ease," I declared.

The room fell silent. He came to life and gave a ringing minute oration on the dedication and loyalty of all the troops. He gave the room a salute and got a hearty round of applause, then went to the door and stepped out. Considerably later, the discovery was made that Colonel Beers had walked into the closet and passed out.

Years ago, it hurt a great deal more at the dentist, or so one would think. May God bless her soul . . . my mother would make the appointments for the dentist and not tell us kids until the day of.

The Dreaded Dental Appointment

But who is making the appointments for us?

There is something you can do to help yourself. Make that appointment for Monday morning. That way, you have all weekend, turn in Sunday night, and bingo! Monday morning, have the appointment and be done with it. The next best option is Friday afternoon. Hey, it's Friday. You are on the glidepath to the weekend.

Usually, when you leave the dental office, you are going to feel better that it is over and done.

I was waiting in a dental office once, and I saw a woman in her mid-twenties or so waiting her turn like she did not have a care in the world. If you can, make small talk with people in the medical offices. I find it helps to relax me. I asked her if she was as relaxed as she appeared. She said she was relaxed. I asked her how in the world she did that?

"I decided not to let it bother me" she said.

Wow! Mind over matter. Further, she said she was more relaxed now that she was going to Arlington Family Dental. She said her previous dentists were finding cavities that turned out not to be there. Wow. Imagine that.

I did not go to Arlington Family Dental for years. It was just down the street, it was convenient, and easy parking. It is in a house converted to an office, which used to be home to a psychic. How good could that be? I was used to seeing Dr. Pain, the dentist forty-five minutes away.

Are You Seeing Dr. Pain?

For years, I saw Dr. Pain. Actually, at first, there was little or no pain, but after the years went by, Dr. Good Guy became more and more grumpy and he started inflicting more and more pain. Very slowly, I decided that not only must he not like me. He really must not like his own life. Not a good thing in a dentist.

One day, I am in the chair for a routine examination. They did the X-rays, always the X-rays. He got out one of those little metal hammers and tapped the teeth on the upper right. "Does that hurt?" he asked.

"No," I said.

He said I needed a root canal.

"Say what?" I said. I think he drove a Buick. Maybe he wanted to trade up.

"You almost jumped out of the chair," he said.

"No, I didn't."

"Yes, you did."

I went to a new dentist, you know, the root-canal type. He did the little silver hammer thing.

"Does that hurt?"

"No."

"You have an infection. Take these antibiotics, and you will be fine."

And so I was. What a great guy. He could have done the root canal. How would I know? I sent him a gift basket for Christmas.

Many years ago, I had a dentist I really liked. He examined me one day and said, "It looks like you have a cavity in your tooth number this or so . . ."

Who knows these numbers? Oh no.

"Does it hurt," he asked?

"No," I said.

"Well forget it then. Don't worry about it."

But The "Numbing" Part Hurts The Most!

Later, that dentist retired and sold his practice—probably because he was not making the money he could have. The guy who bought the practice (I remember his name. First the same as mine). Real personable guy. Too personable. You know how the good dentists kind of hide the needle with their hand before they jam it in?

Woody Allen once said that he is only afraid of two things: needles and cancer. He says he is not even afraid of death. He just does not want to be there when it happens.

How long can you remember a single visit to the dentist, especially one a few decades ago? Don't you love it when they say they are going to numb it up? Hey, that is the part that hurts the most. So, Dr. B. has this needle that I seem to remember to this day must have been like four inches long.

Show Me The Money, Not The Needle!

He brings it up in his right hand. It is sticking straight up in the air as it's glistening. I can't take my eyes off of it. He holds it there and holds it there. He seems to be thinking.

He finally says, "Brian, why is it that the sleepiest you are all night is when it is time to get up in the morning?"

"I don't know," I said.

"Why is that? It seems like you should be more rested in the morning." The needle is pointed straight in the air, it seemed to be a foot long, glistening in the bright light.

"I don't know. I just don't know," I said.

So, a couple suggestions. If they don't kind of hide the needle with their open hand, that's a clue. But better yet, look how you can avoid the needle. Like, do I need the numbing? How about you try it for a while, and if it really hurts, I will go with it.

You know how they put those bright lights right in your face? Take your sunglasses in there. Put them on before they swing you back. Maybe they have their own shades, or not. Yours are probably more comfortable anyway.

Sometimes it is easy to miss the obvious. Make sure they put that gel on the little cotton stick on your gum in advance. Sometimes they forget, like Dr. Pain started forgetting. Hey, if they pinch your cheek and push it in and out, that helps, a kind of forgotten art. Some still do this, though. If you have one who does the gel and the cheek thing, you likely have a good dentist.

Teeth Extraction: Being Forewarned Is Being Forearmed

The reason I wrote this book, dear reader, is to make a positive difference in the lives of others by offering up techniques I have learned through hard experience. Learning about dentistry has been one of the biggest challenges I have experienced in the area of taking care of the body, the temple of the mind.

Try to conduct online research on the treatment after teeth extractions. There are almost as many different suggested variations of routines as there are links. For example, one link to a dentist's office says to use a cold compress on the affected area for thirty minutes several times on the first day. Another says use this for twenty minutes, take a twenty-minute break, then do it for ten more minutes. Still another says ten on and ten off, and so on. Each suggestion is good, but I found that ten and ten was the most workable for me.

Now, allow me to share a couple more stories about extractions from which I learned first-hand experience. I went to a dental office recently, and among everything else, they said first up, I needed an extraction of a back tooth. I shared with the dentist a very distasteful episode I experienced in graduate school at Michigan State University. I got an extraction, and the gum did not stop bleeding for three days. I was in bed, with blood all over. And I had blood clots that seemed to grow to almost as big as a golf ball.

A very kind housemate had seen enough, and one night, he took me to a Lansing hospital Emergency Department. The good folks there could not help, and they reached the dentist at his home. He came in and did something that must have been so awful that I have repressed the memory. Then, for the next week, I had to go back to the same dentist several times because I got several dry sockets (no clot), and he had to prick the gum to get it to bleed to form a clot.

Anyway, I shared this experience with the dentist, and he said, "That doesn't happen."

I politely told him that I was sitting in his chair, and it happened to me.

Later, I saw another dentist for his opinion and he agreed that I needed to have the tooth extracted. I went back to the first because they offered nitrous oxide, and the other did not.

Remember, "Fool me once, shame on you. Fool me twice, shame on me." Here is where I messed up, not with the same dentist, but with two different dentists on the same issue. I went in for the extraction, could not feel the Novocain much, the extraction even less.

Home free! I thought. I told the dentist it was well done, and we shook hands before he walked out.

Then I started checking the barn door after the horses had already escaped. I asked his assistant if they put in any sutures. She said they only do stitches for bottom teeth, not the top, which made no sense to me. She gave me the "Instructions After Extractions," in tiny little type that said I was destined to bleed a little. She made a point of telling me how to gently rinse my mouth with salt water.

I had gauze in my mouth over the gum, got into the car, and noticed I was bleeding all over my chin. I had a couple handkerchiefs and they ended up bloody all over. Thereupon began a very frightening dental saga. As you probably know, the idea is to develop a clot in the gum pocket, but the gum kept bleeding. The clot would fall out and start bleeding again. One is not advised to try to sleep with the gauze because of possible choking. The preponderance of advice is to leave in the gauze for thirty minutes. Have plenty on hand because the dental office will probably not give you enough.

I slept that night (somewhat), and the next morning, I got up and found blood all over my chin and caked inside my mouth. I opened my mouth and a deluge of blood poured out. My immediate concern was not so much the current condition but what was going to happen in the future and what I could do about it. I knew the dental office was closed for the weekend.

Here is what I learned. I recalled, after the fact, that I had extractions after that first college episode and I'd had no problems with clotting, I believe because I had gotten stitches and they were the kind that dissolve in several days and do not have to be taken out. Don't be like me this last time. Be assertive about the possibility for stitches.

Do not start the salt water rinsing until twenty-four hours after the extraction. That was in the written, but not the oral, instructions. No matter what, do not spit. With a teaspoon of salt in warm water, just hold it in the mouth for a few seconds a few times and let the water drop from your mouth, do not swish it around. This routine is recommended about four times a day.

If you are having problems with getting a clot, try folding a wet black tea bag up in the pocket. It helped me on the way. Do *not* drink hot fluids or food for a couple days. That information was *not* in the instructions. Neither was information on keeping your blood pressure lower, which helps with the clotting that should be more or less stabilized within twenty-four hours. After a full day of these treatments, I was out of the woods.

There are also fairly new prescribed liquid medications, which can be soaked in the gauze, which is supposed to bring about that all-important, more permanent clot in thirty minutes! I did not try that, but I am thinking that remedy could do no wrong and might actually help.

A final word on extractions. Make sure your dental office is open the day after the extraction. Many are closed on Fridays. Also, check to be sure the home phone number of the dentist is listed on the release instructions. A local dental office relates the home emergency number of the dentist on their voicemail—a strong indication of a good dentist.

Dreaded Dental Decision: Help To Pick The Right One

Choosing the right dental practice can be quite a dilemma. Just like with medical doctors, one can receive far different advice from two different dentists for the same condition.

And, like other doctors, they can frighten a patient without even trying or maybe even thinking about it. "Look at all these X-rays on the big screen. You have twenty teeth needing various different treatments!"

Like the doctors, they are the dentists, though they are called doctors as well. Different dental practices sometimes have far different approaches from each other.

I have dealt with a family practice where the staff called the dentist by their first name. Really! And the office actually called me on the phone to confirm an appointment, rather than sending some text to my phone. Yet, the patient-friendly office may not have the full services you are looking for.

Find out in advance exactly what you are getting by asking plenty of questions upfront. For example, one practice might provide an evaluation and a cleaning in one visit. A more assembly-line type of practice might take a full hour with the consultation and then not be able to schedule the cleaning until three months later.

Let's face it, as my wife says, if a dental office finds you have good insurance, they will be more inclined to offer you the Platinum Plan for endless procedures just because they can. Just human nature at work. For some seniors, they may offer the Platinum Plan for teeth that will last decades, while the patient may have a tin can body already playing in overtime.

What to do? Ask plenty of questions at every turn and compare the answers. One dentist told me I had a diseased gum and I needed an extraction and then probably an implant. Of course, this was not my first rodeo.

"How about an antibiotic?" I suggested.

"It will come back with a vengeance." he said.

"I had this before (different tooth), and it never, ever came back."

"It will come back," he said.

All this was not my opinion. It was based on empirical data, meaning based on my real experience.

"How about a water pick to help remove the pockets in the gum?" I asked.

"No," he said. "It will only remove debris from between the teeth."

But only several months before, another dentist suggested I buy a water pick for the very same condition.

I took that dentist's advice and based on my own research, I added a few drops of what is called "under the gums irrigate" to the hand-held pick, with good results. The water pick is a bit awkward. You have to lean over the sink as the water comes out of your mouth and probably fill it up two or three times for each use. The directions say to point the pick at the front and back of the teeth on both sides, up and down, but I found that only the front was practical in my case.

Just like with doctors, we patients have to be patient, try to get other opinions, add a bit of research, and decide for ourselves. I's our teeth and gums, our budget, and our decision. We are in charge.

What's The Deal With "Sedation Dentistry?"

A near-by dentist runs display ads in the local paper. Above his name, which is in ALL CAPS, it says, Sedation Dentistry, which could be a very good thing. The copy in the ad asks if your smile conflicts with your "vibrancy and positivity." A bit goofy. But who wants pain? So I checked out the practice.

The practice was big and thriving and inside was a flyer that said, "Sedation Dentistry . . . a reason to dream." I checked it out. Inside, it asked, "Are you scared, even terrified, to pick up the phone to schedule . . . overwhelmed by the thoughts of repeated visits to the dentist?"

A bit overdone, wouldn't you say? At the bottom, the name and address of the dentist was stamped on. Perhaps this flyer was put out by the Association For Sedation Dentistry?

I checked it out, asked questions, and read the fine print. Another term they use is conscious sedation. First of all, the nitrous oxide (laughing gas) is offered when you breathe it, which takes effect immediately but only lasts a couple minutes or so. They put it over your nose, and you get happy and relaxed. It can be used for extractions, root canals, scaling (which removes plaque from under the gums), and other painful procedures. A friend told me you still sort of feel the pain, but you don't care!

Another method of sedation dentistry can be a tablet sedative. Typically, the dental office will give you a prescription to take the night before to get a good night's rest and then another one before the procedure. One example is Triazolone, which I'm told really takes all the pain away. This is a super benefit, but you need a designated driver to take you home.

I have found by checking around that most dental offices do not provide this full sedation dentistry. A few more offer nitrous oxide, yet insurance will often not cover it, but if that is the case, in my opinion, it is well worth the out-of-pocket cost.

Why Our Overall Dental Health Is A Big Deal

Studies indicate the overall health risks from poor dental habits that can ripple through our body that are truly scary. While uncommon, people can get an inflammation inside the heart, caused by germs from the gums. Poor periodontal health can lead to chronic kidney disease. And those with gum disease are much more likely to have Alzheimer's disease.

Taking care of one's teeth and gums can obviously save money on dental costs. Look out, men with erectile dysfunction (who came up with this term?), you are three times more likely to have periodontal disease. Imagine how that research was conducted!

Okay, this dental health is really important to overall health. How many times has the dental hygienist told you that you have gingivitis or you are on the way to periodontal problems? Plenty, right? What they do not tell you is about the best way to prevent it.

Sure, you floss at least once a day. They always tell you that.

Beyond that, buy those battery-operated toothbrushes. Brush your teeth morning and night the usual way. But during the process, hold the vibrating brushes just above the gum line for one second, above and below, top and bottom. What this does is to oxidize the gums, enhance blood circulation, and help take toxins away.

Difference Between Toothbrush And Teethbrush

A friend of mine lives in West Virginia. He occasionally asks his out-of-town friends how we can know that the toothbrush was invented in West Virginia. Answer: If it were invented in another state, it would have been called a teethbrush.

In the rare circumstances that you have to see the dentist and the periodontist on the same day, in the same office, you can offer a friendly competition like I did once.

"Okay, guys," I said to each before the action. "Whoever inflicts the less pain, gets one hundred dollars in cash." The dentist seemed like he was a sure winner. After two injections, there was not much pain.

Then he put on the temporary crown. "You are good for two or three weeks until the final crown comes in."

"Wow! You could be the winner," I told him.

For a "pocket" in the gum, before the "scaling" (try to avoid this). The periodontist did one injection and then another, and then another, and then another . . . hold on. Still doesn't hurt much though, I thought (see the Chapter on "The Law Of The Universe").

"Anymore?"

There were at least eight.

"One more."

"Holy Moly!" He'd stuck the needle to the roof of my mouth. I thought I had revisited Dr. Pain.

On the way out, I told him he had lost the competition, so no one hundred dollars.

He laughed and said, "Yeah, that's the pallet shot."

Tell them to stop before they get that far.

But payback is good. The periodontist is a graduate of the University of Michigan, and I went to Michigan State University. So, when MSU beats our big rival, Michigan, I call up his office and leave a message about how his team lost, thus giving him the needle.

Meanwhile, the same day I went home, sitting there doing nothing but working on the computer, the temporary falls out. I had to go back the next day, a Saturday to get the temporary put in again. I declared a draw between the doctors. I didn't pay either.

Biggest House Gives Out The Most Candy

The biggest house in my neighborhood is owned by, you guessed it, a dentist, and an implant specialist at that. It costs $2,000 to $3,000 per implant. The guy never seems to be there. He's on vacation to London and France. The only ones around are the endless number of home maintenance people.

He is friendly enough, though not much on the small talk, which is probably why he picked a profession where his patients can't talk much because there is always something in their mouth. But you have to give him this. He and his wife hand out more candy to the kids in the neighborhood on Halloween than anyone else by far.

I guess it's good for business.

Chapter 7

Your Dog Loves You!
The Vet Loves Your Money

You have no doubt heard the famous saying by President Harry S. Truman: "If you want a friend in Washington, get yourself a dog."

Politics is a blood sport in Washington, and if you are not controversial in Washington, it's because you aren't doing anything.

But you already know, there is fierce politics everywhere you go, on every street corner: office politics, campus politics, labor politics, politics in the professions, and on and on.

My suggestion? If you have not done so already, get yourself a dog and a whole new world will open to you. If you already have a dog, check your signals with a fellow dog-lover, me.

Dogs are famous. There are White House dogs. There are YouTube dogs who get the paper and a bottle of beer from the fridge,. There are dogs who are trotted out during the University of Nebraska basketball games, trotting on top of the ball, moving it down the floor, and getting the frisbee midair.

Maybe that's why there are so many sayings about dogs. Here are just a few (add some more and give yourself a prize!):

- I'll be doggone
- Dog tired
- Sick as a dog
- Dogging it
- That dog won't hunt
- *Dog Day Afternoon* (good Al Pacino movie)
- Three Dog Night, a 70s band

- It's not the dog in the fight but the fight in the dog. *Roger that!*
- Be the kind of person your dog thinks you are
- It's a dog's life
- Junkyard dog lawyer—the kind you want, not the one to be facing
- You can't teach an old dog new tricks . . . but who says so?

How about in your neighborhood? You see all these people walking, but what percent have dogs with them? My neighborhood is at about 70 percent. Just for fun, I counted for a few hours one day.

Now the real question: Is the person walking the dog? Or is the dog walking the person or people?

Another saying for us is walking the dog. I'm not sure exactly what that means, but I've heard it often.

"I will dog walk you," Rapper Cardi B said in a Twitter (now X) feud with conservative Tomi Lahren.

Let's say you are out for a walk. You see someone walking the dog. They say, "Fido doesn't bite."

What do you say? Try this. "Does Fido know that?"

A Child Or A Dog Or Both?

If you have a dog, you already know this. If you don't, you may have heard this. Having a dog is like having a small child, kind of. You let the dog out, then let the dog in, then let the dog out, and so forth. A couple could have children or dogs, children and dogs? If so, you are super multitaskers. Special awards go to you.

When I think of awards, I occasionally think about former Senator Al Franken of Minnesota. You may remember he starred in Saturday Night Live many years ago and was hounded (another dog word) out of the Senate for inappropriate behavior toward women. Anyway, his book was called *Al Franken: Giant of the Senate*. See my chapter on "The Law Of The Universe" because he violated it just with that title.

He was in the middle of a book tour when the scandal drew him back to Washington.

Anyway, the soon-to-be-former Senator Franken had a chapter in his book devoted just to awards. He thought it was funny, all the awards Members of Congress accrue, from every interest group imaginable. They put them on their office walls, of course. So, at the end of his awards chapter, Al gives the name and phone number of a staffer and invites the reader to call her if the reader wants to give the boss an award.

So, I do have a "Wall of Respect" (as they call it in Washington) and I do accept awards, but then who would offer?

And the protocol for dog walking, wow! It's a world unto itself. In our neighborhood, I am certain there are dog watchers—people who peer out of the window and see you scoop the poop after your dog. Some houses actually have warning signs or friendly admonitions such as scoop your dogs' poop and others with eye-catching pictures.

So, what to do when you walk the dog? First, I have found that one does not need to buy all those little plastic bags from the pet store. You can just use the plastic bags that wrap the morning newspaper. Put it in your pocket, walk Jasper, your dog along, and bingo! Your dog does the job. Careful! Those dog watchers are watching.

Now, I am not saying I have ever done this, but I may have seen people who have leaned over and just pretended to pick up the poop. Do you hang on to it? Put it in your pocket? This is important stuff, obviously.

I Know Who You Are: Come And Get Your Poop

Do you belong to a neighborhood association? I do, and the association sends around all these emails that people post about everything imaginable. There is also a post of the day. I think my favorite from about a year ago was something like this: come and pick up the poop!

A woman posted her name and street address, and said she saw a guy walk by with his dog who did a poop, and the guy kept on walking! She said she was waiting for him to come back and pick it up. He knows who he is.

Then she added another line or two to say that this was not the first time it had happened—probably different people.

Then she related something that went like this. "Another time, I saw a man with a dog who did his business on my lawn and the guy came up and knocked on my door and confessed but said he could not pick it up because he had high blood pressure, and then he ran away."

Present For A Secret Agent

Along the same lines is one of those GEICO commercials, I believe it was. The husband is sprucing himself up in the bathroom, looking at himself in the mirror, seemingly thinking he is some sort of a super being.

His wife intrudes and says, "Hey, Secret Agent Man, come and clean it up. Your dog just left a present for you in the hallway."

There is another side of dogs that you need to know about if you do not already. One of the biggest cash cows an entrepreneur can get into is the veterinary business. Do you know what I mean? Most of the employees get into the clinics because they really love the cats and dogs, that is surely clear. The owners of the clinics, not so much.

This sounds obvious, but like lots of things, it's obvious after you have already been initiated. They will run up your tabs to unimaginable heights unless you make it clear you will do what is necessary and not one more thing. I know of a guy who takes his dog to the vet, and every time, he gets hit with hundreds of dollars of charges to send away the blood or cultures to a special lab, do a sonogram.

He just pays and says, "Thank you very much."

How To Keep Your Vet Bill Low

My wife takes the dog to the same vet and her bill is always under a hundred dollars. How? She makes it very clear to the people at the desk that she will pay for what she brought him there for and nothing else unless she specifically approves it in advance. This sounds like a standard business practice, but the word seems to get around, and her bills are always far smaller because of her forcible mentality.

The potentially worst are the urgent care vet places. Be careful when your dog has a serious ailment. If you take him there in the middle of the night you will find some technician will come out with some clipboard to show you all these potentially outrageous costs.

And pay right then and there, otherwise no service, so "buyer beware."

But in extreme cases, where one of these clinics may have ripped you off, there is a recourse. Some of these shyster urgent care for pets places could provide all sorts of treatments, never give a diagnosis, and keep running up the tab because they didn't do the right thing from the beginning.

Say your dog is diagnosed with inflammatory bowel disease. The standard treatment for that is commonly steroids. But the urgent care place may never even suggest it. I know, it happened to me.

The Licensing Board Is Their Hot Button

Recourse! For veterinarians there is a Board of Veterinary Medicine or a similar such name. You issue a complaint or provide a warning or a promise to the vet, and your complaint will be investigated.

But, more importantly, we know that taking time to make friends (see Chapter 22) is one vital key to a fulfilling, happy life. We have our dogs, and they love us unconditionally. When we have a bad day, we are still the same great person when we go home.

In my youth, I knew guys who had dogs just so they could walk on the beach and meet more women. You are a dog person, you know. You walk in the park and many of the other dog people will take time to chat about your dogs. It's always a conversation starter.

Protect Your Dog From Identity Theft

Our dog, Jasper, the King Charles Cavalier, needs to take special medication for his heart condition, but it is not so bad because his prescription is actually for, get this, a generic

Viagra. I call up the pharmacy for a refill of his prescription, and the guy asks me his date of birth. I tell him that Jasper is a dog, look for Jasper K. Hampton.

The pharmacist says, "No, we need his birthday."

I say, "We don't know his birthday. In fact, I remember this issue came up before, and you just gave him an arbitrary birthday." He asked me what it was. I said, "I am not sure I remember. You picked the date."

He said he was sorry (right), but I'd have to give him the birthday—that it's for privacy reasons. "What? For Jasper, our dog?"

Luckily, after several guesses, I got lucky and picked the big day. Later, I went to the pharmacy counter. The pharmacist was on the phone so I could not give him the message in person. I addressed the woman behind the counter and said, "Please thank Vic for protecting the identify of our dog, Jasper. Not a day goes by that someone is not trying to steal his identify."

There was a blank stare, of course. One has to amuse oneself in public sometimes.

I think it was Nick Nolte, the star of movies and TV, who was interviewed a year or so ago. He had moved to Hawaii where he is semi-retired. He said he was happy. Why?

In order, he said: "I have my dogs, and (long pause) I have my wife."

What? He might have been put in the doghouse for that!

Chapter 8

Watch Out! Protect Yourself From Crazed Drivers

They're everywhere! They're everywhere! Like Chicken Man. They're everywhere! They're everywhere!

Bad drivers. Crazy drivers. There are impatient drivers because of more congestion and commutes are longer. Road-rage drivers . . . what to do?

You know the deal. There are two lanes merging into one. You have the right of way, but a driver tries to cut you off from the rear and pass in your blind spot on the right side. What the heck!

You wait patiently to make a left turn at rush hour. There is no helpful little green arrow. The good news is you are next in line to turn. You venture into the middle of the intersection, and, being a good driver, you turn on your left directional a block before. They keep coming. The cars behind you are honking and honking.

Then you crane your neck, the light turns yellow, you edge out, and the cars keep coming. You know you are turning on red now, but you go for it. The bad news is the driver streaks through the intersection from the other way. You escape, but barely.

You have taken an access road to get on a main highway, and you know the intersection well. There's very busy, speeding traffic. There is one of those old, yellow yield signs. Being a good driver, who doesn't want to have a fender bender, you come to a stop—or you try to come to a stop.

You are still moving and craning your neck, and that's when the car behind you starts to blow their horn.

The Dreaded Tailgater

You are going thirty miles per hour in a neighborhood with a twenty-five mils per hour speed limit. That's kind of okay, except there is a tailgater behind you. They get closer and closer. Do you speed up? Do you slow down? Do you pull over? Do you drive the same speed and curse out loud? You brake check—that is, you touch your brakes so they slow down. Or maybe you turn on your lights, so they think you have done a brake check.

The car in front of you went really slowly—so slowly that they just made it through the yellow light, but there is no time for you. But you are a good citizen, so you stop and wait. It's one of those long lights. You know where they all are. The light turns green and you get ready, but the car behind you honks its horn.

They say the shortest period of measurable time is the time between when the light turns green and the car behind you honks.

What do you do? The one-finger salute? We know that's a very bad idea. The Second Amendment of the Constitution and all. Let's compare what you do to what I do. First, I want to introduce you to Brenda. She used to work for me in an office where I worked.

Brenda has a wild sense of humor. She will say anything to anybody. She is fearless. On her back bumper she has a sticker that says, "Graduate Road Rage School of Driving." It's better than the ones that say, "If you can read this, back off, buster!"

So, one summer afternoon, Brenda and her husband are out for a drive. Their windows are down. It's a lovely day. Some driver nearby does something bizarre and offends Brenda, something that no one should ever do. Her husband told me what happened.

Hot Coffee In The Crotch

Brenda is riding shotgun. The highway has four lanes. Brenda and her mild-mannered husband are in the left of the two forward lanes. At a light, the offending car of guys pulls up to the right of Brenda and jeers at the two of them. Brenda has just bought a cup of steaming hot Dunkin' Donuts coffee. Brenda gets out of her car, walks over, smiles, bends over, and pours the scalding coffee in the guy's crotch. When the light turns green, my understanding is the offending car stands still at the light. Sudden and extreme pain will do that to you.

I don't suggest anything like that. But should you be in a situation where you really need to get away from someone pursuing in the auto from behind, the formula is to make a series of left-hand turns. Leave them back there. Makes sense, doesn't it?

So what do you do to deal with these crazed, bad, and offensive nuts behind the wheel? When someone honks unnecessarily from behind me (it is always unnecessary for me) I wave my hand. That is the full hand, back and forth, all the fingers and thumb showing. What am I signaling? I don't know. They don't know. In my mind, I am saying, "You had no reason to honk, so you must be a friend of mine. I'm wishing you well. Howdy."

Just A Wave Or The Evil Eye?

When I do that (about every time), my wife says, "Brian, are you crazy? Do you want to get shot?"

I say, "Not today. I am just waving hello." It makes me feel better that I did something, and nothing has happened (yet).

A friend and I had a discussion about this. This is important, obviously. What she does is glare at the driver. For example, someone stops right in the middle of the street for no reason. She will pull out around them, slow down, and glare at them. I do this too. It is strangely satisfying. What do you do?

I read about a rich guy once who became so infuriated with bad drivers that he made it his hobby to do something about it when he retired. He bought an old car and when a driver made a mistake driving, he would not avoid the fender bender. If it wasn't going to be serious, he would just let it happen. Then, he would jump out and take a picture of the scene. He bought a new old car and repeated this again and again, happy in his retirement.

Think of all the untoward things people do in moving cars, other than that, I mean. They eat. They text. How many odd things can you name? Recently, I read in the paper that for some people, their moving cars are a place where they break down crying? I went to a heart doctor, and one of the questions they asked was whether I fall asleep when I am driving the car. Wow! I guess people do that.

Have you seen people get dressed for work in the car? I have seen men tie their neck ties when behind the wheel. That usually takes both hands. You could drive by and give the guy the thumbs up. "Hey, you are looking good!" Or not.

One "Line" You Do *Not* Want To Cross!

I discovered a safe driving technique that I knew from experience but did not exactly know that I knew it until I thought about it later. Maybe you know this technique? Allow me to share it.

I was driving on a twenty-mile stretch of road between two cities. The countryside was very pleasant but had no chance to really look left or right because there was lots of traffic and the highway was only one lane going either way.

The highway was hilly, and of course there were the yellow lines indicating where one should not pass along with the Do Not Pass and Pass With Care signs. I was driving the limit of fifty-five miles per hour, and you guessed it. Cars started coming up close to my rear. The formula is supposed to be that a driver should be one car length behind for every ten miles an hour they are going.

But wait! They were closer than that in many cases, occasionally passing on the yellow line and even passing two cars at a time, narrowly swerving back and missing the oncoming traffic. A normal inclination would be just to slow down. But the problem was that if there was a two-car crash in front of me around the top of a hill, it may end up being a three-car crash with me running into it.

What to do? I instinctively found that with cars close behind me and closely approaching a yellow line on my side, I nudged up on the accelerator about five miles per hour to take away the urge to pass me. Once, I hit the peak of the hill and had no yellow line. I slowed down by a few miles per hour. It worked well, but I don't want to jinx myself! See Chapter 26 on "The Law Of The Universe."

Put Your Hands On The Wheel

If you get stopped by law enforcement, do not get out of the car. We know that. Instead, put your hands on the top of the steering wheel where the officer can see them. There's no room for confusion. Let the officer know you are cooperative.

So. This is a big deal. If you drive like a bat out of hades and you save four minutes a day, what do you do with those minutes? Ever notice how many of those folks on bikes and scooters keep passing you by?

One thing you don't want to happen is for someone to steal your car and then drive around crazy. Worried about the old Slim Jim? There is one newer, high-tech way they can get your car. Your key fob. What? That keyless fob that helps you unlock your car sends out constant signals right out of your house. Crooks can use an amplifying device to get in your car and drive it away.

What should you do? Well, you can put the fob in a steel box, wrap it in aluminum foil, or put it in a Faraday bag. Seems like a lot of trouble for probably your neighborhood or mine. But, along the same lines, here is something you don't want to do. In case bad guys are around, put a check for a bill in an envelope for the mail person to take when they bring your mail around. What could happen? Bad guys drive up, get the outgoing envelopes of checks, wash off the payee you indicated, and put in some bogus company of theirs.

Back Off: I'm A Postal Worker

Years ago, I had a friend who worked for the US Postal Service. They always joked about "going postal." So, just to test things, we put two bumper stickers on the back of the car. On my side, it said Vietnam Veteran and on her side, Postal Worker.

Nothing. It had no effect. US Army stickers? Nothing. The drivers are impervious—maybe only the coffee or one finger salute can get their attention. But if you try this at home, remember how to get away from a crazed driver who is after you. Make that left-hand turn, another left-hand turn, another left-hand turn, and if you are still not in the clear, pull into the parking lot of the nearest fire station.

Dealing With Backseat Drivers

I always drive my wife, who, of course, is in the passenger seat—or riding shotgun. She constantly does the backseat driver thing. I tell her she is in the wrong seat to be a backseat driver. She is not amused. What do you hear from backseat drivers? Here are some of the things I hear from mine.

- Don't look at the scenery. You can't do that and drive.
- If someone honks at you, it is always your fault.
- Driving through the neighborhood, don't look at the houses. They may be watching you watch them.
- Don't adjust the radio when you drive. You cannot look at the road and move your hands at the same time.

See Chapter 23, "Love and Marriage on an Ocean Cruise."

Chapter 9

Exercise: How To Get The Most Out Of The Least

Have you worked out this week yet? Have you worked out two or three times? Or none? Chances are, if the answer is none, or not what you think it should be, you feel guilty. I know I do. Yet we know with few exceptions that the most important thing we can do all week is to exercise. How do we find the time? The motivation?

As an old Army Infantry Officer, over the course of several years, I developed an exercise all on my own that I found was outstanding for my body and mental state. I call it the Pretzel. I am excited about sharing with you how to do it and the amazing benefits I receive from it as well.

First, I would like to share my history with exercise. Compare it with your own as I go along and get back to the Pretzel.

What I am going to offer up is a mixture of all sorts of exercises, with the idea you'll fit some into your own lifestyles and get the most out of it for your body, doing it with an economical use of your time. We have to take care of our bodies. The most important thing we are likely to do all week is the workouts. The goal is to fashion your workout weeks to make them more enjoyable.

Getting The Sense Of Control and Empowerment

Good exercise gives us a sense of empowerment and control, to say nothing of the mighty need for fitness. But how do we fit it all into our busy schedules and motivate ourselves? I don't see too many joggers out there with big smiles on their faces.

In Chapter 10, I will share techniques for getting organized, including how to prioritize for your physical and mental health. On the physical side, what do you do? I have learned a thing or two over several decades and can pass on what I learned in just a few minutes of your reading time.

I have learned by decades of experiences and experimenting and can offer the best of it all for you to get the most out of it. I started learning as a pledge in a fraternity, then as an Infantry Officer, and then later, I taught myself in the work-a-day world.

In college, I pledged a fraternity. The pledge period was eight weeks, topped off by the most fun of all: Hell Week. Any time, without warning, during the first eight weeks, the actives could call the pledges into the House for Happy Hour. (See Chapter 25 for the happiness without the exercise.)

"Hell Week" Now Banned

Doors locked, curtains pulled, lights down low, the actives would get in a big circle in the living room yelling a number of names at the pledges, who were center circle. One set of exercises, among many that I fondly remember, was directed by the head tormenter, the Pledge Master. It was called Top and Downs. We had to jump to try to touch the ceiling, get down, do one push-up, then jump to the ceiling two more times, get down and do two push-ups, and so on until we were lying in a silhouette of our sweat on the floor.

Don't try this exercise at home, not even if there is nobody there to call you these really nasty names. Actually, pledging (this type of hazing is now universally banned) prepared me for army training, especially the nasty names and for all that went after them. I learned it was all a game, and I learned to play.

Do What Your Body Tells You To Do

I walked out of the sports medicine doctor's office in Phoenix, the Valley of the Sun, where I had gone to get some help on my aching left knee. "Do what your body tells you to do."

How inane, I thought. What a waste of time and money. But over the course of many years, I realized it was some of the best advice I ever got. It just took me a couple decades to really put it into practice.

I am no stranger to a lot of exercising, but I know for almost a year of my life, I wanted to be a stranger to it. Army basic training is for eight weeks. So much exercise that at six feet, one inches, I weighed all of about 150 pounds. I think when I took a shower, the water didn't even hit me.

Another eight weeks in AIT, Advanced Infantry Training.

"I want to be an Airborne Ranger: I want to live the life and danger."

"All the way, every day."

Then twenty-three and a half weeks of crawling through the mud at Infantry Officer Training at Fort Benning, Georgia. But wait! If not crawling, we ran everywhere. But that was easy compared to trying to get into the chow hall in the morning, when still dark of course.

"Drop down; give me fifty."

"All done? Give me fifty more."

Repeat, repeat.

"Candidate, run around that airborne track."

Time for breakfast yet?

"Push that tray through, candidate. You have one minute to eat."

We often ate while pushing the tray along in line. Then, done.

Lowest Whale Dung At The Bottom Of The Ocean

All this because, as they reminded us, we were lower than the lowest whale dung at the bottom of the ocean. We were so low that a pregnant ant could not crawl under us. "Those were the days, my friends, we thought they would never end . . ." What did I learn from all that PT (physical training)? I learned that I really hated it.

So, after a much needed, ten year break from it all, I got back to it but did so in a way I more or less liked. You can too. Let me pass on to you what has taken me a few decades to figure out and refine.

As we get older, one thing we really need is flexibility. Sounds obvious, right? Stretching, right? Yes, but with a difference. I started to do my own formula of stretching years and years ago. It evolved over time. Now I can pass it on to you in minutes.

Let Your Body Take Over From Your Mind

In the back of my mind was that sports medicine guy: "Do what your body tells you." But what is that? The key I found is so elusive and yet so simple. Get one of those tranquility sound devices. These Brookstone stores have all this incredibly nifty stuff—foot massagers . . . all kinds of great stuff for our bodies.

There it was right on the front of the sound box: relax with underneath ocean surf, thunderstorm, serenity, unwind, sleep, and under there, white noise, rain, celestial, summer night, renew, and under that, stream, mediate, focus, and rejuvenate. I never paid much attention to the names of the sounds, just the sounds. Over the years, I have settled on "unwind" under "relax" for my showers and cleaning up and the "rejuvenate" under "renew" for my Pretzel exercises.

I just gave that name to my favorite, head-clearing, relaxing, and renewing exercise. But it is not even an exercise as such. I count it as one of the three or four workouts I aim to get each week.

The tranquility machine goes on, the lights go down way low. I take off my shoes, lie on my bed, and *presto*: do what my body tells me to do. What is that for you? That is for your body to decide. I'm not kidding. You let your body take over from the mind.

You start stretching, turning. Whatever feels good . . . not at all like OCS. I do it for an hour or so at least once a week. Whatever you do is right. Here is one way I occasionally start. I lie flat, with my arms stretched above my head and flat. I turn to the left. I turn to the right. All the while, whenever I feel like it—it is not to be planned—my left leg stretches out, then my right. I roll back and forth on my shoulders. *Pop, pop, pop!* I can always hear those little noises from the bones when the air escapes from them.

No Need To Figure Out Perplexing Directions

Over the years, I have carefully looked over directions for exercises I found online and even in old magazines. Is it just me, or do you get confused trying to figure out where all the limbs go?

The problem with all that is that it is not relaxing.

Anyway, here are specifics of what inevitably I end up doing: lie on the bed, turn on your right side, stretch your arms out straight above your head, but parallel with your body, put your hands close together, bend your left knee around thirty degrees, whatever feels comfortable, left knee on the bed.

Now put your left shoulder back to the left. Feel the stretch. Rock back and forth. You will feel the stretch in both arms, both legs, and up and down your spine, especially the small of your spine from which most of our neck problems could originate.

Now reverse the process. Feel the stretching, muscles and bones. Rock back and forth. Then forget the knees, just lie with the arms stretched on your left side. Bend your right knee thirty or forty degrees as it rests on the bed. Then push the right shoulder back. Feel the stretching, muscles and bones. Rock back and forth. Then forget the knees, just lie with the arms stretched out straight above your head, straight out not up, parallel to the body.

Rock back and forth and back and forth and back and forth. You can do this for thirty minutes alone and still get optimum benefit from it. Bored with that? Do the legs up straight in the air, hips flat on the bed. Rock your legs all the way to the left and to the right. There you go, now make it up from there. Let your body take over from the mind.

The results of the Pretzel I have found to be amazing: far greater flexibility, along with the mental relaxation, letting the mind wander as it might. I tend not to focus on any worries during my stretching time, and I seem to get some of my best creative ideas during the process. But if I don't, I never give it a second thought. It's a "To You" exercise, and I think the best of the lot of all I do.

This is good stuff. You are not thinking about anything really, certainly not what you are doing. Your body has taken over from the mind, and your mind is at peace.

Pop, Pop, Pop Without The Chiropractor!

Pop, pop, pop! You know this is good with those little pops, the kind you don't have the chiropractor for. Loosened up? Out of pops for a while? This time, put your feet up in the air, cross your legs in front of you, grip your right foot with your left hand and your left foot with your right hand and pull down. You can feel the stretching. You can feel the loosening up, the energy flow. Re-cross your feet and do it again, or don't. It doesn't matter.

That rejuvenation music is on. But strangely, you do not hear it. It's all part of the unwinding. Do the back and forth, you move one way and the other another way. Feel the stretch. Feel the back get loosened. Feel the neck muscles get loose. Move your legs while they're in the air, to the right and then the left. Give yourself a couple sessions and don't think about what you are going to do afterward at all. Just do it. No thinking. No worrying.

Keep rolling around, keep stretching, keep pulling, keep popping. I find it truly amazing, and I bet you will too. You don't need the music, but that and the low lights set the mood. Have you cracked your toes before?

A good time to do it is while you are at it here. With your thumb and first finger of your left hand, reach up and pull three or four of your toes. You pull them out of course, then pop, pop. Repeat with the right hand and left foot. You will find you can do this for an easy hour. Your mind and your body are going to feel just liberated. Free at last!

I used to count the pops, always getting well past fifty, but after a fashion, that made it seem too goal-oriented. Just relax, stretch, and feel the stretch along your spine and all your joints.

And congratulations! The Pretzel, or whatever you want to call it, counts for me as one full exercise for the week. If you have a dog, the chances are you can see them doing a variation of the Pretzel, rolling completely over. They know how to act! Then, with some cross-training at your pace and at your time, you are going to knock out your three or four weekly workouts.

Okay, you with me here? This is actually fun, easy, and good for you. Doing four in a week is fine, but cross-training is needed, especially the cardio exercises. Be sure to remember the earlier you start in the week, the better your chance of hitting three or four for the week.

Weekly Goals Are The Best Yardstick

We need to count weekly. Weekly goals are good. They're not on top of us and not stretched out too far away. Remember how many work-outs you have had to hit the weekly allotment. I always count Sunday as a part of the just completed week, although it technically is the first day of the week. That is our catch-up day to hit our weekly quota.

Next up? You decide. Are you a jogger? You can hardly top that. Some joggers get a negative addition, meaning if they miss a day, they feel really bad. We don't want that. Jogging is great. George Bush II used to own the Texans Baseball Team. He took losing hard. He reportedly asked his doctor what to do to get over a crushing loss. "Run until you can't go any farther," he supposedly was told.

Joggers also know that, over the years, jogging can cause knee problems. Hence, President George Bush II took up riding trail bikes. He used to have a couple buddies and, of course, all the Secret Service, and go from Washington, D.C., to Maryland and ride for an hour or two—in the middle of the afternoon!

Presidents Take Time And So Can We!

Wow! How can you take a couple hours out in the middle of the day two or three times a week while president of the United States? (And only one of seventeen presidents who were elected to two terms). Because of the stress. The exercise helps beat the stress. One has to do it to stay in the fast lane.

President Bill Clinton used to jog all the time as one of those seventeen. For many decades, President Jimmy Carter stayed fit by swimming just about every day.

With swimming, you get the cardio but you don't beat the knees, and get the flexibility. But where to go? And how to work it into your busy schedule? Your nearby high schools may have aquatic centers where you can pay by the day, or get maybe ten sessions or a yearly membership. The Arlington (Virginia) Aquatic Center has a yearly membership for about $240—good motivation to use it more often. Knowing when to go is a fine art.

The centers around Arlington have the early bird that starts at 5 a.m. What? It concludes a few hours later and has a midday session from around 11 a.m. to 2 p.m. and then the evening from 5:30 to 8 p.m.

Beware Of The Shark Tanks

Swimming is great but beware of the sharks and not the fun ones on the TV show, *Shark Tank*, an acquired taste in my opinion. The sharks are the very strong swimmers who splash up a storm. With slow, medium, and fast lanes at some pools, these creatures are to be avoided. But then there is the pool etiquette you may know, when you have the lane to yourself, and you are in the middle. Great! Two people and you may know the two are to split the lane. Stay on your side, backward and forward.

Three in a lane is a real challenge for a slow swimmer like me. The three are supposed to go counterclockwise. The challenge is, as you may know, that someone is always faster, and you get lapped by the sharks. Better to go to the pool when you can have no more than two in a lane. Go toward closing time of any given period. If the mid-day hours are until 2 p.m., then plan on getting into the pool about 1:15. It's always thin at the end. Saturday, for example, if it closes at 7 p.m., be there at 6:15 p.m., because there is barely anyone around.

Swimming has to be the single best exercise there is. It's great cardio, helps flexibility, and builds strength in the legs and arms, with no trauma on the knees. But swimming has challenges: etiquette and the swimmers going in and out of lanes, to say nothing about how the lifeguards often close off your lane for classes and a multitude of splashing young people.

Get your own lane? Feeling good about it? See the Chapter on "The Law Of The Universe." You might look up and some big, really fat guy (who still deserves credit for trying) starts stretching at the end of the lane. You know he is going to be a splasher. Is he going to show common courtesy and ask if he can share the lane? That's not required, but it is courteous.

Sometimes, There Are Jerks In The Pool

No, he says nothing. He jumps in with a cannonball-type jump, making a huge splash, and thereupon, heads straight for you. You are probably doing the backstroke at the time, so you have to crane your neck to see if he is going to collide with you. Does any of this sound familiar? If you are a swimmer, it will. If you are not a swimmer and thinking of it, keep it all in mind.

So, you think you can live with that, just so long as he just takes only half of the lane. You crane your neck backward while doing the backstroke and indeed he is taking half of the lane. But he is right in the center! So, his half is in the center and there is a quarter of a lane on each side of him.

There you go. That's lap-lane swimming. What do you do when you go to the pool and all the lanes are crowded? I am going to pass on something that took me three decades of swimming to figure out. Like a lot of things, you tell people something, and they say they knew that because it makes common sense, and they figured they already knew it.

If you go to the pool and the lanes are jammed, what do you do for the cardio workout? Like I said, I did not figure this out until I found, "necessity, the mother of invention."

I went in the deep tank, the seven feet to twelve feet deep, no lanes area. I tried doing laps and was slip-sliding around and started to think I was going to sink.

Does Swimming In The Vertical Position Work?

I got the brilliant idea that had never occurred to me before. I climbed out of the pool and got ahold of one of these floatation devices, and a kind woman helped me buckle it on. I got back in the water and *presto*. I kicked my legs, pulled up my knees back and forth, and got my swimming cardio done in the vertical position! I talked to people and had actual fun.

I thought the belts were just for old people. Wow! Now I had a formula where I could go to the pool any time and not worry about getting a lane, which meant I got to the pool far more often.

Sounds easy, right? Everything is easy if you know how to do it. It just took me decades, but now, if you were not before, you are good to go right now.

A bit of a secret is that hotels often allow non-guests to use their pools, usually for a daily fee. I used to go to a local Marriott. They only had one lane for lap-lane swimming. I almost always had it to myself and when I did not, one can swim just on the other side of the rope and be out of the way of the regular guests.

Many hotels have pools that were just never made for lap swimming, as if none of their guests would think of it. Of course, you are looking for an indoor pool. If you are shopping around for a hotel pool, make sure it is not three feet everywhere. You'll scrape your knees.

Scout Around For Free Pools

For years, I went to an indoor pool at a Quality Inn where I could go in a side door to get to it. Nobody was ever in it. There were like three regular lifeguards. I made friends with them, telling them I was friends with the owner. I never paid, and rarely were there other guests around.

Do you travel? The fitness centers of hotels are usually empty. You have the bed for the Pretzel, and you could use your room creatively for something else. A few years ago, I had a business meeting in Las Vegas (yes it was). I think in the New York, New York Hotel. What was I thinking? I asked if there was a pool, and there was! You guessed it. It was packed with drinking partiers.

So, I put on my swimsuit in my room and did what I did for many years, the Primordial Walk. You get down on all fours with your back arched and walk around on your hands and feet. Sounds easy? Try it for a while. But this is one great exercise if you can take it. You are in that hotel room, or some room, and you do the Primordial Walk to the hotel door, turn around, go to the end of the room, and repeat.

You will quickly figure out you can't do these for long. Do sets, like around the room twice. Then lie down and get your breath. Do this for thirty or forty minutes, and you will have done a super workout. The sweat will be dripping from your forehead. It is big-time cardio and good for the arm and leg muscles—right there in your hotel room, or wherever.

Primordial Walk: "Cruel And Unusual Punishment"

I used to have an office with a long hallway and I would race a young colleague back and forth down the hall just for laughs. I have never seen this exercise done in an organized fashion, except once, when driving by a high school football field where the kids were working out. Wow. The Primordial Walk. Later, I found there is another name for it—crabbing. A university coach in Virginia had the jocks do crabbing. The university let him go, saying it was "cruel and unusual punishment." Be careful doing this at home!

What else can you do to get to three or four workouts a week? Walking is superior. Go out your front door, walk around for about forty-five minutes or an hour, then you are back home and you have another workout done for the week. Swimming takes me really almost two and a half hours door to door. With walking, there is no car time and no this and that in the locker room.

Flexibility and adaptability are the keys to your good health through exercise. If you cannot do one thing, do another, or another, but keep moving and pumping. Here's another one that's usually overlooked: dancing. Gear up iTunes, or whatever you have, and pick some workout tunes for right there in your living room, or bedroom, or what have you.

Dancing For Fun And Fitness

This can be fun stuff. No one has to be around to see how you shimmy and shake. Move anyway you want, getting that pulse rate up there so when you slow down, your heart is stronger . . . plus you get all the other benefits of a cardio workout.

As an old rocker, for years my favorite song has been "Miss You" by the Rolling Stones. I just really get into it, starting slowly and then speeding it up. "Start Me Up" is another one that you hear in all those sports arenas. It just makes you want to get moving. More of my favorites are Linda Ronstadt, CCR, Fleetwood Mac, Chicago, Johnny Rivers, 70s music, the Golden Oldies, and all the Motown classics. Most TVs have the option for different music channels. Whatever you like is good.

Some people have a negative addition to exercise, especially with jogging it seems. One feels great guilt if one misses a regular session. I was a jogger for a couple decades, which I found can really mess up your knees. One of your big keys is that a regular routine is fine for every week but things happen every day and we have to improvise. So, your potpourri of exercising can vary from week to week, just so each week ends up being the optimum amount.

Yoga: Some Like It Hot!

Yoga counts, and yoga is good. Reports were that during her campaign for president in 2016, Hillary Clinton tried to stay fit by doing yoga in her various campaign hotel rooms. Nobody I saw ever asked her, but I can imagine that while she was doing the Scarecrow and Half Moon poses in her hotel rooms, she was also probably chatting and getting briefed by her staffers. Multi-tasking . . . I would not recommend it.

I was taught yoga by a student of the famed Bikram of California. He has studios throughout the country. Maybe you have been to some. The room temperature has to be eighty-two degrees. Why is that? I don't know.

It's more door-to-door time if you go to a class. You can easily do this in your living room or bedroom. According to the famed Bikram, each of twelve and more poses have to be done in the same exact order every time. Sounds a little too organized for you? It always did for me.

I studied yoga, mostly from afar, for several years. I try to do a set of these exercises once a week, but I do it all at home. It saves time, and time is money after all. The idea, as you may know, is that you put your body into various poses, stretch the muscles, create some dynamic extension in the body, and maybe even meditate at the same time. All good.

Finally, after reading and practicing for a few years, I finally found out how yoga is supposed to help you stay fit and young. The idea being that after you get in these poses for thirty seconds or so, then you lie down for another thirty seconds.

The reason for lying down is you have these extensions and when you lie down, the blood circulates throughout your body—full-body circulation. Ahh! When I understand why and how something works, I am more motivated to do it because I understand how it works. We want to take care of ourselves for the long haul, not depend on someone else.

Improvising: Those Stairwells Were Made For Walking

Do you live in a house or an apartment? I lived in a nine-story apartment for years. There was a pool, outdoor and good for the summer. There was a workout room, but it was always crowded, and they never really maintained the exercise equipment. Sound familiar?

The apartment, of course, had a couple of elevators, and it also had stairwells meant for emergency exits like during fires. The signs on the doors to the stairwells said so. Nobody used these stairwells, but I saw them as a blessed opportunity.

I would slip on some shorts and a sweatshirt, grab a bottle of water, and up and down I went. Walk, no need to run. Down nine or whatever you have and then up nine flights. Walk around on the top landing until you catch your breath and repeat. In my younger days, I would do it ten times. Wow! I counted the number of steps a few times. It was in the thousands. Talk about a cardio workout, right there outside my apartment door!

And surprise! In years and years, never once did I see one person doing this stairwell exercise. I did see some people occasionally access the stairs between flights to get out or into their apartments. I ignored them and they ignored me. In years and years, I don't recall anyone who had the same idea, or if they did, who actually wanted to do it. Door to door, no time at all. And remember, swimming may be well over two hours.

Live in a house? That works too. Have an upstairs or downstairs? There are maybe twelve steps between floors. You have your exercise right there. Go up and down ten times and then walk around a bit. Repeat the sets three, four, or five times. Great cardio.

Mancave Cross Training

Now, here is a variation I use to change it up. We have an exercise bike in the basement rec room. I do about five minutes of the bike, then up and down the stairs five times, and repeat the bike and stairs a full five times. We are talking about a forty-five-minute full cardio and cross-training workout.

Have a TV set in the Mancave? Turn it on to sports or various other programs. Talking political heads are not good for the psyche!

If you are especially fit to begin with, you most likely know about the exercises you can do at home: the push-ups, the sit-ups, and the pull-ups with one of those bars you can buy that sets up at the top of a door frame. Squat jumps are when you squat and jump and squat and jump. Add in some isometrics like that, and you have a full workout at home

Pumping iron is always good, and, you likely know, a good way to lose weight. It helps your metabolism burn more calories. Gold's Gym? Doing the pendulum lifts, the calf raises, the squat rack, the bench press, the deadlift, and as many weights as you can take on the plate bar. You know all about these and you are way ahead of most of the rest.

They Are Running Their Mouths, But You Are Getting Fit

Your living room can work. Speaking of these talking heads, you know the chattering class on the cable news? Lie on the rug, watch and/or hear the noise. That will pump you up to lift those weights. Or sit in the chair and use those smaller weights, pumping those biceps back and forth. Every bit counts. Try to get to at least four full workouts every week. If you do half of one, give yourself half credit.

So, there we have just the short list. Take your pick and mix and match: walking, swimming, jogging, exercise machines, stairwells, pumping the iron, yoga, biking, and maybe golf, pick-up basketball, or whatever—oh, and yes, the Primordial Walk. You could do this once or twice and tell your friends you do it. They will think you are strange, but invite them to try it. The first couple minutes are a piece of cake, then the pain begins.

There you go. Every week, all the way. When the going gets tough, the tough get going. The variables in our lives are extremely challenging to control, yet when we exercise, we feel more in control. And the exercise, we can control.

When life throws us all these challenges, that's when it is extra important to do the fundamentals. Be fit for life.

PART 3

How to Power Up Your Career

Chapter 10

Time to Get Organized, But Who Has the Time?

H ow do we find the time to get organized? How many times have we said, "I'll get all organized, including all these files that have not been digitized, but I don't have the time right now. Maybe later"?

"One minute of organization is worth an hour of work."
—Benjamin Franklin

We have read it and heard it all. Everyone has the same amount of time in each day, then they count the hours, minutes, and seconds just to make us feel better, but we probably feel worse.

How do you organize your work or study days? Your personal life? Your relationships? How much time do you plan to allot for them? Through several decades, I have certainly learned how it can and does work to make oneself more productive and have the time for rewarding pursuits as well.

Be Your Own Boss And You Won't Get Fired!

First, let me establish my bona fides. I worked for a time management firm in Phoenix. I learned quite a bit. Then, I got fired after about seven weeks. Truth to power, kind of a thing.

My dad told me early on, "Son, with your kind of personality, you better be your own boss."

A backward compliment? I did take his advice when I finally figured out that he was right. I was my own boss for three decades, and I never fired myself.

> "When I was eighteen, my old man didn't know a thing, but by the time I turned twenty-five, I was amazed how much he had learned." —**Mark Twain**

It was kind of that way with me, which is good to remember if you have children, especially teenage children.

This fun-loving, time-management firm had this insidious and extremely effective way to make people accountable and, thus, really more productive. This was for their own employees. We/they gave these regular time-management seminars. That was how the money was made, but the most strident tactics were reserved for employees.

Here is what they did. The ownership management was one of these incestuous groups, husband, wife, brother-in-law, and probably some hidden relatives as well—about a dozen all told.

Every Friday about 4 p.m., we would gather in the living room of the owner's house. Everyone of course would start to get happy, full of renewed energy and optimism (see "Happy Hour," Chapter 25). Thereupon everyone (not the owners) would write down about six projects that were to be individually achieved within the next week.

Everyone was thinking, "Next week, I'm going to be great. I can do anything next week, that is after Friday night, all of Saturday, and of course Sunday. I am not even thinking about next week, so anything is possible."

The Insidious Weekly Goals

Everyone was required to write down their projects, in some cases, the number of sales calls they would make and other quantitative stuff. That was the second half of the Friday meeting. The first part is where you had to read aloud all your goals for the current week and confess your shortcomings.

This is a simple but brutally effective technique for time management. The idea is that a week's time is the optimum time for the measurement of progress. One day is too short. One month, and certainly a year, is too long, at least to generate ongoing accountable performance.

I have used this technique where I have been the boss, especially where I wanted to hold some slackers accountable, sort of holding a mirror to their face and letting them see themselves. Many times, people got more productive or quit. Quite a few times, I discontinued the process because I was the one who came up with all these weekly goals for myself that I couldn't keep either. In those cases, I just wouldn't have the report meeting on Friday. Do as I say, not as I do.

So, anyway, back to the firing. I was meeting all my goals and enjoying the seminars, including my part in them and even the sales. I was learning quite a bit in spite of myself. As I said, it was an insular group. One Monday, the scuttlebutt around the office was that a young woman was going to be fired on Friday. Everybody knew it but her. The brother-in-law, the hatchet man of the operation, did the deed in front of us all at 4 p.m. on Friday.

I thought about the cruelty of that for a week. At the next Friday council, I raised my voice and, in some detail, related how this was a bad practice. It was bad for company morale and ultimately bad for business. I was relatively young and I thought, at least to some degree, that the bottom-line impact argument might have some sway.

"No Real Happy Hour On Friday. You Are Fired."

You guessed it. The next Friday at 4 p.m., the hatchet man brought me in front of the dozen or so others before retiring to the living room of the esteemed leaders. This, I saw coming. It was one of those, "You're fired. Here's a box. Clean out your desk and give me your keys."

I had actually planned in advance what I was going to say. I had seen my coworker's kind of looking askance during the week, especially Friday. I knew what to expect.

(By the way, this part could be in "Some People Have To Be Told," Chapter 3, but since I am relating my prowess in time management, I saved it for this one.)

We were kind of standing no more than a couple of feet from each other, right in the middle of a relatively small office. I put some extra weight on my rear leg so I could move quickly if he decided to take a swing at me.

"Alex, you should know that everybody knows."

"Knows what?" said Alex

"That you wear a rug." It was obvious. You know, half his hair was one color, and suddenly, it went halfway down the side of his head and it's another color.

I was ready to pull my head back when he took a swing at me. But he didn't. There were a couple seconds for his recognition, and he said, "Is that supposed to be funny?"

I ignored that and said, "Alex, you should get a better toupee. Everybody knows."

"Get out." said Alex. "Pick up your check on Monday."

Axman Recommends A Bonus!

Monday came and I went to pick up the check from the owner.

"Here, she said. "Alex recommended that we give you some extra money for severance, even though your contract doesn't call for any of it."

Wow! I learned about time management and one of my first lessons in how some people have to be told. Of all people, Frank said I should have more money. Was he afraid of me?

Did he respect me more? I am not sure, but because I "told him," so to speak, it was, without doubt, the reason I got more money.

So, in managing the time in your life, how do you do it? A to-do list for the day, the year, or a to-me list? How do you go about getting organized to get the most out of all facets of your life?

First, I can tell you that of the literally hundreds of people I have supervised, the ones with the messed-up desks at the end of the workday (that is, the disorganized ones—as in files strewn over their desks) were the least productive people in the office. I do not recall ever experiencing an exception to this reality.

The most organized and productive people (the far smaller number) invariably leave their desks completely cleared off at the end of the day—or at least with a minimum of papers in the in/out box and others in vertical files. I don't care how paperless your office is. You'll have papers until you scan them or get rid of them.

It's like garbage. You show me people who are living without garbage, and I will show you people who aren't living.

Clear Off Your Desk Before You Leave

Clear off your desk before you leave. You'll have good karma when you show up the next day and it is cleared off.

Filing? Wow! Who wants to do that? Who does it on time? A long time ago, some unknown wag in the office put up a picture of St. Anthony, the patron saint of finding things above our filing cabinet. Say a prayer to St. Anthony if you can't find some file. I think it works.

In one office I oversaw, we were always looking for files. And one guy, his name was Fred. You know, you might know some people for a year and only remember one thing they said?

Fred would say about some unfound file or object, "Well, it didn't get legs and walk out of here."

Heard that before? Feel free to use it yourself. I actually found it strangely comforting rather than annoying when it was said. He was right. It had to be someplace.

In some offices where I have worked, we had a Finder Award. Whoever found the most lost items got it.

Better not to lose all that stuff in the first place. Yes, I know, put it all in the computer. But if you have enough turnover in your office, new people are always using new systems for their own organization, new folders with names you would not use, or folders you can't find.

Keep Your Office A Mess And People Out?

Quite a few years ago, I knew a guy at the national headquarters of the US Postal Service in downtown Washington, D.C., who could find every single file he wanted, without fail. How did he do it? He had at least a hundred pieces of paper, some a page or two together, and also separate files. He put these all over his office. Everywhere. I mean everywhere. All over the floor, in every chair, on every windowsill, everywhere. And you may not be surprised to hear he was a high-level manager. But he could find everything! If a coworker named a certain document, he would pick it up and hand it to that person.

According to friends I knew there, his system had the added benefit of keeping people out of his office. There was no place to walk in and sit, and they didn't want to step on his piles.

Maybe you are so organized that you have no paper files. But if you are in the likely majority, you do have files and the files get disorganized. The files might be hard to find, and the papers inside may be disorganized and belong in another file because you picked the nearest file and put the papers there. Yet you know to keep your desk clear and organized.

So, the most highly organized among us are still going to have these pesky paper files. Without a shadow of a doubt, the most productive time you devote all week long is to go through these files and organize them and relabel them. And the most important part is to *throw out* the documents that have been updated or outdated and, for sure, those not needed.

Take Time to Get Organized And You Are Gaining Time

Do you know the Japanese art of tidying up? Don't keep handling the same document again and again. Pick it up once and do something with it so you don't keep picking up the same document over and over. The same goes for household bills. Try to handle once or twice, no more, or extra time is involved.

I obviously did not learn any of this from Alex at Time Management School, though I did get the weekly accountability brainstorm there. I was a leader of national operations where we had a very lean staff and a very big operation. Does this sound familiar? By nature, it was constant organized chaos, a kind of professional guerrilla operation.

Part of my job was to help people be more productive because the bulk were constantly disorganized because of the massive number of variables and changing priorities by the hour.

So, I taught a system. How does this compare to yours? First, the old one week of objectives, the six to eight middle-sized projects to complete and/or take a big bite out of. Here comes the precision. These weekly objectives have to be put on a single piece of paper with a header, such as "Objectives for the Wk. of July 20th" That always starts Monday.

Then, preferably at the close of one day or at the beginning of the next day, make out the old reliable to-do list and put the day of the month and day of the week for precision. Slack off on that basic and it is all slacking. But you look at these weekly objectives when you make out the daily to-do list. It is your guide and helps you remember what needs to be done. If you don't look at the weekly list to make up the daily list, one gets lost in the weeds.

Make a list of the ten, fifteen, or even twenty things to get accomplished that day, in random order, with no thinking. Just put them all down as soon as they occur to you. Obviously, some timing has to be done before others can be started. Some are more important, and so forth. But the key is no one can be expected to decide exactly what needs to be done, and in what order, the first time through.

Since this is key, get organized. Decide exactly in sequential order what should be done first, second, third, and so forth. You will find you may go down the list and come up with number one through number fifteen. Then look at it again to be sure. You probably got the numbers out of order of what they should be. That's why you do this list. Since you don't want to renumber every fifteen of them, then what you do is add a letter or two to each number, like 3a, 3b, and 3c.

Why go to all this trouble? It's not trouble. It's organization.

Here's the big deal. How many times during the day are you doing something and you have the nagging feeling you should be doing something else? That's how I motivated the people in the office to use this system to get organized. I would ask them that question, and they would say, "All the dang time."

You Now Know You Are Doing Exactly What You Should

This organizer allows you to know you are doing exactly what you should be doing at any given time because you have already thought it through. You have already organized it!

Tuesday? Look at your weekly objectives to be the guidepost for what you need to do that day to chip away on those weekly goals. Don't be like us in Time Management School. "It's Thursday, My gosh, I haven't gotten hardly any of the stuff done I wanted to."

Now for the holistic approach. The old line, "Do you live to work or work to live" is important. For too many of us, it's the former. So, get out that weekly objectives list and divide it into three categories. What do you want to accomplish by the end of the week? You have the three categories, the business, which we have covered, and then two more: personal and relationships.

First, I decide what should be the rank order of those three for the week. Too often, we make business or work or career, or whatever you care to call it, as the top priority. So, let's give some top-of-head examples of the types of things I prioritize.

One Page For One Week: A More Fulfilling Life

Relationships:

- Show the love to my wife daily
- Pick out a movie to see with my wife

- Call my sister
- Call my two daughters
- Make an appointment for Jasper, the dog (he thinks he's a cat, but he's a dog)
- Call the neighbors and ask them over for the game Saturday afternoon

Personal:

- Swim twice and find two other exercise days: yoga, exercise bike, stairway, or walk (as in up and down the basement steps)
- Make a dental appointment
- Meditate at least three times
- Get that empowerment book from the bookstore
- Take the car to the shop
- Bring the diary up to date (don't have one, but for me it could be write one more chapter for the next book)

Business/Career/School:

- You pick the five or six

And there you have it—your integrated, entire plan for the week. Look at it every weekday before you get started on the day.

As they say, even the super-rich have no more daily or weekly time than we do. Make the days count and just maybe we can work less hard and smarter and have a more fulfilling life.

Chapter 11
How To Interview And Get The Job

Do you have a job now? Great, but as we look around, we realize we could be out of a job next week. Don't like your job? The vast majority of people don't. Are you looking for a job now?

Sooner or later, you will probably be interviewing for a job, and interviewing is a skill not taught in school. Or, maybe you got the job and now you have to interview others. That skill is every bit as challenging.

You probably have some job-interviewing experience. I have more than I ever expected to have, having interviewed several hundred people for work and having interviewed dozens of times for jobs myself—yes, indeed. Every few months, I tell my wife of another job I once had.

Her reaction is always the same. "How long did you have that one?"

But when I became a consultant and became my own boss, I had long-time job security.

The Biggest Interview Mistake

In my "Path to Success" seminars on job interviewing, I start by asking, "What is the biggest mistake people make during a job interview?" No one has guessed it correctly yet. They guess not being prepared or being late for the interview. Both are deal breakers.

In another category of its own is not being able to find the office when it is on the main street! No kidding. I ran an office on a main street of a town for a couple decades. Many people called and said they could not find the office, like they did not know the odd numbers are on one side of the street and the even are on the other, or that there is a difference between east and west.

It's Talking Too Much!

People like to talk. They don't like to listen nearly as much, even when they are doing the interviewing. Talking is easier than listening, after all.

Years ago, I was working for Norman, Navan, Moore & Beard Advertising. My boss, Jack Norman, told me to go out and find some new clients. "How do I do that?" I said. "Do I talk about the services of NNM&B?"

"No," he said. "Get them to talk about their advertising."

Now think about that and relate it to the job interview.

I have interviewed a great deal of people who talked themselves right out of a job. I would ask them a question, and they would go on for two or three minutes, which is way too long. With few exceptions, answers should be about thirty seconds long. That's about how long it takes before the interviewer will start thinking about the next question to be asked. Talk too long, and the interviewer gets impatient

Keep The Answers Short

Answers that are concise reflect a well-organized, disciplined, agile mind and a person who is good at communicating. Rambling is a losing philosophy. It is actually more challenging to make answers shorter.

Harry Truman once gave a two-minute speech. The media loved it and asked how long it took to prepare. "Several weeks," said the thirty-third president.

"What!" said the media. "How long for a fifteen-minute speech?"

"A week," said the President.

"How long for an hour-long address?"

"I am ready now," he said. Being concise pays during the interview.

Take too long to answer any given question, and the person doing the interview might think, "If they are taking so long to answer a question now, I can only imagine the time this person will waste if I hire them."

Interview buster? Unnecessary explanations. "Well, the boss really didn't like me, and I didn't like the mission of the organization." No job for you. You never have to say anything negative about yourself. Don't volunteer mistakes you made. And only maybe disclose how people took advantage of you. Don't come across as a loser.

Say What You Are, Never What You Aren't

Don't say what you are not. Richard Nixon famously said, "I am not a crook." What did people remember? The last word. The former Attorney General Jess Sessions said, "I am not a racist." He should've said, "I am benevolent to all races."

A former head of the IRS non-profit division testified before Congress and said, "I didn't break the law or break regulations or lie to Congress." She should have said, "I upheld the law, worked within the regulations, and told the truth."

A man says, "I did not cheat on my wife." People remember the word cheat. He should have said, "I have always been faithful to my wife." These are semantics that are vital in all walks of life, but especially good to remember when trying to get a job.

The idea is to always tell the truth. But if someone asks you a question, there is no law you have to answer that question completely. Successful politicians make a living at this. They use the question for a segue to make another point.

Decide How You Want To Come Across

How a person comes across in an interview is every bit as important as what one says. The interviewer will ask themselves, "Does this person have character? Confidence? Intelligence? Are they likable?" This is probably the most important of the four.

When I look at a person's resume when interviewing them, I will ask something like, "I see you were an executive assistant at the Aardvark Corporation, and I see what you list as the duties. Please expand on that." I know what they said they did is on the resume. I am simply asking the question to see how they come across, as in assessing the above qualities. A good interviewer will do that.

Then, of course, you might get a bad interviewer, which happens with regularity and really makes it more challenging to give a good interview. An interviewer like this might say, "Tell us about yourself." Be ready for that one. Also, be ready for the usual "book" question: "What is your biggest strength?" Know what the job requires and be ready with those qualities.

Your biggest weakness? Don't give a weakness. There is no need. But don't be too cute either, saying, "I work too hard," or" I should take time for lunch more often," though that is not bad. Saying you're a perfectionist is pretty fair for an answer to that one.

I had a young woman in one of my seminars who said if she didn't say something, that it was a weakness. She didn't think she'd have any credibility. There are two problems here: first is the interview itself, and next is if one gets the job.

So, she said, "I try to do too much and am not as good at time management as I should be."

The problem with that, I told her, was she might get hired and then in a couple months, the boss will think, "Gosh, that Sally has bad time management skills. Maybe she needs to go."

A better answer along those lines would be, "I tend to expect too much of myself for what I can accomplish in one day, but I have learned the art of daily time management." It's the best of both worlds.

The Incredible Power Of Body Language

At these seminars, I ask what sort of body language can contribute to a positive impression. No one has gotten it correct yet, and you will not see this anywhere else. Body language contributes very strongly to how a person is assessed. A big smile at the beginning and end of the interview contributes a great deal to a successful interview—that is a given.

But a very effective technique, used by the pros and neglected by the others, is head nodding. When the person being interviewed occasionally nods their head slightly up and down, it signals, I understand. I am with you, and I trust what you are saying. You have struck a responsive chord with me.

An amazing number of people, the majority, sit during an interview stone-faced, like a sphinx, and thus unreadable. They strike no rapport with the person talking to them. Hello? Hello? Is there anybody there?

Merely nodding your head occasionally when the other is talking, interview or not, is a very powerful technique to make a very positive impression. Try it at your office or during a Zoom call and you will sense how powerful it is.

At the "Farm," the CIA training facility in Virginia, reports are they teach the art of head nodding when trainees are questioning friendly foreign assets, to keep them talking and interested.

We Manipulated The Psychology Prof.

I first witnessed a variation of this technique in college during a psychology class. One of these lecture-style classrooms with a slanted floor and the seats in a row from close in to the higher in the back.

A few of us in the front row got together on a wager, had fun, and literally passed the professor from one end of the front of the class to the other. Those on the left started nodding and looking straight at him. The prof went to them. They kind of fell off and the other side of the class picked him up. Remember, there is power in the head nod!

Preparation: decide in advance how you want to come across in the interview. First, I recommend, is professional, then prepared. But more than that, know the key traits you will exhibit, such as relaxed, confident, enthusiastic.

Consider and practice, without memorization, answers to potential questions (at least a dozen should be considered). Remember, do not memorize them, just remember themes, and the words will flow (see Chapter 13).

How To Be At Ease At The Start Of An Interview

When you go into the interview, put the preparation behind you. It's all ready for you to call upon when needed. Keep it simple now. Just think of how you want to come across. As related in the speaking before a group in the public speaking chapter, start talking as soon as you enter the office.

Say whatever comes to your mind. It will help you relax and get into the flow. "Everyone looks so busy here." "What a great view." It does not matter. That way, you have shown you are at ease and do not have to start from nothing and get to something right after you are seated.

Remember, a key tenet to negotiating is that you care but not too much. In other words, you want the job, but you are not desperate. You believe in yourself, and you are a find for them. Besides, you may find that you don't want the job.

Now for the end of the interview. Have one, no more than two, question(s) prepared to ask. Here is one about as good as they come: "I always make it a point to adapt to my boss. So how would you describe your management style?"

They are going to love to answer this one, and the idea is you let them know that you will adapt to them, and you don't expect them to adapt to you. Some people on the job have never figured out this simple concept.

You Go First On The Money And You Lose

Let's say you have really scored, and they talk about money. Maybe there is a set salary, but very often, there is not. The key here is not to go first. If they invite you to give your required salary level, do not do it.

It sounds counterintuitive, but the person in a money negotiation who goes first is at a disadvantage. If you go first and it's too low, you lose your value in their eyes. If you go too high, you could price yourself out of the job. They will know that if you come down, you will never be happy there.

When I interview, I ask, "What is the lowest weekly salary you would be willing to accept and still be happy?" Watch out for this! If someone answers this question by saying they don't know, it means they don't know what they are worth. That's a deal buster too.

So, you have the job, and now you are doing the interviewing. Here are about the best generic questions you can ask—or conversely, if you're still looking, be ready to answer.

Be Ready For The Questions With Your Answers

- "What motivates you and gets you excited about work?"
- "Tell me about a time when your workload was heavy. How did you complete the tasks on time?" (Be ready for examples if you are asked.)
- "How do you accept direction and instructions, and at the same time, apply your own ideas and values?" (These are sharp questions from very experienced interviewers.)
- "We are looking for people who will be indispensable to our company. What skills do you have that make you indispensable?"
- Finally, here is a question I got from John Dozier, the vice president of Kalamazoo College, when I applied for the job of director of Development: "Have you ever fired anyone?"

The answer was easy. Early in my career, I had already fired a few people. The last two were a staffer in a congressional campaign and a wealthy volunteer. The campaign was successful. I know why John was asking me that question. Since I had to hire a staff, would I have the guts to fire someone who couldn't do the job?

Even though I never had any formal fundraising experience (unless one counts being a bill collector), I got the job and, indeed, I hired someone I later had to let go.

In my career, I have had to fire a great many people. Maybe if I had been a better interviewer, I would have weeded out all the slackers and shirkers. But, like a line in *Forrest Gump*, "Life is like a box of chocolates. You never know what is going to be inside."

Chapter 12

Key To Wealth:
Your Own Mastermind Group

Think and Grow Rich by Napoleon Hill is one of my favorite books by those who have become successful, at least by monetary measurements. Written decades ago, Hill was commissioned by Andrew Carnegie to devote about twenty years of his life to interview millionaires (only billionaires would have qualified today, of course) to see what could be passed on in a book—what they all had in common.

Think and Grow Rich has sold over 150 million copies. First published in 1937, it remains a best-seller today. Mr. Hill offered a boatload of great motivational ideas. This is one great book.

All the success stories were different, but all the millionaires had at least one thing in common: each had established their own Mastermind Group. Hill described the purpose of the groups (be successful) but was a little short on exactly *how* a Mastermind Group should function. I am going to pick up where he left off and share with you some of the vital *how* to do it.

Over the years, I have created and led Mastermind Groups that I found very helpful to me and all the members. I want to share with you what I learned, how to do it, how not to do it, how to set it up, the people who should be in it, and how it functions best.

Knowing The What Is Good. Knowing The How Is Better

First, while on the subject, do you read self-improvement books? This book you are reading is really a different genre because, as you have already seen, I start where almost all the others have left off and get to actual techniques for good living, the all-important how to do it.

The most famous and most read is the first book by Dale Carnegie, *How to Win Friends and Influence People*. If you have not read this one in a long time, consider reading it again.

Carnegie's second book, which did not sell as many copies (how could any such book?) is called, *How to Stop Worrying and Start Living*. Notice the *how* in both titles. The *what* is the simple part. The *how* is the key.

Carnegie was a great writer in that his books are very readable, with lots of anecdotes and self-effacing stories about trying to figure it all out, the many mistakes, and more. Carnegie set a high standard, spawning training classes and Dale Carnegie trainers—very hard to top that.

A book that came out several decades ago was thought to be a ground-breaker too, *How to Win Through Intimidation*. For a year, it seemed that every wannabe was reading it. The author's success turned out to be small potatoes, though he did have the lead on a potent idea. (See Chapter 3 on "How Some People Have To Be Told.")

Speaker, coach, and leadership expert John Maxwell has written a whole series of readable books that are fast-paced and filled with examples of people who were successful sports coaches or generals.

Things Successful People Do is right up there, as is *How Successful People Think* and *How To Be a Leader*. There's that *how to* again. What do you do exactly, and how are you supposed to do it?

Seven Traits of Successful People Revisited

The late Stephen Covey's *Seven Traits of Successful People* has endured. Have you read that one? Two traits that he mentions stand out to me. The Ratchet Effect, meaning when things have not gone well for you in almost too long, you need to turn on the ratchet, like the teeth on a wheel, knowing when to stop and go in a new direction and cut your losses. "Never give up" has to be changed to know when to try a new tact in a certain facet of your life.

Another Covey tenet is that successful people are by nature pessimists—but not in the usual sense. They are always figuring out in advance what can go wrong and trying to plan to get around it. Remember, Murphy's Law.

How about those negotiation books and tapes? I have finished quite a few. A couple tenets I remember . . . in a negotiation over money, never go first with a dollar figure. You are at a disadvantage. You may be too high or too low, and you could get boxed in. Let the other party go first and take it from there. Hopefully, you remember this strategy as was related in Chapter 11, "How To Interview," it is worth repeating.

Classic Negotiation Dodge

Here is another favorite to remember: take it to the committee. You are negotiating, you don't want to be hedged in, so you say you have to take it to the committee, whatever that might be.

Now here's a good one to use as well: what is your counter to this committee subterfuge? "You will recommend it to the committee, won't you? Your stature certainly carries great weight in the final decision."

As in life, over and over, best to put the ball back into their court. Like in tennis, don't let them leave it on your side.

Now It's Time For Your Mastermind Group

In short, a Mastermind Group is a loose affiliation of peers you know, not family nor business-related colleagues (this is important), but high achievers who are motivated and full of energy, just like you.

So, these people could be those you met through a more formal networking group (a leads group, some are called), a service organization (the Rotarians own the businesses, the Kiwanis run the business, and the Lions do all the work, or so some people are fond to say), your church, swim club, or neighbors, what have you, just not family or people who have direct business ties with you.

Now for the why. What is the point? The payoff? Your Mastermind Group, or a loosely organized group, is a sounding board for business ideas. It is a source of news and information of techniques learned, and of mutual personal support, for business and personal life. Also, it is a forum that helps build confidence and gives its participants a sense of success and confidence.

Now the all-important *how*. I have set up Mastermind Groups (call them whatever you want) in The Valley of the Sun in Arizona and in the Northern Virginia area, both of which met over the course of many fulfilling years.

Here is what I found: no drinks or happy hour-type format (see that in "Happy Hour," Chapter 25) so no meetings after work hours. You would think that lunches would work but really in no league with breakfasts. You try the lunches. Something happens to busy people eight times out of ten. Attendance is not "required" like with the Rotary Club.

People Are Happier On Friday!

I found that breakfast always works best on Fridays. On Monday, people feel they don't have things under control right off. There is pressing business that must be handled. On Tuesday, it's much of the same. Wednesday is only slightly better. Thursday, no, better yet Friday, is best of all.

Everyone looks forward to Fridays. Start out with a power breakfast with your mastermind colleagues and you will be fired up and ready to roll out Friday, finishing the week with a bang. Lots of coffee we are talking about here. Daylight in the swamp, time to get up and have a husky cup of coffee, or two or three.

How often? Every week? Is that too much? Every fourth Friday? Maybe too far apart? Make it 7 a.m. every other Friday morning, 7:30 a.m. at the latest.

You pick the meeting spot. Obviously, there should be no loud music in the background. That would eliminate many places right there. We are talking about a middle of the road, family diner or hotel restaurant.

Now, the all-important agenda. What do you talk about, how is it organized, and how many people are we talking about?

Let's start with the number of people. Harvard University did a study about twenty years ago to find the optimum number of people that make the most cohesive and effective team. You can ask people this question yourself, and you may be surprised by the answers. The more seasoned professional will have a good idea of the number spread we are talking about. The uninitiated will not. They may say as many as you can get. No. No!

Number Of People That Make The Most Efficient Group?

The answer is three to five people, which is the optimum number for the most efficient group to perform. That's what you need at all the meetings. Two is not enough, and more than five starts to be dysfunctional. But with that spread in mind, consider people who develop conflicts for your every other Friday meeting (people will not forget a meeting, as it's just too energizing and motivating).

You need six or seven people who are affiliated because, invariably, a couple will have some serious conflicts that come up. Only two people might show up, so it doesn't work. So, you can pretty much pass on your usual format. Five or six is okay.

How do you organize the Mastermind agenda? If you do not have a stated agenda, it does not work! It falls apart. The most loquacious person (See Chapter 14 on "Word Power") takes over the session. If your agenda is too detailed, the session is too constrained and does not flow with the brainstorming, which is what a lot of it is. So here you have it, an agenda with three items:

1. News and information
2. Business brainstorming
3. Social time

News and Information: after no more than ten minutes of greeting and how's it going, it's news and information time. Everyone is expected to kick in some useful information they know about. It could be about an upcoming seminar or conference.

It could be news about the markets, or it could be items in the news that are of value to the people to know. It could be about a useful book, and it could be about some contacts a person has developed.

Information is power. Everyone should share information that adds value for the participants, whatever it is.

Business Is The Heart Of The Mastermind

Business: the heart of it all. Here is where individuals share techniques that have helped themselves professionally, talk about lessons they have learned, and talk about new business prospects.

Then one participant every session has the floor for a full ten minutes or so to share some business move or deal they could be considering, or some job change, or something for which the person wants to have the others be a sounding board. The Mastermind Group is, after all, your sounding board group.

During this time, our groups have had people talk about office politics, what is really raking them over, and not in a good way, and what to do. One person may talk about a major investment they are thinking of making. Someone may share some financial challenges they are having. This is all privileged information, and people understand the confidentiality. This number two, Business, is the heart of your Mastermind Meetings.

Social Time: this part of the meeting is good for bonding.

"My husband and I are thinking about going on a vacation. What about to Italy?"

"My wife and I are going to Figaro's for dinner." One participant shares how he assures he gets a good table from the maître d'. Another relates that he tells them if they send him to the bar while he is waiting too long, "They won't like me anymore." Another relates other plans for the weekend. And so on.

"Are You Talking About Me With Your Masterminds?"

Your Mastermind Group is extraordinarily empowering, easy to set up, with little to no maintenance, and the payoff is enormous—just like Napoleon Hill found from all those wealthy people he interviewed. But now you know just how it works.

Your MMG is not secret, just what is talked about is confidential. You will find that beyond the great ideas and support you get, a side benefit is that when you mention it to select family and friends outside of the group, they will give it some mythical power because they will kind of wish they were in on it. They might want to be like you!

During my bachelor days, I had more than one gal pal who asked me, "Are you talking about me at your Mastermind Group?" A gentleman never tells!

Chapter 13

Public Speaking:
Path To Power And Influence

T he fastest way to influence, power, and success, is through effective communication with people. We are talking verbal communication here—a lost art! Facebook, Instagram, X, texts, emails . . . our fingers do the talking, but nothing surpasses our verbal ability, which is far and away our most important skill.

Nine out of ten people are frightened to speak before a group, and it's higher with men than women. The vast majority of men would rather jump out of a plane than have to give a presentation to a group of people.

Be honest. How do you rate your personal communication skills? How do you think others rate your verbal skills?

Let's think about how often our personal communication skills, especially speaking before a group, come into play. Such skills include speaking to a boss and peers at business meetings, speaking before a service club, talking for a minute at a networking group, speaking in a hall, at a convention, at a conference, or giving a sales presentation. It even can include being called upon to give the prayer at an important dinner. Are you ready? Do you shine?

Can You Own The Room?

When was the last time you gave a "speech?" When is the next time you will give a talk? If you are moving on up, you will be called upon. Do you know how to be ready? Do you know how to *Own the Room?*

I have given literally hundreds of speeches before groups of a dozen or so to well over 1,000. I have introduced over one hundred Members of Congress and other national figures at venues around America. First, let me say, if a person is not nervous before an important presentation, it's because they don't know any better.

I have given all these endless speeches and taught public speaking at the university level. Allow me to share what I have learned in the next few minutes of your time, which, added to your natural gifts and those you have already developed, will be the key to opening a whole new world for you and help you achieve your goals in life. Let's set the stage for you.

Your Mindset

First and foremost, *total confidence*, total assurance, is your key to the castle. Work on your mindset, so that you are prepared to Own the Room. Second, prepare your fullest and loudest voice. We are talking about *projection*, speaking with a full voice, with lots of force and authority. Let your voice boom to the back of the room and bounce all around it, for you Own the Room!

In the university public speaking classes I taught, 95 percent of the students made the same mistake. They do not speak up! Feel the power in your voice. Feel the power your voice gives you, and speak up! Have total confidence because you will be prepared. You will have a compelling message. You will be assured, and you will Own the Room.

When speaking before a group or on the phone for a business type call, the volume of your voice is vital. I have supervised several hundred people in the business setting, and the rarest quality to find is assurance. People should be assertive—maybe that's why there are full classes on assertiveness training. By speaking up, you command more respect. You can say all the right things. But if you talk like a mouse, you will be treated that way.

Mental Preparation For Every Speech And Talk

Well before any presentation, start with the Big Picture so you do not get lost in the details. When the presentation is over, you will have achieved your goals.

Think in advance about how you want to come across to the audience. Visualize how you want the audience to react to you. You make those decisions. You and you alone have the power to decide those outcomes. Visualize how you want to come off and then make conscious decisions about how you will make it happen.

For example, how do you want to come across? Inspirational? As a leader? Smart? As part of the in crowd? How you decide you want to come across should be the first item on your agenda. When planning your presentation, it should be the last thing you think about before you go on. In the middle are all the important details, important, but details.

After you have completed your outline and you are all set to stand and give your presentation, forget all other details. You are prepared. Just think back to the Big Picture of what you want to achieve.

Your final instructions to yourself are how you are going to act to get the response from the audience you want. You can give yourself these directions in a couple words at the top of your notes: relaxed, confident, have fun, get audience response, take it slow, or any other way you want to come across to get the audience's response.

Do you know why very successful speakers like to come across like they are having fun for almost any type of presentation? Because if you seem to be having fun, you must be confident, and if the audience sees you having fun, they will have fun too.

When I have been called upon to make an inspirational speech (that's most of them), I like to let the audience feel they are glad they are alive. I mean, you can fire them up! You are a consummate professional and you are about to Own the Room!

Detailed Preparation

If you are prepared, really prepared, the chances are overwhelmingly good that you will be successful. I recommend practicing the presentation five times.

We are talking here about true practice: stand up and use a full voice. Go to the site of the speech if possible and practice there. You can usually make arrangements. Be a professional! Do what the others would not even think of doing.

Feel the room. Stand where you will be standing. Look out over the room. Visualize the people. Get comfortable. Be prepared to be in control. Determine where you will sit. Practice sitting where you will sit and walking to where you will be standing.

At the height of World War II, the great British Prime Minister Winston Churchill rallied the English people from the depths with his immortal "Blood, Sweat, and Tears" speech. Churchill practiced for several hours on just how he would rise out of his chair, approach the lectern, and look out over the audience before he'd say a word.

During the speech, Churchill lost over five pounds because he'd put so much into it. So be a pro. Do it right!

Bad Form For Notes = Bad Speech

Figure out in advance where your notes will be—where on the lectern or in which hand, or wherever. During my instruction in public speaking, I always asked the students to show me their notes after they gave a speech. In a few cases they would try to write out the whole speech, a receipt for disaster in 99 percent of the cases. The 1 percent is when only a few key words to outline the key themes are present.

People talk about extemporaneous speaking. They think that means, "off the top of your head." It does not. That is impromptu speaking. Extemporaneous speaking is actually speaking from notes. Speaking situations differ widely, obviously, but the best way to prepare for a passionate and compelling speech is to put down only four or five themes on one piece of paper, and put those themes into about four words each.

You do not want to have to look down too long, or you will lose eye contact with the audience. You do not want to concentrate on the words, or you will read them. Concentrate on the themes, and the words will come.

Do you remember the late Senator Fred Thompson (R-TN)? Probably not, and here is one of the obscure reasons why. He ran for president in 2008. He waited longer than most to make his entry into the primaries. He gave his maiden speech in Orange County, California, which was highly anticipated and greatly panned. They showed it on TV again and again because he gave a "bad" speech. What was the major reason?

Consider Everything In The Walk-Through

He and his advance people had not done their homework. Senator Thompson was a tall, commanding figure of about six foot, four inches. But when he spoke, he never seemed to make eye contact with the audience.

Why? He had a lectern made for a person about five feet, ten inches, and had to keep looking down at his notes. His staff should have found another lectern or adjusted the one at hand. There should be an almost straight line from the eyes to the notes to the heart of the audience. Checking out the setting in advance is called the walk-through and is a must for success.

Do you usually memorize your talks? Don't. There are rarely exceptions. If you try to remember the words, you will forget your train of thought. If you forget the next words you had memorized, you are lost.

That very thing happened to me long ago in the eighth grade. In biology class, we had to give an oral report every week. I was so glib about it, and the teacher picked me to give an oral report on oral reports during parent's day.

The "Best" Speaker Froze—Me!

In the first hour, I cut through it like a hot knife through butter. In the second hour, three minutes through, I froze up. I mean froze! My teacher probably didn't know whether to laugh or cry (Mr. Ballentine—I still remember his name). He finally coaxed me out of it. I threw away the notes and was later undefeated every year in a very competitive high school varsity debate in the state of Michigan.

Think of the last time you made a standing, or even a seated, presentation. Can you remember what your notes looked like?

Organizing the outline of your speech is separate from practicing and is best left for separate days. Organize your thoughts and print them onto paper. Pay special attention to how you will transition from one theme to the next. A smooth transition between every one of your points makes for a smooth presentation. So, deal with transitions, which is where a lot of speakers flub. Get your talk tightened up!

Get away from your notes for a day and then see if your notes still make complete sense. Much to your surprise, you will probably find that what you were thinking of when you wrote down a couple words no longer makes sense to you.

To eliminate any speech problem areas, refine those notes. Ensure your understanding of your own meaning is clear. To easily make changes, on your index cards or paper, make your notes in pencil so that you can erase and readily make smooth changes, without starting over.

You Won't Get Lucky. You Have To Practice

Practicing the night before the presentation is ideal. With a new, challenging speech and audience, you might want to practice on three successive nights before the big day. You should go from the beginning to the end five full times in total. Myself, I feel more comfortable going over small segments (as in a half-minute or so each) five times each before I get it where I want it, so it flows, and then I move on.

After you have practiced the last time, the night before, put your materials away and forget about it. You have done all your homework. You are relaxed and ready to go.

When thinking of the presentation, go back to the Big Picture. How do you want to come across? Relaxed? Knowledgeable? Passionate? Think Big Picture so there is no need to fret about the details. You have already handled the details. Everything will fall into place.

Please remember, if you are not on tap to give a speech or presentation of some kind, you will be in the future, especially as you get to be more successful. And the stronger of a communicator you are, the farther you will move up the ladder of success. So, with all that in mind, here are some further details on your way to influence and success.

Warning On Jokes: A No-Lose Way

Most often, jokes are not worth the risk. If you tell a joke, it is obviously a joke. You get a laugh, and it's a slight plus. When you finish the punch line and there is silence, you lose. Early in my career, I told jokes that I thought were hilarious. Often, the audience was unimpressed.

Afterward, my friends would give me the needle for unfunny jokes. Anecdotes, about some real event or happenstance, especially self-deprecating things about yourself, are far more win-wins. They don't laugh because they don't know they were expected to.

Showtime

How can you help yourself relax? Remember, when you come across relaxed, the audience will be too. Thus, you never say you are nervous. But here is something that will help you take the edge off to get into your remarks. Do not memorize the exact words that you will use to get started, unless it is "Madam Speaker" or "Mr. Vice President." Let it play out.

On the notes, maybe I have a page of five themes with the four words to remind me of each theme. At the top of the page, I have my two words that tell me how to come across, like "Relaxed, Confident." Then, at the very beginning I always write "Intro" and that reminds me it is off the cuff.

Secret Technique For Getting Relaxed

I never decide what my technique will be until I get up there. I say the first thing that comes into my head, based on the circumstances. Maybe I will thank Joe for the introduction. Maybe I remark about how hot the room is. Maybe I say hello to someone who just came into the room. The key is to take the pressure off yourself. No matter what you say, it'll be fine and since the audience will know it's spontaneous, they know it's unrehearsed and you are in control.

Hecklers And Sharpshooters

Gotta love 'em. Make them your friend, kind of. The first rule is to acknowledge them. If you try to ignore them, the audience may come over to their side and/or think you are intimidated. So, acknowledge, have a segue, and move on. Though, sometimes some hecklers need a bit more time than others.

I was having a problem with the audio system once at the beginning of another big speech and mentioned it to the audience in passing. That's when a guy in the audience yelled out, "Man up!" I happened to know the guy (my buddy, right?) and knew he had probably done some front-loading at the bar, so I quickly responded, "Proof that there is an open bar." Some people use, "I remember when I had my first beer." But I have never needed it.

If someone is having a quip, a joke, that is clearly in good fun, you laugh, point and say a couple words, and move on. Whatever you do, you don't give them the mike. You just might not get it back on your time.

Working the Crowd

It's one thing to get the crowd impassioned. But a step above is where you work the crowd, get them to respond in a way you can predict, and create a back-and-forth energy for your message.

Close It Out

It's one thing to get the crowd up on their feet at the end. That is a bar I have always set for myself. MSNBC keeps rerunning a video of Jeb Bush (a very decent guy from a family of most distinguished Americans) in 2016, from when he was running for President.

He finishes the speech, and nothing. He says, "Please applaud." They do. Maybe they did not know the speech was finished. Your job is to let them know when it is over. So really punch it up at the end. So here is the only place you memorize a few lines. You plan your cadence for each word and phrase and end on a very high note.

When I arrived in Vietnam, I got what I considered to be a lucky break. Rather than leaning on my supposed skills as a "trained killer" (how some of my fellow infantry officers with a macabre sense of humor referred to us) the Army decided to lean on my supposed brains, and I was assigned to the 4th PSYOP group.

I was a few days into my tour, and I kept thinking, "This is great. This is great. I might actually live through this." So, there was a Hail and Farewell Party at some BOQ in Cholon, the Chinese section of then Saigon. It's where you say farewell to the outgoing officers and greet the incoming ones. There were officers from the four battalions—a group of one hundred or so in my memory.

Surprise! "In one minute, you are going to rise and give a rousing speech."

First there were drinks, of course, then there was dinner and more drinks.

I am sitting there, thinking, Wow! This is unbelievable. I never thought I could have this much fun in the US Army.

The dinner was about done and LTC Deputy Commander Barker, who was sitting opposite me, leaned toward me and said, "Hampton, in one minute, I am going to rise and introduce you to speak, and you are going to get up and talk about the great job CPT Thompson, Lt. Jenks, and Lt. Haus did, and why they are great Americans."

I certainly cannot remember their real names, but he named the three of them, and I most certainly knew I had never met them. I recall that was one long minute. I believe I may have sobered up considerably in that time. At any rate, I cannot remember what I said—other than I spoke for maybe four minutes. After I got rolling, I was really enjoying it all.

After that, at the monthly officer happy hour meetups, LTC Barker would simply say, "Hampton will say a few words." Just me and the Commander spoke. I was the warm-up act, I suppose. I remember one time I was addressing the would-be exploits of some officer, relating how he had been surrounded on five sides on Pork Chop Hill in Korea and all he had was a Korean's leg swinging around his head.

I remember that one. I had gone on for several minutes when the Commander interrupted me to say, "Are you done yet?" I told him not quite, and I "talked" a bit longer. Amazing I was ever promoted!

Introducing Presidential Surrogates

Over the course of many Presidential campaigns, I have traveled to the early primary and caucus states to host programs/rallies. Acting as the MC in places like Cedar Rapids and Des Moines Iowa; Manchester, New Hampshire; Columbia, South Carolina; Tampa, Florida;

Las Vegas, and many other locations, I had the honor of introducing surrogates who were appointed to speak for the candidates.

The Presidential candidates included Barack Obama, John McCain, George Bush, Mitt Romney, John Kerry, Hillary Clinton, and many others. Friends and family of the candidates rose and spoke of the virtues of their supported candidates. Some people I remember well, others I do not, and for many, I cannot remember what they said.

But one surrogate I will never forget. The program/rally was in Philadelphia. With the full crowd and the cameras rolling, this particular surrogate was about five minutes into a really unremarkable speech. Then suddenly, his lips stopped moving. He didn't talk but just stood there amid the eerie silence.

People held their breath. What was he going to do? He stared straight ahead. After about a minute that seemed far longer, he continued like nothing happened. For that minute, like me in high school when I froze up, he Owned the Room—not the way you want to do it, though.

Back in the day, we had videos of all the programs and speakers. This particular speech took on iconic notoriety. The top on everyone's list to review was this "mesmerizing" speech.

No wonder some people would rather jump out of a plane than give a speech!

Chapter 14

Be A Power Player With Your Words

What is your most valuable personal skill? What is your most important career skill? Think it over and give yourself honest answers.

Answer: no matter what your skill levels are, your verbal skill is your most important personal and career skill.

You have probably heard the old saying, "Never use a big word when a small word will do." Little could be further from the truth. You know the people who say that? The people who don't know any big words.

There are notable exceptions if you are in league with Abraham Lincoln and have a Gettysburg Address in you. Then there is an exception. The sixteenth president gave one of the most memorable addresses in history, with all small words.

We are talking in everyday communication, with business people, friends, you name it. Longer is better. It is worth repeating: our verbal skills are our most important skill. (See Chapter 13 on Public Speaking, for just one aspect of it.) The fastest way to influence is through the spoken word.

Three Got To Be President And Never Sent An Email

You may know that in the age of computers, there are three living presidents who never sent an email.

Our fingers are important—as in the keyboards to our computers. Probably the most valuable class I took was typing in high school. I was one of thirty students in a class of only two males, and the other guy assuredly never earned a varsity sports letter. I was terrible, but I picked it up after a couple years of practice. I have always been able to do about seventy words per minute.

But here is far and away the best part: you don't have to have a big vocabulary (i.e., all the extra, most tedious study time) to seem like you have a big vocabulary. When people think you have a big vocabulary, they impart special powers to you.

People hear you use a couple words they don't really know and they instantly believe you come from a great background with a good education, whether you do or not. It's the reverse of what knowledgeable people think of you when you use poor grammar.

Not convinced? I understand. Let me give you just one example. Years ago, I was a junior Account Executive for an advertising agency in Grand Rapids, Michigan, the second largest agency in the second largest city in Michigan.

What a great job—not like Mad Men, but way up there. Trips on private planes to far away cities to roll out of some of our advertising campaigns. My boss, Jack Norman, President of Norman, Navan, Moore & Baird (the best boss a guy could have) was on the Board of Directors of this bank. They were changing the name of the bank. I was assigned to put together a broadcast and print campaign to roll out the new name.

Two Big Words and They Thought I Was a Genius!

One Saturday morning, the directors convened in our conference room. I gave the full pitch for the entire campaign. They like it? Great. If they don't, it's back to the drawing board. After my presentation, the directors convened with Jack in his office. Later, Jack came out and told me they liked it. All systems a go!

Wow! I was new at the agency and off to a good start. What did Jack say about the content of my presentation? He said, "You used a bunch of words they didn't know the meaning to. Way to go!" I was not conscious of my big my words at all.

That was it. That was all. I didn't know what to make of it for a long time, but having reflected on it, clearly, if I knew some big words, I must be a smart guy and it must be a strong ad campaign. They were not advertising people, after all. I did have the Master's Degree in Advertising and another in communications experience, but they did not know that.

This can really work for you, but in a very time-economical way. I did not even think of myself as a guy with a big vocabulary at the time, but like a lot of things in our lives, my parents made me do it.

How many tests have you taken? How did you do? I have taken far, far more than I ever wanted to. Have you ever taken an IQ test? I have. Another case where my parents made me do it. You may know that young people taking IQ tests typically score higher than they might in later life.

At any rate, here is how I was forced into learning a great number of big words, which I still have knocking around in there despite the hard times I have given my brain. I am going to come back with a real short cut for you. The little time you invest to have a "large vocabulary" will continue to amaze your friends and confound your adversaries. We are talking verbal vocabulary here. If you have them, you don't have to go to the thesaurus.

I Misspelled My Name During An IQ Test!

My parents were university professors. They wanted their kids to be smart, and if we were not, they wanted us to get smart. So, they took us junior high schoolers from Albion, Michigan, to Northwestern University to have our IQs tested. We were in the waiting room, and my sister Charlene took it upon herself to introduce herself to everyone who came in the door and invite them to take a seat. I doubt that points were added to her score.

They certainly were not for me, for after I filled out the form, they came out and asked, "We don't usually ask people if they know how to spell their name, but is your middle name *Author*? Like someone who writes a book?"

I said, "No, it's Arthur." But I did not know how to spell it because I'd never used it before. Off to a running start.

Anyway, here is the bottom line to all this: I scored pretty high overall, but they said while my math skills were good, my verbal skills were weak. My parents were appalled. They instituted a remedial program. I was made to take a couple dozen vocabulary building learning courses, turning in answers to these questions about what all the words meant after looking them all up in the dictionary. You will not have to do this!

I was paid a couple dollars for each of the tests I was required to hand over to my parents. I cheated by going two doors down to Becky Bennet's house where we both worked on the answers. I gave her part of the money.

So, there you go. That is the only reason I still have a good vocabulary after all the Happy Hours (see Chapter 25).

Only A Handful Of Words Needed For A "Big" Vocabulary

Okay, here we go. I have been telling people this for years but never made it happen until this book. You only need to master ten big words or maybe even half of them! That's all! Then spring them on people. Nobody is with you all the time so sprinkle them in here and there and *bingo*! People will think you have a large vocabulary.

This is going to be some of the very best time you have ever invested in yourself. We are talking the absolute minimum of your time for the absolute maximum return, but you have to do the minimum.

I have thought about this quite a bit over the years and now for you, dear reader, I am going to pass on the Top Twelve, which is all you will ever need. You probably know some of these already. The big key is to not just know them but to add them to your working vocabulary. Add them to the ones you likely already have, and it will be a bonus.

Here is the guide: the "big words" should usually have four syllables to qualify, those ending in -ous seem to have the biggest kick. When I put my mental list together, I also found that some words starting with *P* also deserved special merit.

Now, these words can be in two categories: words you know your friends and colleagues have never heard of before and, maybe even better than the first, words people are going to hear *you* use where they know what they mean, but they are not in their working vocabulary.

That's why the Dynamic Dozen are largely the second, but if they fall in the first category, that's fine because people will hear you say them and of course not know what they mean. That's a good thing. They can mean anything to the listener—so much the better. See number twelve for that.

The Dynamic Dozen: Top Words For Your Personal Power

Obsequious: (ob.-see-kwe-us) adjective. In a bit of a coincidence, I had planned this chapter in my mind when my wife and I saw the hit movie *Night School*, a very good movie starring a very funny guy and great actor, Kevin Hart. His character is in high school, taking the final exam to graduate, I believe. The first word on the test was *obsequious*, and Kevin's head swims, the word gets all blurry, and he obviously does not know the word. He drops out of high school and goes back seventeen years later to "Night School" to get his degree.

Laughter is an instant vacation. This movie was a full vacation. Anyway, this one is in most people's vocabulary but not their working vocabulary, meaning they know what it means but never really use the word. So, people hear it and think, "I know what that means, but I never say it." But you should use it if you don't already.

So, its four syllables and ends in -ous and means, "excessively attentive, fawning, sycophantic," and the behavior of being a suck up. Usage? You are speaking of a politician or maybe a disliked coworker behind their back.

"We know that Joe is just being his obsequious self."

Doesn't it just sound like something very distasteful? Great for your word arsenal.

Perspicacious: (per-spa-ka-sous) adjective. Here we go again with four syllables and ending in -ous, perfect for your working vocabulary. Now, this word is one step up (more obscure) from sagacious—you know, the quality of being smart—but perspicacious is better. It's one more syllable. This can be used in any number of ways, such as when a person tries to impress you with how bright they are and you say, "I can tell you are really perspicacious." Maybe you mean it and maybe you don't and you're being facetious or sarcastic, a word that can be used for many occasions.

Propinquity: (pro-pin-kwa-tee) noun, as in the "Law of Propinquity." Okay, I made that up. At least, I have not heard it elsewhere, but there is a "law," the Law of Proximity, as in

Woody Allen and President H. W. Bush said, "Ninety percent of life is showing up." You can see all the uses. Look for them. They are everywhere.

You might say in casual conversation, "Remember the Law of Propinquity?"

More than half the time, they will pretend they know what you are talking about, which is what makes it especially fun.

Peripatetic: (per-a-pa-tet-ic) adjective. Another word starting with *P* but it has five syllables, meaning you get more credit. This one can come into play all the time. It simply means, "The act of moving around a lot, traveling from place to place." As opposed to *being there*, this one is *moving around to be there*.

Know a person who travels a lot? They are peripatetic. I talked to a lawyer (see the Chapter 4 on protecting yourself from lawyers). He was in Baltimore and from downstate Virginia.

He traveled a lot, and I said, "Bob you are very peripatetic."

I am quite sure he did not know what I meant, but he knew I was talking about traveling a lot, so he said, "I wouldn't say a jet setter." Maybe a coverup?

Perpetuity: (perp-pa-too-a-tee) noun. Another *P* one and another of my favorites. It means "Something that will go on and not end." That is a long time. I was head of an organization, and we gave plaques to Members of Congress—the usual certificates of appreciation, explaining why they are great Americans (they all were with only a couple exceptions). The bottom of the plaque stated, "Your contribution is inscribed and will be honored in perpetuity." Gosh, I loved to read that word aloud! I would drag it out.

Inexplicable: (in-ex-plic-a-ble) adjective. There are five syllables. People mostly know what this means: "Having the quality of not being able to be understood." They know what it means, but it is not in their working vocabulary. People hear you use the word and can't help themselves.

They think, "I know what that means, but I never say that word out loud, but obviously Sally here is using that word . . ."

The back of their brain is probably saying, "Gee, she probably uses a couple hundred that I don't."

Not checkmate but check.

A lawyer writes up some contract. It is inexplicable, not able to be understood by anybody. "Frank, what you just said is inexplicable." Of course, if they use that line on you, your answer is "What part don't you understand?" (see "Some People Have To Be Told," Chapter 3.)

Languorous: (lan-guor-ous) adjective. Meaning, "listless, inert," as in the head, possibly. Here we go. Don't employ short words like stupid or even dull-witted, empty-headed, or vacuous, which are okay, but a longer one like languorous is better. Sock it to them! Repeat these words and make them your own.

Supercilious: (sue-per-sil-e-ous) adjective. Why say someone is arrogant when you can call them supercilious? People have heard the word, but what exactly does it mean, they ask themselves. I got one OER (Officer Efficiency Rating) where I was written up.

The grading officer said, "This officer is arrogant and aloof." He could have said, "supercilious," but I was in the Army. Later, I read a Nelson DeMille book where he wrote, "Infantry Officers are arrogant and aloof." Word for word of my OER! I was supposed to be that way. Okay, arrogant, but who wants to be called supercilious?

Sanctimonious: (sank-ta-moun-e-ous) adjective. A top favorite of mine that means, "The quality of a person being way too pious." Boy, have you all met many of these types? It has the -ous and five syllables.

Vexatious: (vex-a-ous) adjective. It has only three syllables, but it's in category number one. Who knows what this means? You do: the quality of being annoying, but ten times better. It comes in handy at dinner parties, receptions, and state dinners

Loquacious: (lo-qua-sous) adjective. Why call someone wordy or verbose when you can call them *loquacious*? You can see all the cases where this comes in handy. "They are being loquacious, and you are being the opposite, laconic, saying a lot in a few words."

Contumulous: (con-tum-u-lush) an adjective again. There are four syllables, ends in -ous and means . . . nothing! I made it up. It has no meaning, which means it is the best of the lot! The twelfth "word" is added to the eleven words for good measure, like Humpty Dumpty in *Alice in Wonderland*, who said, "What does it mean? It means whatever I say it means."

Try it yourself. "You are being contumulous," you say to some vexatious person. They either let it go and change the subject or, as has happened to me when I pulled it out, they deny it. "No, I am not being that way." This really puts the ball in their court because they know they want to deny whatever it is you are saying, but they know they will probably mispronounce the word when they try it. Gotta love it!

A final word on the Dynamic Dozen and this word power exercise for your personal power. First, this works. Second, it can work for you in short order. But don't make work out of it. This is fun and rewarding. There are twelve of these, so I suggest you go over them a couple times, at least. Maybe there are only half that you really feel comfortable with—that includes being able to pronounce them. Look at the phonetically done part.

So, you could pick only five or six that you feel comfortable with, ones that you can fairly easily see fit into situations where you can call upon them.

Once you have added these words to your personal repertory, you will never lose them. They will always be in the back of your brain, just waiting for the front of your brain to call them out and through your lips.

This is what it is all about: you are now ready for all the ups and downs in life and the jerks in-between!

Chapter 15

How And When To Reinvent Yourself

Are you happy or at least satisfied with where you live and what you are doing? If you are part of the work-a-day world, do you have the feeling that you are working your tail off but experiencing nothing but grief and aggravation? You have lots of company!

Do you remember seeing that GEICO commercial? The guy gets up in the morning and exclaims, "Not another day of this terrible job. I can't face another day." Then the guy's parrot says, "Not another day. I can't stand another day." Then the guy says, "I can't stand another day." These GEICO ads are funny, aren't they? With most funny TV commercials, you forget what the product or service is. GEICO makes it work. What a fun company.

Quick: can you count how many different places you have lived? When were you satisfied? Did you move on if you weren't? How many different personas have you made for yourself? Can you do it? Do you need to do it? Do you know how to do it?

I am not the leader of the class in knowing exactly when to make a serious life change, but I surely have established some sort of land, sea, and air record for moving and reinventing myself.

How Many Times Have You Moved?

In my family of origin, we moved eleven times by the time I got to high school. We are talking about a father who just liked to move—still not sure why. In graduate school at Michigan State University, I lived in six different locations in two years. Apples do not fall too far from the tree. I have moved all around the country many times.

Years ago, I was living in a venerable desert and things were not going so well, And not going well, and not going well, and so on. I kept telling myself I would end up crawling through the desert, out of food and water, before I would give up.

Well, I kept that mentality for a couple years before it finally got through my thick skull: You know what, Brian, you deserve better than this, and you can get better than this." There

129

began—or rather continued—a long process of reinventing myself so many times that the U.S. Patent Office could issue at least a dozen different patents on me.

Having to reinvent yourself is not necessarily a good thing but being able to reinvent yourself most certainly is. Let's start with the former.

Knowing when to make an important change and cut your losses is crucial so you may find a very important attribute . . . and doing so could be a very good thing.

Have you been trying and trying and trying on some career path?

Are You Ready To Employ The Ratchet?

If so, take stock of yourself. Are you happy with where you are professionally? Are you happy and successful in the job? The location? The satisfaction? The compensation?

Successful people know when to employ the "ratchet," meaning they stop doing what they have been doing, which is not working, and go in another direction.

Let me share with you some of my reinventions and tell you what I learned so you can compare it to your situation. You will see that I reinvented myself to the maximum that would seem possible, and am still doing it. But I have learned more than I thought possible along the way. You have read about those couple billion people, such as in India and elsewhere, who believe in reincarnation?

You probably know about the beliefs of reincarnation. We pass away. Our spirit survives and passes into a kind of mental place in the cosmos. Then, when we are getting closer to reentry, we go into the Astro Belt.

From there, we wait for our new body to be conceived, into which we are put and kind of get born again. The thinking goes that the entire purpose of life as we know it is to gain knowledge and understanding.

The more we have to learn from one life, the faster we go through the process—maybe a couple hundred years—and the more we are required to go back and try again to learn more. When our spirit is finally evolved into the highest possible form, we are evolved into Nirvana.

What does all this maybe mean? For me, I guess I had an overwhelming amount to learn. My gosh, can I even contain it all or even understand it all? It's reincarnation without leaving the planet. At any rate, to reinvent or not to reinvent, that is the question. How you reinvent and what you get from it and learn from it is another question.

Think. When Did You Last Invent Yourself?

When did you last reinvent yourself? What did you do? What did you learn? Did you do the right thing? Do you feel like you moved forward, depending on what that means to you? Life is uncertain, and nobody gets through it without plenty of challenges, so at least we have established the ability to reinvent ourselves can come in mighty handy.

At the age of four, I collected newspapers in my little red wagon on Cherry Lane, right next to the campus of Michigan State University. It's my earliest memory of life, going door to door in the rain at night and until my wagon was full. I can only imagine that my father had set me up in business . . . you could do those things way back then and there.

What did I learn? Well, I learned how to work and learned, looking back, that I didn't know enough, including when to get out of the rain.

Next up was a lemonade stand a couple years later, featuring my sister and me. What did I learn? That I could run a business. Remind you of the slam of one politician to another? "He couldn't run a lemonade stand." I learned I could run a business but I couldn't save any money. Still working on that one. How about you? That's a very good one to learn and stay learned.

So, enough of the making lemonade from a lemon. Want a career change? Want a location change? Want them both? Make a real assessment of your skills, then assess your skills on a resume. They may be different.

Decide What You Are Willing To Settle For

Decide how much you are willing to gamble and risk in reinventing yourself. No risk, no reward is largely true. Do you want to live your life to just extend your life? Is your goal just to be comfortable? Never get out of your comfort zone, and then some day—or maybe for a long time—ask yourself, is that all there is? You don't have to be either bored or scared. You can challenge yourself and be neither. I have never been bored, but I sure have been scared. Try to find a balance so you can live a wonderful life of passion and personal fulfillment.

I worked my way through graduate school as a bill collector. It's probably why I moved so many times. One guy had taken out a loan from "the Associates" and never made a payment. None of my predecessors could get a payment out of him. That's why they were my predecessors.

He worked nights at Oldsmobile. I went by one morning and his car was in front of his boarding house. He didn't answer the door upstairs, but I knew he was there. I borrowed a ladder from a couple houses down and put it against the second-story roof.

Some guy who must have been the landlord yelled at me when I was on the way up, "Get my money while you're up there."

His window was partly open, and I knocked. No answer. I opened the window, and there he was, lying in bed asleep. There was a chair propped against the door, and there was a deadbolt lock and a chain lock as well on his door.

I went around the bed and tapped on his shoulder and said, "Mr. Dietricts, it's Hampton from the Associates." No response. Louder, I said, "Hampton from the Associates."

He sat up in bed with a start and stammered, "How, how did you get in here?" Then he looked out the window and saw the ladder. I explained to him that I was collecting on a consumer loan that was six months overdue.

He was speechless. There was a wallet on an ironing board. I reached in and got forty dollars and wrote him a receipt. Then I told him I expected him not to be late again and exited the way I had come in.

Another time, I ended up chasing a guy through a warehouse, both of us on forklifts. He had lied to me at least six times about paying a bill. I finished off this excellent adventure in consumer affairs by being the Regional Recovery Manager.

There Is A Far Better Way To Make A Living!

I was the guy who would knock on people's doors and say, "Mr. Hopkins, I am Hampton with the Associates. You know that Chevy that was repossessed in the middle of the night for non-payment? Well, it was sold at a public auction, and I am here to collect the $800 deficiency balance."

I survived those two years working my way through graduate school by the skin of my teeth. But my out-of-body experiences proved valuable in reinventing myself and getting a real job. I was hired to be the Director of Development at Kalamazoo College, though I had never raised any money in my life before, except if one could count bill collecting.

I was so full of myself. I never even remember telling my great new boss these stories. But now and then, with a big laugh, he would say, "It's Hampton from the Associates."

You can make more money, if that is what you want, by repackaging yourself: the same skills with a new presentation. It's possible. I once tripled my salary because I had the skills, gave a good interview, and, of course, they didn't check or ask how much money I had made before. It's possible. I had to move across the country, but I landed the job before I moved.

Another time, I quit one of the best jobs of my life which I had previously mentioned, working for an advertising agency in the penthouse suite in Grand Rapids, Michigan. What a great job. I resigned, had no more than about $400 back then and a credit card with a low limit and drove to Washington D.C. to get a job with the forecast political consultant of the time. I had picked him out and talked my way into his office.

Get In The Door And Get Liked!

This man ran the foremost political consulting agency in the land at the time. I guess he liked my *chutzpah*. You can employ it, too, when called for. He took me to dinner with other consultants, and he liked me, so I was hired. I did have some, but not very much, political experience. Please remember: when you reinvent yourself, it's almost better to be liked than to have the deep experience.

Would I do that again? Wow! What was I thinking? I had no plan B. So be bold, take a chance, but have a plan B.

It is always easier to get a job if you already have a job. Why is that? Because with no job, at the interview, the person doing the interviewing cannot help themselves and thinks, "This person is unemployed—what a needy person." (See Chapter 11 for how to land a job through the interview.)

You can fix that, though. Enter one of the most time-honored professions there is and become a "Consultant." How do you do that? You establish your business platform online. You have some cards printed up. That's it. You are the head of a sole proprietor, such as "Hampton Enterprises: Political, Communications, and Fundraising." Your clients? You have a few. Stay vague—confidentially, you know. Bingo, you are not unemployed. That business card is for the job interview. Maybe you will get some clients in the meantime.

Be Sure To Get This Clause In Your Contract

You make that big move, land the new job, find a new place, or not. But always, always get a severance agreement, as in, "If this contract is terminated for any reason," you will get a severance of, say, six months of your salary. You never know what is going to happen when you walk into a new job. The boss might be a dreadnaught, they run out of money, they get bought out—who can say?

Here is another one: remember that great job at Kalamazoo College I had before I did another reinvention to a would-be politician? On a Friday, I resigned from my great job at K College. On Saturday, I announced my candidacy for the US Congress. I moved from a restored mansion on South Street to a boarding house, with a tiny bathroom and kitchen down the hall. The rent way back then was one hundred dollars a month.

But campaigning would have to wait for two weeks. I was Commander of an Army Reserve Company. On Sunday, the company got on a few buses bound for Pennsylvania for operations training in the Poconos Mountains. I ended up carrying the total vote in nine of ten counties, but lost the tenth, the most populous one by a sizable margin. Close, but no cigar!

So, this part you already know, but to reiterate: when you are reinventing yourself, try not to quit your day job!

PART 4

How to "Scheme" the Systems

Chapter 16

There Is Always A System: Make It Work For You!

Everywhere we look, there are systems, the organization, the SOP—call it whatever you like.

Remember the old saying, "Better they are inside the tent doing their business out, then outside doing their business in." This refers to co-opting your enemies and/or other outliers. Abraham Lincoln said, "Do I not destroy my enemies if I make them my friends?"

The old Mafia line is to "keep your enemies closer than your friends." If you don't have any enemies or serious detractors who would not mind helping to bring you down, then you have lived a charmed life, so far.

Politics is everywhere, federal, state, and local. Vince Foster, who died by suicide when he was General Council early on in the Clinton Administration, said, "Politics is a blood sport."

There Are "Systems" Everywhere

How about the "politics" where you work or even in your own family or maybe your neighborhood association? It's everywhere. It's everywhere. You could be performing way above average in your job but don't do the office politics and be out on your rear. You better devote a considerable amount of your time, even if it doesn't seem right, to protect yourself from those who might stab you in the back if they can't get you in the front.

While Kelly Ann Conway was in the Trump White House, she famously said she didn't stab people in the back, but that she does it in the front, so, "They see it coming." It's a dog-eat-dog world (see Chapter 7).

Talking about tough politics, there is the elective type, the labor politics, and the campus politics—some of the most brutal there is. If you are in college or went to college, you have a fairly good view of the campus politics. The professors who have tenure, who are the most sanctimonious of the lot (see Chapter 14 for when to use this fun word). My parents were college professors, and they told me so at a young age. It was not them, of course.

One of my favorite bosses (I have had too many to count), John Dozier at Kalamazoo College (a World War I fighter pilot, which was good preparation for the campus), told me once that one of the deans was out to get him. He said if the dean did not pull it back, that he would, "Slit his throat and he won't even know who did it."

Wow! That is politics. He was speaking metaphorically, but you get the idea. He knew what he had to do to protect his job. Do you? Are you ready to do what is necessary?

How To Make The System Work For You

First, you need to learn the system in which you operate. Then, after you learn the system, you turn the system back on itself. The idea is rather than throwing rocks at the system, you get the rocks to build something for you.

A few years ago, a buddy invited me to join him at a meeting AT what was then Jessop Federal Prison. I don't think it had a number of fellow veterans. All the inmates who were veterans were afforded the benefit of inviting their wives, girlfriends, or what have you to a kind of luncheon in the general area. It was truly a scary place. My friend was like a counselor to these inmates. A chaplain went with us. Those two were expected to address the group. I intended to say a few words myself.

We were led from one secure area to another, the barred doors closing behind us. Further and further in. At one point, my buddy turned to me—I had probably gone pale—and he said, "Are you alright?"

I said, "Oh yeah. I'm great."

There they all were, about eighty inmates seated at a separate row of tables, with their women friends right next to them. No women inmates in this part of the prison.

A mic was set up. My buddy, a real street-smart guy, talked. Really inspirational stuff, but he was basically ignored. Without a doubt, these guys were a little busy under the tables. The guards were respectful, keeping their distance, but at the ready inside the catwalks.

Imagine Giving A Speech In Prison

The chaplain spoke, and maybe a third of the guys looked up. Those two were wrapping it up. The mic stand was pushed aside. I said I wanted to say a few words and pulled the stand in front of me. I only remember a couple of the themes I delivered. But I had sized up the kind of crowd that would be there well in advance (see Chapter 13 on "Public Speaking").

I had campaigned for Congress in Black Baptist churches. I grew up in Albion, Michigan, which was then industrial and about 35 percent African American. My friends who came to my house (to work on the Jack Kennedy campaign, play cards, and play pool) said they always felt welcome at our house. I had never given it a thought in the first place until it was mentioned one day.

I thought I could really get the attention of these guys and maybe give them some hope. I spoke for a while but was totally ignored, so quickly I realized I had to change the dynamics.

I remember a couple themes were that life is not fair, some people are not treated the same by the system, and it was time for them to rise up (meant in a figurative sort of way).

I had one line in mind all along.

"It's time to get some!" I yelled it out, and half took notice. I yelled it again, "It's time to get some!" Now about two-thirds looked up. Whatever I meant by that, I'm not entirely sure. I think I was saying it's time to stand up and speak out or something. Time to be empowered.

They Were "Getting Some" In Prison!

About that time, about half of the guys were on their feet yelling and shaking their fists. "That's right! That's right. Right on, brother."

Now I was getting really scared. The scene was wild and maybe about to go out of control. Then, all around me, glamg, glamg, glamg! The prison was put in a lockdown.

What have I done? What will I do? I improvised and said something like, "You know what, guys, there is plenty of injustice, but we have to work within the system. Get to know the system and turn it back on itself."

They sat down (half had certainly heard me but were otherwise preoccupied) and order was restored. The three of us were quickly led out of the secure areas, which were many. When we got to the fresh air, I thought my two attendees would comment on my ability to inspire/incite a crowd.

Instead, the chaplain said, "You know, Brian, I think they were getting some."

In what systems are you operating? Do you understand the system? Do you really understand how it works? Knowing what you know, are you making it work for you? There is a difference, of course, between knowing and doing something about it.

Take the United States Army, for example. It's the biggest organization in the world, with more systems and regulations than humanly imaginable. It took nearly a year to get working within the system of the Army through my thick skull. I wanted to do it my way (you can surely imagine). But I did pick up a few things along the way.

Organizations May Be Different: Techniques Are The Same

The United States Army is one of the most regulated and rigid organizations in the world. When you learn to operate there, you can operate almost anywhere. So, I am going to give you many real examples of how I did it, so you can get the drift of how to adapt parallel techniques throughout your life.

You most likely know this: the ones who did the most courageous things in the military talk about them the least. But I am going to be sharing something different while relating some lessons for life I learned in the Army. There are strong parallels that you can draw to make your life far easier as you perfect the vital art of making the systems work for you.

I learned some of these lessons only after I asked myself, "Why in the world did I do that?" You can learn some lessons from my experiences and probably be really entertained as well.

Basic Training was for eight weeks during the winter at Ft. Dix in New Jersey. On the second day, Drill Sergeant Nascimento (the flyweight boxing champion of the entire Army—one always remembers the names of such people) caught me shaving after breakfast in the latrine. You were supposed to do it with everybody else, before breakfast. He was even-tempered (this time), but he gave me the eyeball-to-eyeball stare and told me to wake him up every morning, 5:30 a.m. or whatever, knocking on his door, so he could escort me to the latrine, where I would dry shave. You know, shave with just the razor.

Sergeant Butt Kicker made me his personal project. He showered me with attention. Part of our physical training (PT) test was the 250-yard man carry (now outlawed). He lined up the platoon of forty-three recruits by height and then assigned a man for each to carry.

I weighed 150 pounds, but I was six foot one inch, so he lined me up with another guy who was the same, but wait . . . he weighed at least 220 pounds! I barely got the guy on my back. I did the 150 yards kind of staggering the whole way.

We had pugil training, done with wooden sticks with pads on the end. The platoon would form a circle and the contest would begin. They pretended it was like bayonet training: parry left, parry right, and so forth. Fancy stuff. The reality was that you got in the ring with a wire mask on your face and a groin cup and then proceeded to try to beat your opponent senseless.

Is A Ruffian On Your Case?

The platoon commenced competition on pugil training. Guess who I got matched up with? Yep, the biggest guy in the platoon. It was two out of three each round of three minutes. The first round, I did well and put out an enormous amount of energy, but the big guy had clearly won. Sergeant held up his arm in victory. For the second round, I was furious in my attacking, and I did a little better, but the guy had clearly beaten me. I was totally exhausted but also kind of exhilarated. I had shown up before my fellow soldiers. I was glad it was over.

But then, Sergeant Butt Kicker unexpectedly held up my arm. I was the winner of the second round! Oh no. This is not over! What a sadist.

In the third round, my considerably less weight was in my favor, and I beat him convincingly. Sergeant held up my arm. Thank goodness, it was over.

But wait, again!

Sergeant says, "Okay, you are representing the platoon in the company platoon competition, and that starts right now."

Holy cow! Some guy comes up to the Sergeant and says, "Why is he representing our platoon?"

"Because he beat the biggest guy in the platoon."

I knew I was sunk for the next and final round. I said, "Sergeant, I left it all out there in the field. I have nothing left."

He ignored me.

So, there are about 120 guys in a bigger circle. I am up first.

My opponent gives me the bull rush, beats me senseless, and in a little over a minute, has me on the ground, with the bugle pointed at my throat. First round was over. Second round was the same but shorter.

Afterward, a couple guys came over to console me. "That's all right, Hampton. That guy is a mad dog."

After that, the drill sergeant essentially left me alone, except during drill and ceremony (which I could never quite get), where we had to present arms—as in our M-14s. I never got it quite right.

A couple times, he would come over and kind of push the rifle back and forth against my chest. "You're going to be an officer, right? You're going to OCS, right?"

The idea that one day I might be an officer, the kind he would have to salute, really annoyed him. I totally understood.

What's The Game Where You Work?

Do you know the games going on where you work and play? Like much of life, some of these big questions, like what's happening within the government, are serious, but still basically games. Do you know how to play the game? It's good to know and do it.

Toward the end of our eight weeks (we got one day and one night off) the NCOs had obviously gone out for drinks. At twenty-four, I was older than almost all the trainees, who were mostly eighteen and nineteen. Still, the training was such that come Saturday at 7 p.m., you would lie down in your bed and be asleep when your head hit the pillow.

At maybe 2 a.m., the NCOs turn on all the lights and yell the usual, "Formation in the company streets." We all rush to get dressed and then line up in formation in the dark in the company street. Looking straight, heels together, waiting, waiting, and waiting for some kind of doom.

Some NCO yells, "Fall out!"

We troop back to the barracks and go back to bed. About five minutes later, the lights are turned on again, and one NCO yells again, "Formation in the company streets!"

Same thing. Five minutes, two minutes, and then, "Fall out!"

I thought to myself, Why go through this exercise again? They are just going to do it again. I am just going to stand here.

In the Army, when I was in training, troops were lined up in alpha order—hence me, Hampton, was next to Haddix, Hunt, Harrington, and so forth.

I am standing there in the dark, thinking I am all alone, and I sense somebody else is there. I turn around in the dark and see one other guy, Huff. It's me and Huff, like-minded guys. We were friends throughout Army training and right into Vietnam. Golly, the trouble we got into. I was kind of learning the system, but I was still too independently minded to just flow with the flow. I didn't stand in the back and not get noticed.

Do You Know And Work Your Office Politics?

How about you? I was involved with some office politics even after the Army, and I let my morality or whatever get in the way of my career. There was a big shake-up in the headquarters office. A new President of the organization was to be nominated.

I had a favorite, and I thought he might get the job, but I didn't do anything about it. After he got it and I knew he knew me and my strong track record of performance, I made no effort to really cultivate him, you could say. I was the strongest performer in the office. I thought he would want to keep me for that alone. Wrong. He let me go.

People later said they thought that he thought I was a threat to him. In retrospect, he was all about loyalty first, and I hadn't realized that. Or if I did, I didn't do anything about it. A slow learner in the office world of politics, I was, even though I finally grasped the Army system. But even that took me longer than it should have.

Are you a fast learner? Do you like to be taught? I like to learn, but I don't like to be taught. And do you learn fast or more slowly? I seem to learn more slowly. We are not talking about book learning here. We are talking about lessons in life. Let me share some more, so maybe you can learn faster the lessons I learned in fits and starts.

When you mess up at work or your personal life, like make a mistake or a series of mistakes and it is most likely not going to come to light, do you fess up or keep quiet?

So, Huff, Hannah, Haddix, and Handcock, were among others who went to AIT (advanced infantry training) at Fort Dix. AIT was everything that basic training was not. That is, really roughshod and disorganized. While the weapons and physical training were there, it was much easier. But still not easy.

Why Hit Yourself On The Head With A Hammer?

Why did the man keep hitting himself on the head with a hammer, he was asked?

"Because it feels so good when I stop." Something along those lines, let's think about after the hammer has stopped.

Our Platoon Commander was a Vietnam Veteran Captain. He was out and out convivial compared to any of the officers we had any contact with in basic. Huff and Hannah and I, but mostly me, were cutting every corner just because we thought we could.

This was 1968, and troops were in and going on their way to the jungles of Vietnam. Get them ready, get them out, was the philosophy. So, we were issued fatigues that were used by soldiers that had gone before us. When they issued the last names of the previous soldiers on a strip on the upper chest, I think everyone had them replaced with their rightful name. I didn't see the point, or maybe the advantage, so I left the original one on there. It said Betwee.

One day, we were in formation, and the CO gave an impassioned command about the "Army Way." He said he had an "Extra Duty List," and if anybody ever gets on it, they will probably never get off it. He said he had one soldier on the list, and at that point, he said, "Private Betwee, step forward."

What to do? I looked around briefly, and all eyes were straight ahead. I ripped off the Betwee label from my fatigues and stuffed it in my pockets. They conducted a search for Private Betwee. He was never found. I told you this was a disordered outfit. Nothing ever came of it. I never made the "Extra Duty List." But in a day or so, I checked in with my Private Hampton label.

If you mess up, you didn't have to lie about it, and it probably wouldn't come to light, would you fess up? Why would you want to do that?

How Not To Show Up And Stand Out!

So, the dirty dozen motley crew, about a dozen of us, head to OCS infantry training in Benning, Georgia. A couple days before we had to turn ourselves in we decided to meet at the Downtowner, a motel with a pool in the garden city of Columbus.

Pick any Army post. They are pretty much the same. We partied down—really partied. It was a couple hours before game time, and we were clearing out and throwing the bottles away and wow, there were maybe five fingers of bourbon left in a bottle. Waste not, want not, so I alone drank it down in short order.

We reported to the orderly room. The yelling began the second we opened the door. "Throw away those clothes, put on these fatigues, and low crawl to the mess hall!"

I was full of you know what and vinegar and bourbon. I led our group of about five and got to the steps first. I climbed up the steps and as I was reaching the door, it burst open and more wild yelling began. A First Lieutenant TAC Officer in a hard hat was calling us names, saying we hadn't colored in our patches and that our laces on our shoes were over when they should be under.

Then it was one of these moments of truth. We were face to face and a foot apart.

"What! What? This candidate has been drinking in my mess hall?"

He was absolutely beside himself with stark fury. Words no longer came out. His face got red.

The memory of those few minutes is hard-wired in my brain, never to be erased. There was like a thirty-second silence.

Somebody in the mess hall yelled, "At ease!"

More silence. He and I faced each other.

Somebody yelled, "Go get the CO."

Finally, words returned to 2nd Lieutenant LJ Smith: "You better hope . . . you better pray that you don't get put in the 3rd platoon or you are a dead man." Those words are hard-wired as well.

Smith was actually led away. The CO was there in a flash. Later, I learned he was only a 1st Lieutenant and another Vietnam combat Veteran.

He was a very calm and cool character. I was at attention. He looked me over from the right side of my head to the left and back again. He quietly said, "Be in my office at 500 hours tomorrow."

Lieutenant Smith was, of course, my platoon officer for the next twenty-three and a half weeks. Those were the days, my friends. I thought they would never end.

You Can Hate It And Still Be Good

I really hated all the training, every minute of it, as you can imagine. But I turned out to be quite proficient in all of it, all the endless weapons training, the PT, all of it. I had a bad attitude and they all knew it. They were on my case day and night to do everything within their power to get me out of the program.

Nobody talked about it, but certainly, we all knew what was in store for us. Around 1968 and 1969, about 40 percent of the small unit infantry platoon leaders would be KIA, MIA, or wounded in their first three months in Vietnam.

Finally, come graduation (even backstage getting ready to walk across the stage to get my commission as an officer and a gentleman), I thought they would give me the hook at the last moment. Not you, Hampton.

I actually got it though. The Full Colonel handed it to me and said, "Are you going to make it through the night, tiger?"

Maybe he said that to us all, but I knew what it meant: the 93rd Company CO had also told us when, after eighteen weeks we finally got a night off, "If you dance to the music, you have to pay the piper."

My newly minted fellow officers and I were still calling all the fellow 2nd Lieutenant TACK officers, "Sir."

I sought out Lieutenant Smith and said, "LJ, I enjoyed every minute of it." I knew that was the happiest day of my life so far. But it was not for another ten years or so that I would realize it was one of the proudest moments of my life, to earn that commission and get through Infantry OCS.

Pick Your Openings Or Be A Wiseacre Like Me

But what is the takeaway here? Some obvious things and maybe some not so obvious things. Think before you drink. That's pretty clear. A minute on the lips and months on the hips type of thing. Don't be a devil-may-care wiseacre. Why make it far harder on yourself? Consider your somewhat close-at-hand objectives, decide what you are willing to do, and then be smart about getting there.

Those Army recruiters all told us, Get into the infantry and you can get a branch transfer, like to AG (Adjunct General), the Shield of Shame, maybe even the far away Artillery.

I never believed that, so I started doing research to find out how I would keep the crossed rifles on my uniform and not die in Vietnam.

I found out about the 4th Psychological Operations Group at Fort Bragg, and only after I sent a letter to the now-late Senator Phillip Hart of Michigan, I was allowed to apply to go there. Before that letter arrived at the 93rd Company, I could never even apply.

Magic Pull with the Federal Government

You want some real pull? Send a letter to your Member of Congress, provide the documents and what you want, and then they'll send a letter to a government office. It'll get put in a red folder and become a "Congressional." In many cases, like magic, you go to the top of the bureaucratic pile.

After six months of me being an instructor at the JFK Institute for Special Warfare, I am a newly minted 2nd Lieutenant, teaching Majors and Colonels in the Special Forces courses on persuasive communications, psychological operations, and radio and television as propaganda media. You had to know your stuff. The sharpshooters were always at the ready.

But I was finally learning the Army Way. I was told to design a course on the Area Study, a course and a curriculum on what officers should do when they get to a new combat area of operations to prepare themselves and get the mission integrated. The Area Study was my special pride and job. Among all others, I really enjoyed standing on that platform and teaching the class.

One day, I concluded the class and a Full Colonel stood up to address me. He didn't have to do that, but he did it anyway. "Lieutenant (said with a hint of derision), are we to understand that you are the one who developed this course?"

"Yes, sir."

"Are we to understand that everything that you passed out is what you wrote?"

"Yes, sir."

"Then why, Lieutenant, should any of us believe a word of what you just said?"

If I would have really thought about it, my military career could have been flashing before my eyes. But I didn't really have to think about it. I was learning about how to successfully operate within a big system, a big organization. So, I said (and you can use something like this at your office), "Because the Army says so."

He sat down without further comment, and class smoothly continued.

Pick your spots and invoke the higher power, "Because that's the way the ABC Corporation conducts its business." Maybe you invoke family tradition, or because it's the law of the pack.

I had gone from the outhouse to the penthouse, at least the Army version. Then one otherwise sunny day, my CO at Fort Bragg ushered me into his office, all seemingly excited for me. My orders for Vietnam had arrived!

I knew it was coming, but I kind of removed the idea. He essentially said, "It even gets better. On the way to Vietnam, you get to take two weeks of jungle training in the Panama Canal Zone."

How could that be topped?

If you get some really unwelcomed news, don't let on that you care and are crestfallen. It's good, whatever, doesn't matter, and so forth. Don't let them see you sweat.

I had leave of three weeks before flying to Panama. It used to be that officers booked their own flights, at least stateside, and the enlisted took military flights.

It was hotter than hot at Fort Sherman. It never stopped raining. Our underwear kind of rotted off in about two days. We slept in hammocks on the side of muddy hills.

Try to take a leak at night by tipping the hammock. You would slide to the bottom of the hill on your stomach. We never saw them, but we heard there were officers who reported to jungle warfare training and told the folks, "We'll go to Vietnam, but we won't go through jungle warfare."

Eliminate Unnecessary Paperwork

That one I didn't do or figure out. That one didn't occur to me, but I picked up on it. The commanding offers at Fort Sherman were beside themselves wondering what to do. I am sure they thought of all the paperwork. So, what they ended up doing was putting them in a room by themselves and after two weeks, told them to be on their way.

We graduated from this place with seemingly more dense jungle training than Vietnam and they gave us our orders for reporting in at Travis Airforce Base near Oakland, California.

I had been assigned to USARV, United States Army Republic of Vietnam, to a holding area detachment in Long Bien.

But wait, there were five full days of travel time between the current date and July 19, 1969, the date I was to turn myself in at Travis. My mind started working overtime. I flew to Lansing, Michigan, to hang out with some friends. I had an idea. I was not keen to go, though I was willing to go, but maybe not so fast.

I called Travis AFB. I went through a number of people until I found the unit that was in charge of outgoing flights. I reached an Airman and asked him if he was in charge of the manifest of my particular flight. He said he was. I told him my name and told him to take me off of the manifest, that I would not be on the flight.

"What is your name again, sir, and your military number?"

I gave it to him. "Okay, so have you taken me off the manifest?"

"Yes, sir."

"Airman, tell me your name again." He did, and I thanked him.

I called my buddy Hannah, who was in Chicago. I asked him if he was willing to go to Vietnam. He said yes. I asked him if he was ready to go in about four days. He said no.

"Here's what you do," I said, and he did.

Know The System And Pull Off Amazing Things

My flight to Vietnam took off the same day that Neil Armstrong walked on the Moon, July 20. I was at the Albert Pick Hotel having gin and tonics around the pool at about that time. About July 21, Hannah and I met at Chicago O'Hare and got a flight to San Francisco. We checked into a motel, rented a VW, and partied like there was no tomorrow with all the new friends we could find.

Come July 27, we decided the jig was more than up. Time to pay the piper. We had heard of cases where officers showed up an hour late and were taken in a backroom and really chewed out by some Major.

We were, frankly, midway between hope and utter despair. The AFB was a very grim place. Loudspeakers, high ceilings, some very happy people (those would be incoming), and the other outgoing.

We found a counter. My heart was certainly pounding.

We laid down our orders and I said, "We'd like to catch a flight to Vietnam."

The airman looked at us, looked down, read the orders, then read them again. He said, "I'm sorry, you can't catch a flight for at least a day."

Oh my gosh! We had saved a card from the motel and laid it down and told him to please call us and leave a message at that number.

So it was that I flew over the Pacific and the international date line and turned twenty-five on an early birthday, July 28. We landed, checked into USARV Transient, and nothing happened to us.

In fact, nothing ever happened, except after a little over eleven months in country, I was catching a flight out of Vietnam and some finance guy was processing my orders. "Hey, that was some good vacation you had there Lieutenant. Sorry, but the Army can't pay you for it."

That thought had never entered my mind. Leave it to those finance people everywhere, the HR and the rest. There's no fooling them.

What I had figured out pre-Vietnam was that every single seat in every single plane going to Vietnam had to be occupied. Send all to Vietnam, no empty seats. I was getting to know the big organization. With no empty seat, the system was not up to it.

Learn Your System First. Work Your System Next

You are undoubtedly in a system in an organization. Get to know the system, then get the system to work for you. Don't fight the system. Of course, there always seems to be more challenges and more systems as we move on. Good to learn them, make the scheme, and let the process work for you.

Another Army lesson in store for me: I was most certainly the last one that any of the Army friends would think of to stay in the Army after my two-and-a-half-year commitment was over. Back then, it was two years for a regular tour, but you went to OCS and they tacked on the training.

One day, about eight years later, I got a letter from DOD saying I had been promoted from a 1st Lieutenant to Captain. What? I hadn't done anything I could tell but stay alive. I'm mighty proud of earning this commission. I think I will get into the active Army Reserve, and if something happens military-speaking, especially with PSYOP, I can be part of it.

I went into the active Army Reserve for twenty-two years and was promoted, despite being "arrogant and aloof," as one of the OERs said. I found out that the Reserve was like a culture unto itself. I met guys who really worked the system. Put in and got these training and language schools, got paid, and didn't have another job.

I was part of an IMA (Individual Mobilization Augmented) unit that met every Monday night in Washington, D.C., at the Department of Transportation. These were three-hour "classes" where soldiers, men and women, would check in to get retirement points. It was only after I got my twenty full years in, twenty-three in all, did I find that I would get this Tricare For Life insurance coverage.

Front Door a No-Go? Go Back Door

For two years, every Monday there was signing in for meetings, even if you tried to escape before the end of the three hours. All for that great retirement pay, you know ($1,200 a month for me).

Then one day, an Adjacent of the unit stands up and says, "Guess what? St. Louis, the personnel office for the military, has no record of any of us attending for the last two years."

This was even though he sent in the attendance log and documents after every meeting.

What the heck do we do? We put together a kitty, and one of us was dispatched to St. Louis, where he camped out for a couple days. He took what records he could find, found a Speedy 5 (a Specialist E-5) and took him out for dinner and drinks. In a month, the records were all undated, and order was restored!

Take care of the system, and the system will take care of you, especially those finance types!

Oddly, or maybe not, a large number of my longer enduring friends in life have been Army friends, even though I have not been part of the Army for a long time.

Occasionally, I will let it out to some that I served in the military.

They usually say, "You don't seem like a military type."

I understand. I once told an Army buddy that I could have made it to Colonel if I hadn't ticked off so many people on the way up. He said he had ticked them all off. My kind of guy!

Chapter 17

Make The Government Work For You

Have you ever had a run-in with the government? What kind of a question is that? Let me rephrase this: have you ever had a beef with the federal, state, county, or city government?

That is meant to be a rhetorical question. Ever had a parking ticket that you didn't deserve? Ever had some pushback from a federal government agency? State, as in DMV, or county, as in your property taxes, including your vehicles? If you can say no to all of the above, say a prayer, cross your fingers, and/or buy some lottery tickets. You are living under some lucky stars.

Some say, "I am from the government and am here to help you." It is one of the three biggest lies they tell. When you face government injustice, what should you do? The old saying is that, "You can't fight City Hall." Pay the two dollars. As Shakespeare called it, "The insolence of office." Or, can you fight back? How should you protect yourself, and when?

I have worked in the federal government and served for over two decades in the active Reserve and military duty. Moreover, I lived in the Washington, D.C. area for about twenty-five years. With those qualifications, let me say that we have a great country, but too often a lousy government.

Your Member Of Congress Works For You

Let's start with the Congress. Most people have high marks for their Member of Congress (How else would they get elected?), but very low grades for the Congress itself. The public gives the Congress as a whole a lower ranking than practically every institution in America, barely breaking double digits.

The Congress is the legislative branch of course. All these sixteen executive departments reach into every part of our lives. With plenty of competition for dysfunctional government, the Department of Veterans' Affairs could be exhibit number A.

A simple Google search of all the scandals at the VA turns up a couple million links. Reports of how far too many of our twenty-one million veterans are left behind could fill several books—and already have.

Not so well known is how the VA squanders billions of dollars through a simple lack of competition during its procurement processes. It squanders billions more by failing to fill out paperwork to collect payments from insurance companies.

Just a fraction of the money saved could allow the purchase of 200 facilities that could house 20,000 and provide for 300,000 additional dental procedures—all this for not a single dollar of additional cost for us, the taxpayers.

Why isn't this happening? Congress has known about these issues for years but has not done its job. Congress has a very powerful constitutional tool through oversight of the VA and all of the Cabinet Departments. Congress puts on a great show for the TV cameras in being shocked and outraged at various scandals, but there continues to be no effective oversight.

Every time some government official or agency does something terribly wrong, Congress or some government agency is going to conduct some investigation or conduct a review. More breaking news, more talking heads on TV, but little seems to get better for us.

Getting Your Member Of Congress In Your Corner

Okay, so Congress is an easy target. Here is something you probably don't know about what Congress does really right—well, not Congress, but your individual Member of Congress.

Having trouble with some federal government agency? Is your pension not arriving? Have you not heard back from the VA on your disability claim? (In past years, they have been backed up over 200 days to respond, with 700,00 waiting in line.) The complaints one might have with federal government agencies could fill another couple of books.

The district office of your Member of Congress (the typical member has about three such offices) is really good at something important (it helps many get re-elected), and that is constituent service. These two or three staffers in these district offices know every single service, government and non-government, that could be available to you as the constituent.

This is like magic, or as close as you will come dealing with the federal government. Let's say you have a problem with some federal government agency, holding up something they were supposed to do or just messing it all up.

Here is what you do. To get quick contact information on your elected Member of Congress, just go to house.gov, put in your zip code, and up will pop the contact with your member.

Most People Have No Clue How This Works Best

Then pick up your phone, call that 202-phone number for the Washington D.C. office, quickly identify yourself as a constituent, name the city where you live, and ask for the district office of the member closest to you. Please remember: less is better when dealing with the palace guard at The Hill, so the less explanation the better. The more you explain, the more they will think you don't deserve the right answer. That's the way it works.

Here is a little technique for the Washington types. Don't ask if you can have the information, as in, "Can you please tell me . . ." You say, "Please tell me the phone number . . ." There is a subtle but important difference between the two approaches. Don't ask. They pick up on that. Just politely tell them.

You then call that district office, where again, less is better, though these people will be friendlier than those in Washington. Whoever answers, say something like, "I am Betty Fields, a constituent. What is the name of the district chair for the Congresswoman (Congressman), please? Please spell that for me. What is your district office mailing address?"

If these people are sharp, they will give you the information right away. If they want to know why you are calling, again, less is usually better unless they are the district chair and you want to cultivate them a bit.

Otherwise, you say, "I have a letter for the chair about a constituent service matter."

Not Time-Consuming, And Very Effective

Then you go to work, but not much is required. You type up a one-page letter, no more, saying:

1. What happened
2. What you did already and where it stands
3. What action you want.

You can attach some basic paperwork, like from the government agency that relates to your case. You address this letter to the Member of Congress, as in "The Honorable so and so" and then the ATT line is to the district chair by name.

When you get ready to send it out, you call again and ask if they would take it by email. Snail mail is better, but both are best. Early on in the process, you will have to write off on a form letter that allows the member to direct a federal agency to take action.

After your package goes out, you will get a return response from the member saying they have received your request for help (They better. Give it about ten days.), and they will advise how it works out.

Then the staffer composes a letter for the member that goes to the appropriate office within the behemoth of offices of these government agencies. When it plops down on someone's desk, it becomes a Congressional (used to be a red folder) and your complaint goes to the top of the pile.

This is the process where Congress usually gets it right, so put these public servants to work for you when the time comes!

Are you or will you be confronted by the awesome power of the government? The chances are, unfortunately, if you have not been already, you will, and if you have already, you likely will be again. What to do? What can a single individual do to protect oneself, right a wrong, and/or make a difference? In many cases, public opinion is a powerful tool.

Take Bold Action And The Force Will Be With You

As Goethe said, "Take bold action and powerful forces will come to your aid." Let me just share one experience I had that is but one example where Goliath can be taken on. I will give you the short version. This is a kind of truth to power that you can employ in your own way, in your own circumstances, though what I did in this case is really beyond most human comprehension.

Many years ago, I worked for a couple years at the Federal Trade Commission at the national headquarters at 7th and Pennsylvania Ave. NW in Washington, D.C. The FTC is known as one of, if not the most, powerful federal agency in Washington, right up there with the Securities Exchange Commission. The FTC regulates and enforces antitrust, competition, and consumer affairs matters. It has regional offices around the country.

Working within the Bureau of Consumer Protection, our small Division team had worked almost a full year on a nationwide initiative to protect consumers.

At the time, some of the hundreds of private trade and vocational schools around the country had been ripping off unsuspecting consumers: selling correspondence courses that purported to teach people how to drive trucks through their books or promising jobs after graduation in computer science that were not really available then.

Your Federal Government At Work

Our small staff worked some very long hours to put together a nationwide consumer education program to educate consumers how not to get fooled by false claims made by these correspondence schools. We developed broadcast public service announcements, which we recorded with national celebrities and a dozen separate educational publications, that advised how not to get taken.

We visited government agencies around the capital and developed multiplier channels to get materials out nationwide, such as to most VA guidance counselors through HUD channels, and even to high school principals around the country.

We worked on this project for about a year. The major brochure was a thirty-two-pager that I wrote and which consumers could get for free after calling the 800-number promoted by the PSAs. We were about to conduct a big news conference there on the second floor of the national headquarters.

At the time, the FTC chairman was a Harvard-educated attorney, appointed to the job by President Nixon. Word came down that there was a problem in the Chairman's office. Suddenly, my boss and my boss's boss were nowhere to be found. So, it fell to me to go up and meet with the Chairman.

I was ushered into his spacious office. He had three fellow lawyers seated on either side of him. This was the only time I would ever actually see him, though three years later, I would come close. I remember that his suit looked very high-priced, it looked like he had a manicure, and even his haircut looked expensive.

"We Have A Problem Here"

He told me there was a problem with the thirty-two-page guidebook. The problem turned out to be that the high-paid lobbyists of the private trade and vocational schools had descended on the FTC and the Chairman and objected to the language in it. They were denied due process, he said. Talk about false and misleading arguments! One did not invite in the regulated to have veto power over the regulators.

The Chairman said, "I would say, you can have your news conference, but you will have to change your guidebook."

What? The guidebook was the centerpiece of the entire program. How can we have a news conference without it? The Government Printing Office had already printed 100,000 copies of the guidebook and delivered them to the FTC, where they sat underneath a couple stairwells. And the lobbyists are going to write it?!

He repeated himself, then I was dismissed.

My boss and his boss reappeared. They were actually decent, hard-working guys. Still, changes were made in the guidebook over our objections, and 5,000 were rushed into print by an outside printer while we had the news conference.

Later, someone leaked the story to a gadfly newspaper columnist who did a column on the exposé and said the Chairman had folded like a Japanese fan at the first hint of lobbyist disagreement.

The whole thing seemed to cool off in short order, as these things do in Washington. About a month later, the building superintendent called me to ask me what I intended to do about the 100,000 guidebooks under the stairwells. They are a fire hazard," he said.

I Resigned In Protest

After a couple more weeks, I resigned from the FTC and put my reasons in very strong language, explaining I was protesting the anti-consumer practices of the FTC. I went back to Michigan, was the campaign manager for a successful campaign for Congress (the guy had lost twice before), and then moved on to take a new job in Kalamazoo.

The Chairman was originally from Grand Rapids, Michigan. Nothing had seemed to slow him down. In my absence, he had dissolved the Division of Consumer Education where I had worked.

Somewhat later, I found out he had moved back to Michigan too. I found out why after another six months or so. Word got to me that the former Chairman of the most powerful regulatory organization in Washington was going to run for the U.S. Senate.

Word also was that a major part of his platform was running to be a fighting advocate for consumers! I was steamed. But what could I do, if anything? I had a great job as Director of Development for Kalamazoo College, the oldest private college in Michigan and the one with the biggest endowment. Why rock the boat with politics?

So. I am not suggesting you take on anything like this, but here is an example where one determined person can make a very big difference by taking action that has the moral force of certainty.

I found he was making three big news conferences to announce and kick off his candidacy. The first news conference was set for the Southfield Inn, a hotel north of Detroit. When I got wind of that, I rented a room in the same hotel.

On the day of his first kickoff, I had taken an unpaid day off and a couple gung-ho teenagers and I drove about the width of southern Michigan to Southfield. He kicked off his campaign in the ballroom to a big media scrum. Right after his conference, the two young men escorted the media reps to my hotel room, where I conducted the first news conference of my life.

Outrageous Truth To Power

I had a statement all written out for myself and the media. After all, it was a kind of convoluted story, even before I started. Some TV guy said, "Just put it in your own words."

Emotion took over, and I said something like, "Before the former Chairman continues his campaign for the U.S. Senate on his platform of being a consumer advocate, he should answer to the voters and tell them what happened to the original 100,000 guidebooks (I held one up) and why he shut down the Division of Consumer Education." There were about a dozen media types, and they apparently thought I was running for the Senate.

It turned out we got more media coverage than he did. We heard some of it on the radio as we drove to Lansing. He was traveling by helicopter.

Our little band escaped without being detected by the candidate's crowd, and we drove to Lansing to do another conference right after him at the old Jack Tar Hotel, right in front of the state capitol. We entered the hotel lobby, and my young friend said, "Here they come!" We hid behind a pillar so as not to tip our hand.

Later, we found out we had gotten better TV and print coverage than he did.

We pulled it off again. They did not even seem to know we were there the first or second time. We drove to Grand Rapids for the third and final new conference. By then, the candidate's crowd had prepared a news release that attempted to rebut my coverage. Neither team got much coverage in Grand Rapids.

You Can Employ The Awesome Power Of Public Opinion

The end of this particular story is that he never got enough signatures to even qualify for the ballot. He dropped out of the race before it even started. Call it truth to power, or whatever. You take bold action and powerful forces will come to your aid. Public opinion is sovereign in America. If enough people want a certain action to be taken, it will happen.

Abraham Lincoln said, "Those who mold opinion do more than those who legislate laws or issue judicial opinions." The sixteenth President was generations before any electronic media. How did he mold public opinion? A staffer took notes on a given speech and used the telegraph to get the words out to newspapers around the country. The message has to get out to be the powerful force.

Let's hope it doesn't happen to you. But should it, once the government gets a hold of you, they never want to let go. You may think you cannot fight back, but you can. The simple formula is to Attack! Attack! Attack! In many cases, it's the only thing they understand or respect.

So a news conference takes real commitment and confidence. But what can you do to combat government injustice? There is social media and prominent blogs and sites, like BuzzFeed, that have several million viewers at any given time.

But how about closer to home? How about your neighborhood? Your city or your county? How do you combat City Hall? When they try to interfere with your lives, just because they can, not because it's right?

One day, I came home from work and found an Arlington County sign staked in the grass between the sidewalk and the street that said: no parking between Monday and Friday. Then it had dates that went for like three weeks. Then, just to show their bully power, there was a drawing of a truck hauling a car away.

Annoying Government In Your Neighborhood?

I thought, Well maybe there will be some county work tomorrow morning along my street.

Morning came and no county workers showed . . . none the rest of the day. The third day, I saw a county truck in front of a house, I think for about a day. The house was a block away. I went over to ask them what they were doing, and they said checking gas lines.

I asked if there were leaks. They said no. They were just checking. Then, for a couple days, the signs were still there but no trucks. I got curious and walked all around the neighborhood.

There were these same signs up and down our street for three blocks and side streets and on a long cross street, and then side streets as well. Same signs, same three-week prohibitions.

I have a driveway, but it is on a steep incline—as in, hard to get in and out of the car and hard on the transmission if you don't do it right. I emailed and called the president of the neighborhood association. She is in the know about virtually everything around, but in a good way. She didn't know anything about it, but said she would have a look around. Later, she contacted me and said yes, the signs are everywhere, and she had no idea what they were for.

So now, I am getting annoyed enough to take some action. How might you handle this or something akin to it in your neighborhood? I went from the neighborhood association to my next step: a member of the County Board. In Arlington County, Virginia, it's about the second-most populous in the state.

How Is Your County Organized?

Board Members are elected at large. So, I called the office of one I knew well. A staffer said she would look into it. She was very bright and cheerful. She got back to me and said she couldn't find out what was going on, and then she told me something I didn't know for all my political experience. This would be at a federal level, that the Board Members did not do constituent service. Your County Board or Board of Supervisors, or whatever may be the same. What do they do?

They attend meetings and preside over the one-hundred-million-dollar county budget, funding streetcar projects that never get built, or twenty-million-dollar aquatic centers that most county people will never use and don't want. But the board does set restrictive measures on people using aquatic centers, probably those to which they have never been.

So how do we "fight City Hall?" Finally, I found through the friendly staffer that the county (amid its 8,000 or so employees) has an *ombudsman*, a person who will go to bat for any of the 200,000 county residents, that is if you know he or she exists. I got his name and email address, described the complaint, and sent it to him. He had an assistant, or maybe more, who responded and said they were on it. Wow! Somebody who might do something.

A Way To Fight City Hall

About three days later, all the signs in the neighborhood were down, except for in front of two houses up the street. Then I got an email from the ombudsman, saying he had done a reconnaissance through the neighborhood and found my complaint was legitimate and the vast majority of the signs were not needed, and how I was responsible for a "process improvement."

I had a bit of an afterglow from that for a half-day or so. Actually longer, especially after I sent the email to the head of the neighborhood association and then she sent out an alert through this Next-Door email chain to the 2,000 or so people in the neighborhood. And she included the name and contact information of the ombudsman. Who knew? I am sure he was an extra busy camper after that.

And all of this because of some really incompetent work by the county. Oh, we will put up these signs everywhere. we can't be bothered to find out which houses are going to be visited and when.

And I only saw one truck, one time, again, up the street.

The Commonwealth of Virginia has over a staggering 700,000 publish sector employees who operate under the auspices of the governor. "We're from the government. We are here to help."

After All, It Is "We The People"

But you know what? You are giving the kind of help we don't need! Right, well, we the people are going to tell you how it is. You will not be telling us all the time.

So, you can fight City Hall. You just have to pick your chances and figure out how the system works and turn the system on itself. Let's go remind them who works for whom!

Chapter 18

Want To Take Over?
How To Win An Election

Many people get elected to Congress, and for a month or two, they cannot believe they actually got elected. Then, after they have a chance to meet many fellow members, they start to wonder how they got elected.

You want to be a Councilman or Councilwoman? A county Supervisor? A State Rep? Or heaven forbid, a Member of Congress? It is both easier and more difficult than you can imagine.

Here is a short primmer in case you want to change the world—or the neighborhood. I have been involved with over fifty federal campaigns, including Presidential campaigns, as a consultant, a successful campaign manager, and a candidate for Congress.

They Don't Know What They Don't Know

Some of the best and some of the worst people I have ever, I met in politics. Here is what you should know. First, should you want to run for any office: candidates don't know what they don't know and that goes for about 90 percent of those I worked with.

Please consider that one can't learn if one doesn't know what they don't know. Let me give you an example. Most everybody knows that you have to raise a considerable amount of money to get elected to office. Raising the money doesn't mean you are going to win, but not raising it means you are going to lose.

I told candidates they have to devote about 50 percent of their time to raising money.

They often said, "Well, I'm not known enough to raise money, so I'll get well-known and then raise the money."

No matter who you are, you raise the money first, then you use the money to get as well-known as the money allows. They often didn't know what they didn't know, and when they did, they dropped out of the race for a lack of money.

You have heard all those people talking about their grassroots campaign, right? You have a strong get-out-the-vote (GOTV) effort, and maybe you increase your percentage by 3 percent at best. And so on.

I ran for Congress in a two-person primary. I probably shook about 1,000 or so hands a day, most of those at factory gates. I got them going in and then going out again. During the last two weeks of the campaign, my opponent poured tens of thousands of dollars into the major media markets in the district.

I carried the total vote in nine out of the ten counties in the district but got beaten in that most populous county about three to one. Money talks and BS walks, most certainly in politics.

I Rode The Campaign Train With Jack Kennedy

I first went door-to-door for a Presidential candidate when I was eight-years-old. I have a picture of it. As a senior in high school, I rode on the whistle-stop train with Jack Kennedy on his successful Presidential campaign.

It was the Fall of 1960. I had recruited a bunch of my friends to work out of our basement as volunteers. We had heard JFK would be coming through Albion, Michigan, on his campaign train. We made copies of flyers and took them to about every household in town to build the turnout.

We made up signs, and I recruited a band as well as "Kennedy Girls."

One day, about a week before the big day, I was called into the principal's office—never a good thing. "Brian Hampton, come to the principal's office," the loudspeakers announced.

Harry Williams, the principal, said I was wanted down the street at Genevie Miller's house. I knew that she was the chair of the Calhoun County Democratic party. She ushered me in and there sat two very well-dressed men. As I remember, they exuded an aura of understated self-assurance.

"We are with the Kennedy campaign. We understand you are helping the campaign, so tell us all about it."

I couldn't contain my enthusiasm. "We have leafleted the town once. We will do it again before his appearance. We have a band, and we have signs . . ." I was quite taken by the whole effort.

They looked at each other, and one said, "Okay, you are going to be in charge of the rally, the crowd-building, and the volunteers. We are in charge of everything on the train. If this works out all right, we will put you in charge of the lower tier of counties in Michigan."

If I didn't already know it, I figured it out later. I was really the only operative they had in Albion. The big day arrived. The bands played. The signs were waved. The Kennedy Girls flocked to the caboose of the train as it arrived and started jumping up and down.

I remember how youthful, fit, and tan Senator Kennedy looked. He jabbed the air with his finger and hand. "We are going to carry Michigan in November and go on to Washington."

I was standing off to the side. I had done everything I could do. After a very energetic ten-minute address, the train started to move. On the caboose, Kennedy continued to speak, still jabbing the air.

They Picked Me Up And Put Me On The Moving Train!

I was facing the train from the side. Suddenly, I was aware of being lifted into the air by my elbows. Two guys had lifted me up. "You will be riding with the Senator," they said.

Wow! The train was moving a bit, and they stuffed me in an open door. There was one other person on board from Albion. Judge Alfonso Magnotta, the Circuit Court Judge and a big, local Democrat.

He and I rode the train to Marshall, to another big crowd. I didn't get off the train. I was too enthralled. Heading another fifteen miles west, the train stopped in Battle Creek, the city of my birth.

It seemed like there were 40,000 people, about the population of the city itself. People were hanging from the second stories of buildings, surrounding the train station. The crowd went crazy. It was the best day of my life to that date.

A couple weeks later, I got a call at home. "This is the Kennedy campaign. Be at the corner of Superior and River Street at 5 a.m. tomorrow morning." Click. That was it. So, I went.

It was dark. A heavy fog had come in. I stood on the corner under a streetlight, wondering what in the world I was doing there. A high school prank maybe?

From down the street, there appeared a big truck. It slowed down at the corner, and some big package was pushed off the rear of the truck, landing on the side of the street. Without stopping, the truck turned the corner and disappeared into the fog.

MLK And JFK

There were several thousand black and white flyers with the message that Martin Luther King Jr. had been thrown into jail in Georgia, that Nixon had done nothing to get him out, but that Bobby and Jack were on the case. I didn't have to be told what to do. The next day after school, the team delivered the flyers.

Come election day, Kenney had eked out a close victory in Michigan and very close elsewhere in the country. Jack's father, Joe, the old bootlegger, had famously remarked that he was willing to buy the election, but he would be darned if he would buy a landslide. But they didn't just get lucky. It was one slick, class operation.

You want to run for office? It is an exhilarating experience. I can say from my congressional campaign. Here are some things you should consider: first, husband your energy. It takes lots of energy to run, though most run on adrenalin. One has to be more fit to run than to serve, by a long measure.

You Need A Simple, Compelling Message

Have a coherent message. It sounds obvious, doesn't it? It is simple and complex at the same time. You have to make the case to the voters that there is need for change. That can be tricky because there are more problems than can barely be even mentioned, but people want a positive message. How do you do both?

"Get America Moving Again." That was the Kennedy slogan. Sounds familiar, doesn't it? But it is far more effective than at first notice because it does two important things: 1) It states there are problems that need to be addressed, and 2) It says hope is in sight. Consider President Obama's slogan, "Hope and Change." Simple when you really focus on it.

So much of the campaign is in the message and its delivery. Remember all those political yard signs you have seen? They are to show support in the neighborhood and to get out the important name. But the downside is that you are in a mushroom war. You have to put them up just to stay even with your opponents.

What is the primary mistake the big bulk of these candidates make with those signs? They have their names, usually their party, and the race for office . . . and that is it. No message. Putting up signs without a message is a waste of time and energy.

There was a guy who ran for Governor in Virginia who was successful a number of years ago. All campaign materials, especially his signs, had a message: "No Car Tax." He won on those three words alone. After he was elected, a possible future opponent called Governor James Gilmore a "one trick pony." That was all he needed, and of course, we still have the car tax in Virginia.

You May Not Win With Money, But Without It, You Lose

So, now you know you have to raise lots of money. How do you do that? One important technique is to recruit an Executive Finance Committee. You have to recruit these people in person. Their job is to raise lots of money for you and report in on a regular basis about how much they have raised.

Want to run for Congress? The limit on individuals for a primary and general election is $4,500. Consider that a candidate for Congress in a rural district of Virginia raised $20 million in a quarter! So, you better have your friends start a Political Action Committee (PAC) for you. Starting a PAC is quite easy.

One applies and gets an EIN number from the IRS and applies online to the Federal Election Commission. You can incorporate in your home state or not, but it is best to do it for protection from any liability. Now, your wealthy friends, or friends of friends, who are wealthy can give to your candidate-friendly PAC.

The unfortunate reality for the public is that the FEC, almost without exception, employs no enforcement measures. It was just not set up that way. The PAC operators can use the money for just about anything, but they have to make full disclosure.

Campaign staff? First, you hire a campaign manager. Depending on how high the office is that you are running for, you may not even have to pay that person. Some people with some experience will do it for free just to run the show. My congressional campaign manager did just that, and he was from New York City. He just heard about me at a national party convention. He was quite effective.

Next, you hire and/or recruit your fundraiser, then your Director of Communications, and next your Scheduler. Then hire your Field Director and your media firm and polling organization.

The Cynics Don't Count. Those In The Arena Do

Should you win, everybody you ever knew will take credit. Should you lose, well, defeat is an orphan. But as Teddy Roosevelt said words in effect, "It is not the cynic who matters, but the warrior who goes into the arena and ends up covered with blood and sweat and dirt."

My old "friend," Chris Matthews, who had the Hardball show, once ran for Congress outside of Philadelphia. I lived with him in an old church in Georgetown when he was a Capitol Hill cop. He never stopped talking, so we put him in the basement, as I mentioned previously, but it bears repeating.

Most of his campaign was to hire high school kids to be human billboards at the side of highways. I did it myself, except I was the human board when I ran for Congress. With 10,000 sets of eyes going by in an hour, maybe your ID goes up fast and cheap.

My sign said, "HAMPTON FOR CONGRESS; NOT A LAWYER." (See Chapter 4, "Push Back! Save Yourself From The Lawyers.")

I did get plenty of thumbs up and happy honks!

Chapter 19

Being The House Manager:
Do It Or Get Out Of It!

Are you the house manager at your house? Or apartment manager in your apartment? Or condo manager in your own condo?

Somebody has to do it, or it doesn't get done. You know, deal with the dishwasher that does not work. The toilet that does not flush—you know, because the little chain in the back always gets twisted or that flapper thing doesn't go all the way down—handle the furnace or air conditioner or something or other that goes on the fritz. Who is in charge where you are?

Here is a short primer on how to manage the most annoying duties and jobs and, most of all, how to delegate them so you don't have to do them. And we'll talk about the all-important, how to save money in cases you otherwise would have spent it.

So first, let me start with some protective measures you can take to avoid being ripped off by appliance repair people. Then I will move to how my first job as house manager almost landed me in jail. And then, for the most fun of all, we'll discuss the ever-popular plumbers.

Don't Get Ripped Off On Appliance Repairs

When the appliance repair person is inside and says it will cost $425 to repair your clothes dryer, it's already too late. You are being held hostage. You can't really negotiate unless you have paved the way with management, and if you tell them to walk, you have to pay the $69.95 fee for the service call alone.

Let's take the example of the clothes dryer that is tumbling but not heating. You and Google go through about five unhelpful links, and finally find one that actually provides useful information. It could be a thermal fuse, a thermostat and temperature switch, a heating coil, a timer, or the exhaust vent. You check for the usual replacement cost of the items.

Be aware that exhaust vents are a "specialty" that most appliance repair people will not do. One has to call a vent specialist. But how do you know who to bring in? Chances are that if the dryer was slowly losing heat, it is the vent. A sudden loss means it is something else.

If you don't have a regular, dependable appliance repair service, and most people don't, you need to shop around not only online but on the phone. First, pick three prospects from online or, even better, from home service booklet guides like "Best Pick Reports" or Five Star Rated (fivestarrated.com). These booklets are mailed to you or "current resident."

A Slug On The Phone Means A Slug Company

When you get on the phone, you want to talk to these people! You say something like this, "I am Brian in North Arlington, and I am shopping around on the phone. We have a Whirlpool clothes dryer that is tumbling but not drying."

It is truly amazing how much you can find out about a company by calling them on the phone. If there is a voicemail, I never leave a message or call back. It's just not good customer service.

What you get from talking to the person on the phone gives a real glimmer of the quality of the entire company. Do you find yourself talking to an obtuse slug? Forget them—politely, of course.

How much for the visit? Often, it's the $70 applied against any possible fee, which is essentially meaningless. They are not going to subtract that fee from theirs. It won't happen.

How do they charge for labor? By the hour or the job? It's usually by the job so they can charge whatever they want. But you ask, "What is a typical cost for labor to fix a clothes dryer?" They will say it varies, of course. Everything varies, but ask how much does it vary?

Then get into the weeds a bit. How much will it cost for the thermal fuse if it has to be replaced? How much for the thermostat and temperature switch? Heating coil? Timer? You already know about how much everything should cost.

You probably won't get many straight answers, but you are going to get the real idea of what sort of a company you are dealing with. You can always ask them to ask a coworker to tell them.

For example, when you go online, you could find that a thermal fuse costs between five and ten dollars, but the total cost for the part and labor is eighty to $130. A thermostat could be three dollars to twenty dollars for the part and about $180 for the part and labor. So, you ask, about how much could it be for the part and labor for the one and the other?

Asking Questions Helps You In Four Ways

This short exercise has four benefits for you:

1. Are the people up front sharp or not? How clear and responsive are they?
2. Are they overpricing possible parts?
3. Should you choose a specific company, the dispatcher will likely pass you on to the technician.
4. When the technician tells you that it will be $425 in parts and labor to replace a fuse and thermostat, you know it should not exceed the $310 ($130 and $180). You have some negotiation points.

They will likely say $425 cost, period. How much for the parts and how much is labor?

"Wait a minute, Alex at headquarters. That should be around $130 for one and $180 for the other or whatever." You know your stuff. "I will wait while you call headquarters." Or decision time, you say, "That is fifteen dollars at Office Depot." See how much room there might be for negotiation.

There is a book, *You Can Negotiate Anything*, and I have learned a great deal since my first stint as house manager, which could not be called a success. I was almost arrested and sent to jail.

I was a rising senior at Alma College in Michigan and was working in the library that summer. I was living at the TKE House, along with about five others. I did not have to pay rent because I elected to be the house manager. What would I have to do, anyway? Moreover, what could I do? Nothing I could think of.

Almost Jailed First Time As House Manager

I turned twenty-one that summer—the golden year of drinking age. I was excited, to say the least. Somewhere, I found a long piece of steel, tied a rope around it, and hung it from a tree in the front yard. I made up this big poster that said "The GPB is 21!"

GPB was short for my nickname, Golden Pooh Bear. For some reason I thought I was clever and got everybody to call me Pooh Bear.

At the bewitching hour of midnight, I was finally twenty-one. I had this big hammer, and I commenced to beat on it for a couple minutes. The noise was earth shattering. Then the brothers who were already twenty-one and I went to the local bar (there was only one in town). A motto for Alma College is in fact, "There is only one."

We partied down till last call and retired to the house. Being full of it, I saw fit to start beating on the steel again. After a couple minutes, we went into the house. We didn't even get to the pool table downstairs before we heard the sirens.

"The Police!" was the cry.

No sooner had we heard the sirens than we look out the window and see two black and whites with their front tires rested on the curb, pointed at the house, with the blue and white lights flashing against the front of it.

The House Manager Takes The Lead!

The house manager has to be the leader of the house.

"Hide!" I yelled. I can't speak for the others, but I found a deep closet and hid on the floor behind some clothes. I waited about an hour, as did the rest. The coast appeared clear. We all decided to call it a night, turned off the lights, and went up to the "sack room," which was in the attic. It had open doors at either end, in the summer or winter.

The coast was not entirely clear because the next day, the phone rang, and the Dean summoned me to his office. The Dean and an associate asked me a true rhetorical question, "Brian, did it occur to you that the neighbors might not want to celebrate your birthday with you?"

No, it actually had not. "Well, Dean, what did you do the day you turned twenty-one?"

"I read reflective books."

I am sure he did. I served as an Army officer in Vietnam but never had any nightmares that I was back there. I have had many where I dreamed I was back at Alma. I got a great education there, it turned out, but getting an education never occurred to me, only getting a degree.

I am sure you can do better if it falls to you to be the house manager or apartment manager. Though several years after I left Alma, the TKE House burned to the ground. They conducted a big fundraising campaign, and it was rebuilt a couple years later. Then a number of years after that, it burned to the ground again. At least I wasn't house manager either of those two times!

First Rule: Don't Do It!

So, getting back to your duties if the job has fallen to you to be in charge. The first rule is trying to get out of it. Let your spouse or significant other or someone else there do it. That way, you have no responsibility and can assess blame when things don't go right. This is really important.

I assumed house manager duties when my wife and I moved into our house. I didn't know any better. I do now. The previous owner had been a very conscientious house manager. Wow! She had this big cardboard box with indexed file folders, receipts, warranties, everything. She even had notes on the days people came in for servicing, with labels on the outside of the file folders: windows, drapes, AC, furnace, flagstaff tiles, and fans. Nothing was too small for a file folder.

If you are the house manager, do this before it is too late. Things get out of hand and all these service notices are stuffed in some drawer somewhere. Do you have a warranty on the TV? Where is that statement? Can't find it? You will need it (see Chapter 26, "The Law Of The Universe").

We had been at the new house for a blissful eight months. My sister-in-law was coming to visit from overseas, staying in the rec room, with a full bathroom and all. Except, two weeks before she was set to arrive, we had a home mini-disaster. The basement was flooded with a couple inches of water. You are the house manager; what would you do? Simple, right? Find the problem and fix it.

Plumbing: The Scourge Of The Hose Manager

Not as fast, the plumber comes, rips out the drywall in the bathroom, looks at the pipes, and says, "No, that's not it. You have a leak from the outside groundwater."

Wait, I got someone else in there. No, that's not it. He rips another hole in the rec room bathroom wall and says, "There is your problem. a burst pipe no more than a foot from the previous hole."

"Can you fix this?"

"Yes, but you have to get some of these special people who drain and clean the basement first."

But you probably know, they have to come out and do the estimate and then come back. Hint: always ask if the team coming out can do the estimate *and* the work, preferably in the same visit. So, you probably know, even for painters and drywallers, the "estimators" come first.

Tick tock, tick tock.

Thereupon began the long education of this house manager. Just maybe I can give you a partial degree from my school of hard knocks.

What they did not tell me was that I could go to Home Depot and buy one of those water vacuum things and short circuit the dry-up process. Later, yes, the clean-up-manager guy said the site guy should have told me that. I'll bet they don't tell anybody.

Accept The Responsibility But Not The Blame

Tick tock, tick tock. The basement/rec room is still flooded. My wife becomes more and more irate with me. "You are doing a terrible job as house manager."

I tried the Richard Nixon rationale: "I will accept the responsibility but not the blame." No deal. I typed up my resignation, signed it, and presented it to my wife. It was rejected.

See, there is the vital key right there. Don't be the house manager if you can possibly avoid it. Just tell the others how it should be done. If something goes wrong, it's not your fault. You are kind of like the de facto house manager. You demand results, but it is not your fault!

A happy ending that time. With a day to spare, I got the rec room dried off and cleaned up and my job was intact. Thank goodness . . . or not!

If you live in an apartment or even a condo where these plumbing issues are handled by management, get happy! Let's try to be happy about all the things that we don't want to have happen to us, that aren't happening to us. There are too many really to even imagine.

Splish Splash, Don't Take a Financial Bath

"Fear an ignorant man more than a lion." —Turkish Proverb

"Plumbing is the worst!"

"Plumbing is the bane of my existence."

These are two quotes from friends of mine. Do they sound familiar?

It's not really that plumbers are malicious or unethical. It's just that, often, they don't know what to do. But they do something anyway and then do the wrong thing.

- You have a leaking pipe. They knock out the wrong drywall
- They snake a drain, break a pipe, and cause a leak
- They say you need a new garbage disposal when a reset might do
- They come to fix a slow toilet flush, leave, then there is no flush
- A plumber messes up, and you get another plumber over

To fix the fix and they mess up too. Back to square one!

What misadventures with plumbers have you had? I will share some of mine and then get right to how to get the best for the least from plumbers. Then, if worse comes to worse, I will share some remedies I have used for redress from plumbing damages.

Oh No, More Plumbers

Have you been fooled by a plumber? I most certainly have. Maybe I can help spare you from all the leaky business. Fool me once, shame on you. Fool me twice, shame on me. I remember a plumbing episode where I was getting ready to be fooled three times.

There was a leak on the kitchen ceiling, over the upstairs bathroom. A plumber comes out to diagnose the problem.

"I have to knock out the ceiling drywall. I see the problem. Yep, leaky pipes right there. Looks like the toilet is leaking."

He fixes it and says the problem should go away, but it comes back in a couple months. Another plumber says the last guy messed up. Really!

"Let me take a look." He has to knock out the ceiling drywall that had been replaced a couple months before.

"It's the shower," he says. "I'll fix the drain." The problem goes away, and the drywall is fixed again. A couple months later, it started to leak again on the ceiling of the kitchen.

Plumber number three shows up and starts calling me, "The Boss."

That was my first inkling that things might not go well. Do you like to be called boss?

He says, "It is not the drain. It's the shower tiles. And if it continues to leak, the ceiling in the kitchen will be damaged."

"I didn't know that," I said. He didn't like me. He kind of stormed out without a goodbye. I didn't like him, either. Goodbye and good luck!

Adjusted Shower Head And Saved $2,000

He wanted me to pay $2,000 for all new shower tiles.

"Wait a minute," said the slow-witted house manager. The shower head is pointed against the shower wall, and there is a leak. How about I point it straight down, rather than against the wall. Bingo! Ten minutes later, there were no leaks.

Some people have to be told (see Chapter 3 on that very subject). So, I sent Joe, the Plumbing Manager no less, a nice text that very day: "Thanks for the diagnosis! I merely pointed the shower head straight ahead rather than against the wall. Ten minutes later, no leak! Beats the $2000 to redo the entire shower. You are the Boss. Many thanks! Brian," I got no response, but I did get satisfaction.

So, keep your wits about plumbers. I made a more lasting discovery that I want to pass on to you.

Let's say you live in a house. The furnace and air conditioner tech comes to the house for the routine maintenance. They will always find something that isn't quite right, which you should buy. They must have sales quotas, so buyer beware.

So, one day, I am sitting at the dining table when the United Air Temp guy goes through all the needs and warranties. Why do they always talk in tongues? What exactly are they saying? Know what I mean?

So, the guy is going through it all and says, "Well you can get a plumbing service contract for $250 every six months."

One Hundred Dollars to Take a Breath

That got my attention. Carl used to charge one hundred dollars just to breathe in our house. He would fix a leaky faucet, being there only five minutes, and charge $155. What? You were only here for five minutes!

Carl, being a clever guy, would say, "You are not paying for my time but my expertise and knowing what washer thing to turn here."

Later, I signed a service contract with an air conditioning, heating, and plumbing company. Wow—guess what? It was one of the best contracts I ever signed. Last week, the plumber from the company came and fixed three sinks and a toilet. He had to turn the toilet upside down and replace about six parts he showed me. (I have to be mighty careful, or I will violate the "Law of The Universe," Chapter 26). It took three hours, but no cost, except the six months maintenance fees.

There, I did it! I did violate the "Law Of The Universe." Why do these plumbing fiascos happen to me? I know, so I can pass on the lessons I have learned to you. So, I am adding on to this chapter.

Make A Record Of The Plumbing Process

Take photos before, during, and after the plumbing process. Taking photos takes very little time, and you can document what it was like before they got started. Even if you have limited damage to start, like a leak on your ceiling, get a photo.

Maybe they rip parts of your walls apart and don't put back a towel rack, a grabber, a toothbrush stand, or even a toilet paper spool. You have to show that it was there in the first place.

They will take photos to show all the mold, damaged pipes, and whatever else, to show all the work that had to be done. They will show the photos to prove their case, no matter what the damage is. Why? Because they are photos, and they mean whatever they say they mean!

You need your own photos for the record. Maybe they did more than needed to be done. Make your own record from the beginning, and every day.

I was just talking to my sister Charlene on the phone, and she was telling me about a plumbing scam that was tried on her. It's a long story, but I will keep the problem short and the solutions more detailed.

Mother Of All Plumbing Disasters, Flooded Home: Manage The Chaos And Confusion

Dear reader, I thought I had seen it all and knew it all about busted pipes and flooded houses. Not even close!

Severe water damage to houses, condos, and apartments is quite common. Mention it to a friend, and chances are they have had at least one experience or know someone who has. My wife and I lived in one house for thirteen years and had three episodes of serious water damage. Yet, one is not fully prepared unless one has gone through it. A massive flood in another house (caused by a bursting threaded pipe on the second story) led to the total demolition of three bedrooms and bathrooms and household chaos beyond imagination.

This house was fully inspected by the insurance company the week we moved in. Everything was up to their codes. The following are some lessons and techniques I learned that can save you enormous grief and aggravation, to say nothing of saving you money.

Disaster Strikes: What To Do First?

Many things become obvious when someone tells you something, but when you are in the throes of calamity, you might not think of them. First, know exactly where in your house the water shut-off lever is located. Sounds obvious, right? This house manager moved to a new house and did not know exactly where it was while the water was pouring all over the house.

Next step? Call the insurance company? Probably not. Take a half-hour of your time right now to find the name and contact information for the nearest reputable water restoration company. Have that information in hand so they can come out fast and start draining the water. Have a Plan B company in mind in case the Plan A company is going to be delayed. My insurance was satisfied to work with the restoration company I chose. While they were doing their emergency work, I called up the insurance company.

As mentioned earlier in the chapter—it bears repeating—keep a timeline on all phases and communications on the drying, demolition, and rebuild phases.

The deafening blowers may take ten days or longer to complete the drying process. The moisture level should be at least 15 percent or lower before they are removed. The demolition could take weeks, and then there is the rebuild.

There is vast inherent confusion and chaos among all parties during this process, which you need to keep straight and coordinated. Yes, you need to have a strong hand in coordinating the process. You will have drywallers, carpenters, painters, hardwood floor people, carpet people, and plumbers, among others—some who may work for the restoration company, or they may be subcontractors. Sometimes they do not communicate among themselves. That is where you step in to make sure they are on the same page. And do not forget the insurance company.

The entire process could take three to four weeks, but if you do not maintain quality control yourself, the process could easily take three or four months, or longer.

Delicate Dance Between Insurance And Restoration Companies

The insurance company, of course, will send an adjuster out to survey the damage in a walk-through and give preliminary feedback on what repairs will be covered. The restoration company must submit their drawings and estimates for the water remediation and the build back.

Watch out for this dilemma: the restoration company could be required to work for a week, two weeks, or much longer without being paid the first payment by the insurance company! They have to pay their workers and cash flow is king. You have to speed up the insurance company while mollifying the restoration company to keep working.

Typically, the second and last payment made by the insurance company is called, "recoverable depredation." Do not be alarmed by this term. It is essentially language that means the insurance company will settle up with the restoration company after the repairs are complete.

In their Property Claim Settlement statement, there may be a statement about Legal Information and how you cannot sue them unless you have done so and so. No surprise there! They know many parties have sued them or would like to for not paying on claims. See Chapter 4 and the section about "How To Win A Dispute With An Insurance Company."

The first day you want to get the cell phone numbers of the project manager, company manager, and the owner if she or he shows up. These people are on the go, so you cannot expect to reach them right away by calling headquarters. Also, get their email address. That seems obvious, but when all your worldly belongings are being thrown into a big pile in the living room or garage, you might not otherwise be thinking of it.

Critical: Documenting All Phases Of The Process

Keep very detailed records of when various aspects of the processes happened: when started, when concluded, and exactly what the restoration people told you was going to happen, and when. Amid mass disorder and pandemonium, you are not going to remember what happened when or what they said was going to happen. You have to write it down and keep it organized! You want to keep everyone accountable and be able to go back and tell them exactly what they said was going to happen and when.

When did the blowers start and when were they pulled? When did all these categories of workers arrive? What were the staggered dates of the demolition? What exact date did the restoration company submit their full estimate? When did the insurance company say they received it? When did the adjuster send the estimate to their boss for approval? When is the first check to be mailed? When was it actually mailed?

The usual SOP is that the check is made out to you and mailed to you, you endorse it, as you probably know, and you give it to the restoration company. Plan B, if the check fails to arrive in a timely fashion, the insurance company can do a stop payment and make a direct deposit to your account. Then you write the check to the restoration company.

If your dwelling is unlivable, such as there are no usable toilets and/or showers, your insurance company should pay directly to a hotel for your stay. They do it through a second party that makes the reservation at the chosen hotel and makes arrangements to pay them.

Two weeks after this last flood, my wife and I were scheduled to be out of state and out of the country on vacation. We kept the schedule, but the coordination of the work when we were not on site, unsurprisingly, proved challenging. One has to be there. Midway through our trip, I found our insurance adjuster had also gone on a week vacation, and the restoration company knew nothing about it or who was taking her place.

We returned a full month after the initial "loss" and found that very little had been done in the meantime. One issue that stalled the entire process was that new tiling and bathrooms could not go in until some new plumbing issues were handled.

I had taken pictures of the pipes that needed to be repaired before I left, but nothing was done while we were gone. In the first week we were back, the restoration workers said they could not proceed until the plumbing issues were resolved. Plumbers had been there, but they'd left the job undone.

"Magic" Technique For Putting Repairs Into Overdrive

Here is what I did that turned out to be like waving a magic wand and having a lightning bolt come from the sky. The plumbers did in two days what they had not done in weeks. I drafted and sent an email to the plumbing company, with copies evident for the owner and manager of the restoration company, along with an email for a local slacker contractor who was supposed to expedite the plumbing.

My email follows. Names of the guilty parties have been changed.

Joe and the ABC Plumbing Company:

Thank you for coming by the other day, but work remains to be done, meantime, most repairs are at a standstill.

1. *A pipe in the master bedroom was accidently cut. It needs to be replaced.*
2. *Pipe on the ceiling of the hallway bathroom appears to be an issue.*
3. *In the hallway bathroom, pipes have to be added because the configuration is being changed from a tub to a shower.*
4. *A cutoff was provided on the pipe at the ceiling of the basement, which I hope and expect is adequate? There is a very corroded pipe next to it that needs attention as well. I did forward pictures of both of these pipes 4 weeks ago.*

We received your bill of $525 which we will settle up on, but would like to pay everything once all plumbing is completed. Also, we would like the diagnostics parts of the bill broken out so we can get reimbursed by the insurance company.

We realize you are very busy and in demand, yet I have called Joe three times this week, have left messages, but have not heard back from him. I called him again this morning and sent a text. At 1:58 pm he sent a text saying he was in a meeting. No response after that.

Later today I left a detailed message on the main line. No response.

You need to expedite this process or we will go to Plan B.

Seriously Yours,

Brian Hampton

See Chapter 3, "How Some People Have To Be Told!" The slacker contractor showed up within an hour of me sending out the email. The plumbing company sent out a couple master plumbers who arrived about 6:30 p.m. and stayed an hour. The no-nonsense senior plumber was distressed by Joe's incompetent work.

Now back to more mundane plumbing issues and after that, how to get a plumbing company to settle up after they cause a lot of damage.

Plumbing Fiasco: "Raindrops" Falling On My Head

The plumber comes to fix a clogged sink in the bathroom on the second floor. He is supposed to arrive between 3:30 p.m. and 5:30 p.m. He gets there at ten minutes to six—no surprise. He is there for about twenty minutes snaking out the sink, and my wife and I are in the family room. We hear something like raindrops. There is no rain outside. It was coming from the kitchen ceiling. Water cascading from leaks in the ceiling and dripping from ceiling light fixtures, all over the floor!

"Stop whatever you are doing!"

Thereupon ensues a spirited discussion about why this was happening. He said it was probably the toilet. There was no water on the bathroom floor, and we had no leaks from the toilet before on the ceiling. He snaked a hole in the pipes.

Then he wanted to knock out the drywall in the center of the ceiling to find the leaking pipes! No way. I pointed out that pipes are vertical and would be in the side wall, spraying water from the leaks.

There transpired a full week of lies and obfuscation from various representatives from the plumbing company telling me what they would do and then disappearing and becoming unreachable.

I'd had enough, and here is what I did that finally produced results. (You can use one of these techniques yourself.) First, I checked online to find the name of the management, the top executives. Then I reviewed the complaints that customers took to the Better Business Bureau. There were forty-nine of them in about a five-month period. Their COO had a kind of full-time job responding to them.

The BBB once really helped me with a credit card company that was ripping me off, but in this case, I knew the state licensing authority was a far more powerful linchpin for bringing heat so they would see the light.

Junkyard Dog Lawyer To Run TV Spots On Your Company!

I decided on a kind of pincer operation. I finally got a customer service manager on the line and told her, "Judy, gosh, I told one of my friends about my situation with your company, with the forty-nine complaints to the BBB and all, and they said the whole deal is ripe for a class action suit. You know the kind where a junkyard dog lawyer runs these TV ads, rounding up aggrieved customers, and then files a huge lawsuit?" Then I wished her a good day.

I found that the Virginia Department of Professional and Occupational Regulation (DPOR), the licensing board, had also received complaints. I called their hotline, and they emailed me a complaint form. Unsurprisingly, I found out that the upper management of the company was very secretive about how to contact them.

Finally, I finagled the name and extension of the executive assistant to the CEO. I called the assistant, got the voicemail, and left a message. I gave my name and number and said that she will want to get the message to Tony right away. I said that, as she knew, the DPOR can take their license to do business away and that my last stop before filing my complaint was making the call. Then I filled in a short description of what had happened and the names of the culprits involved.

Another arrow for your quiver is to "make a record," as they say in the legal trade, by sending emails. From my long experience in looking for the email addresses of "high-ranking people," I have found that such folks don't want regular people to know.

But here is a trick to figure out some of these obscured email addresses. Google "email format We Give Grief Corporation." In many cases, you will see something like this:

- First initial last. JDoe @WGGC@gmail.com: 58%
- First last. joedoe: 28%
- Last first initial. doej: 18%

It's A Warning And A Promise. Don't Get Mad. Get Even!

You combine this information with the names of the top executives, and you have a formula for getting your story out just the way you want it. In Chapter 4, on lawyers, I relate how one can employ the very inexpensive email tool called readnotify.com. You send three emails out to the executives and see which one, if any, opens your email. Recipients do not know you are using this software.

Never get mad. Get even. Positive things happened within hours after I left the message. But remember, only the prospect of filing a complaint is really going to provide leverage. Once it's filed, you don't have much leverage anymore. And if someone asks you the age-old question: "Are you threatening me?" Your response is, "You can take it any way you want." Or, another response is, "No, it's a warning and a promise."

Another option for redress of vendor damages at your residence could be your home-owners' insurance, depending on your coverage and level of confidence in the carrier. Your homeowners' insurance company can start a claim, send an adjuster, and take charge of all the repairs. Then, they could possibly provide what they call subrogation, where they would pursue damages for you from the vender company and/or their insurance company.

Are you the hammer or the nail? Sometimes with plumbers one has to be the hammer. So be ready, if need be, to play hardball.

The Art Of The Tip

The service contract vendors need to be handled with your wits. I used to give them ten or twenty dollars on their way out. It took me a long time to figure out I had it backward. You give them ten dollars on the way in and say, "Let's see how this goes, and there could be more for you on the way out." It's kind of like front-loading in drinking (see Chapter 25, "Happy Hour").

Maybe you are single and live in an apartment or house that you share with others. I have more experience in that area than I ever wanted to have. I lived in a half-dozen apartments and houses in graduate school at Michigan State University alone. Let me share with you some of the ups and downs.

That reminds me of the old elevator joke. "It's not the ups and downs in life that are so bad. It's the jerks in between." Try that the next time you are in an elevator with a group of people. It is always good for plenty of laughs, or not.

Most everyone likes to have some human contact, especially those riding up for the dental appointment. They need some love (see Chapter 6 on dentists). I always get at least a few smiles. Of course, there are some who may think you are casting dispersions. Good to keep it funny and loose (see Chapter 22, "Taking Time To Make Friends").

Okay, living with singles. It is actually better to be the house/apartment manager. First, better sign the original lease and then pick and choose who you may sublease to. You never know what you are going to get, like the chocolates in the box, but at least you have some control.

Cure For Sloppy Roommates

How about you get a real sloppy, even dirty, roommate. You know, someone always leaving the dishes in the sink? Who doesn't buff up the bathroom when it is their turn? I dealt with this with some guy for far too long. He was a real Pig Pen. A nice guy, but one who had disgusting hygiene habits. Verbally, nothing worked, so I finally posted a "Jobs List" in the kitchen. I did it at night, and he knew I was serious. He was gone by daybreak—thank goodness. This does not work with a spouse!

Cash flow problems in the apartment? You signed the lease. You have the new leasers sign a sublease, a simple one-pager. They give one month's rent deposit upon moving in and one month's rent as well.

And you don't pay what the rest pay. You pay less and maybe even break even or make a small profit because you are the house manager.

It's remarkable, or not in the least in the Washington D.C. area, that people move in and people move out often. Plans change. Jobs change. Your sublease says they have to provide thirty days advance notice before leaving to get their deposit back, otherwise, they have broken the sublease. It was amazing to me over the years the number of people who said they needed to go without providing notice. So sad, too bad. You lost the deposit. Cash flow is king. You place another ad and get what adds up to be two months' rent up front.

In over a decade of living in a two-bedroom, one-bathroom apartment in Arlington, I had heard every story known to mankind about, "I don't have the money now," either to move in or to stay. House Rules.

One time, a guy really snookered me. He was very clever, moving in with no deposit, no first months' rent, and no furniture even. The embassy was holding up his money, he said.

One day, two days, three days, four, and I smelled a rat. In the second bedroom, I had allowed him to use the big bedspring mattress on the floor until his furniture shipment arrived. It was one lie after another, and I thought I knew them all.

Sorry, They Have Come For Your Mattress

I was getting financially embarrassed about this time. I had placed a notice in the mailroom downstairs: "As Is, Relatively New King-Sized Mattress, $215, or first best offer. Apartment 919" and a phone number.

About 10 p.m. one night, I got a call. "I will give you $200 if we can pick it up now."

"Good to go," I said.

Knock, knock.

"Show me the money."

"Show me the mattress."

There is no light on underneath my apartment mate's door.

Knock, knock. "Abdula, they have come for the mattress."

He opened the door, the buyers took the mattress, and I was rid of the deadbeat the next day.

Hint: as apartment house manager, have a locksmith at the ready to change that deadbolt.

PART 5

How to Deal with the Ups & Downs and Get Happy!

Chapter 20

Living With And Overcoming Depression

"Everyone has a plan until they get hit in the jaw." —Mike Tyson

---

A re you depressed? Have you ever been depressed? Do you expect to be depressed again? Who hasn't been? Who won't be?

But how can you deal with the ups and downs that come into every life?

In one of his many iconic songs, "That's Life," Frank Sinatra parses about the ups and downs in life—how he had been up and down, riding high one month, put down the next, and then back on top the following month. The point is, he gets back up and gets back into the race.

Have you read some of these seemingly endless books on attitudes? It's all in the attitude. Like the ABC theory of life: it's not what happens to you (A), it's how you react (B), and thus C is what you decide to feel about it. That determines your all-important mental state. There is something to that.

Your Three Billion Brain Cells

We have about three billion brain cells and a trillion synapses among these cells. What!? With all these cells and all the things going on, it's no wonder we might feel overwhelmed on a regular basis, or just occasionally.

Do you see couples holding hands and laughing and feel envious? Do you know of friends going on great vacations? Do you get annoyed and unhappy when you see all these happy people in these TV commercials, even the ones with those bad health maladies?

How can you not feel that way, often or occasionally? You would not really be human, a sensitive person, if you did not feel that way once in a while. But what should you do? How should you act? How do you get through these severe challenges we all face in life?

If one has a vivid imagination, one can always imagine everything that could go wrong. Life happens while we are planning something else. The future comes one day at a time.

Often, it is helpful to put the skids on thinking about what we don't have and take a few moments to be grateful for what we do have. Have a spouse or partner? That's one. Have a roof over your head? There is another one. Have a job? There is another. Have retirement income? There is another.

No matter what you are experiencing, compare yourself to others, and you can even eliminate those with life-threatening health ailments. Consider the case of the late John Ehrlichman.

You likely don't remember him, at least not by name. Ehrlichman was the White House Chief of Domestic Policy during most of the Richard Nixon Administration. Talk about being at the very top at 1600 Pennsylvania Avenue and going right to the very bottom—but actually surviving and thriving.

Watergate was in full swing the last two years of the Nixon Administration, before he resigned. Going down himself, he first fired Bob Haldeman, his other right-hand man, and then gave Ehrlichman the ax. They were both thought to be ruthless.

Ehrlichman was a devoted Mormon who did not drink. Personally, he was nice enough of a guy that he would attend Georgetown parties thrown by his White House staff. These young women lived up the street from me on 33rd St. NW in Georgetown. They told me he would drop in, just to be friendly, stay a few minutes, and then leave.

Fired, Divorced, Homeless, And In Prison

First, Ehrlichman is out of a job at the White House. Then he is tried on criminal charges and found guilty. Then he loses his house. Then his wife leaves him. Then he ends up for a while staying with a friendly couple but is eventually asked to leave. Finally, he faces prison.

How low can one person go? Of course, the higher one is up, the bigger the fall. You can hardly be that low. Later, he serves his time. In one of the bestselling books he later wrote, he says that it occurred to him his entire life had been stripped away and it was an opportunity to build another one. Talk about having a positive attitude for bouncing back.

He moved to Santa Fe and became that bestselling author, including writing a couple books about his White House years and fiction, *The China Card*.

What did Ehrlichman do to pull himself up from the darkest depths? At a certain point, he relates in one book, he knew he had to do something physical so he would have the smallest feeling of accomplishment. He took out some trash at the friend's house, then he did his own laundry. After that, he felt a little better.

How Can We Even Keep Up With The Losers?

Sometimes, you have to get up early in the morning, just to keep up with the losers. So, let's say you are lying there depressed in bed, and you just cannot face it. What do you do? Do one thing: brush your teeth. Do another: make your bed. Take out that trash. Clean off the clutter from your dresser. It's the action that is going to make you feel better.

The only real cure for grief is action.

Keep getting up! Keep getting up! Never face facts. If you do, you will never get up in the morning is an old amusing saying. You may not feel like it now, but the trials and tribulations of life are what make us stronger people. Just tell yourself, "More trials? Every day in every way, I am getting stronger and stronger."

Maybe like you, I have been fascinated by people for all my life. What do they do when they are up? What do they do when they are down?

I have been especially interested in finding examples of those who have been way down and then brought themselves up again. How exactly did they do it? You can study people in the same way.

I had read most of Ehrlichman's books when I literally came face to face with him at the Republican National Convention in San Diego in 1996. I was working the crowd, in front of the Convention Center, passing out advocacy newspapers. Though they were free, only one person in five or so would even accept them.

Who's The Man Behind The Bushy Beard?

Even though he had a hat and a beard, I recognized him right away and said, "Did you get one of these?" (Our line for trying to give them away.) He took one right away. As he walked by me, I said, "Mr. Ehrlichman, I have really enjoyed all your books, especially *The China Card*."

He turned around and gave me a slight smile. He had a handsome woman on his arm. I like to think I made his day. Probably not though. He had already rebuilt his entire life.

He did it. Others have done it. There is an old book out called, *Been Down So Long, It Looks Like Up to Me*.

Considering the ups and downs in life, we might well want to remember the immortal words of Vice President Spiro Agnew, who was forced out for corruption when Nixon was President. "Be good to all the little people on your way up because you may be meeting them again on your way down."

You have most likely not been as far down as Ehrlichman. He came back up. You can come back up. We all can take the ups and downs.

It's a great life if we don't weaken!

Chapter 21

Time To Get Happy!

"**D**aylight in the swamp, time to get up and have a husky cup of coffee." Those were the words that woke up we three kids in high school, when our mother would rap softly on the door to our rooms to wake us up.

These days, I go downstairs and I say these same words aloud every day to our King Charles Cavalier, Jasper, as I fix the morning coffee. Then occasionally, during the day, I try out the affirmation, "Time to get happy!" I say it out loud.

Do you worry? How can anyone not worry? But do you worry too much? My dad told me, "I found that it is pointless to worry because you always worry about the wrong thing."

Will Rogers said, "I have had many troubles in my life, most of which never happened."

First, Let's Try To Reduce The Worry

What can we do to reduce the worry? First, we can stay busy. Another thing we can do is cooperate with the inevitable. Worrying about the past is pointless. We can decide just how much anxiety a matter may be worth and give it no more. As to the future?

The future comes one day at a time.

Let's not allow other people to get us down. If we actually expect ingratitude, we will not be disappointed in people. Often, unjust criticism is disguised compliments to us.

The Perception Becomes The Reality

I was in the small airport in Fayetteville, North Carolina, just outside of Fort Bragg, when a student of mine came up and said those words to me. I was quite familiar with the complete concept. I had been teaching classes at the John F. Kennedy Special Warfare Center and he had been in my classes, where I taught coursework such as "Persuasive Communications," "Psychological Operations," and "Using Broadcast Media for Persuasion."

My students were Majors and Colonels, mostly in Special Forces. At Fort Bragg, I completed a long tour of duty of instruction and was brought back three more times for active Reserve duty assignments.

The mantra in short is that when persuasion can be used to change people's perceptions, they will act on the new perceptions, and there is a new reality for them. Classes were anywhere between two to four-hour blocks, so I gave plenty of details about how to change people's perceptions and plenty of examples about how people can change the perceptions of others, creating a new reality in action.

But changing people's perceptions or mindsets about core beliefs, or even about an individual or cause, is probably easier than changing our own mentality, and thus creating a new mindset.

Start Getting Happy Right Now!

"Showtime in thirty minutes! It's time to get happy!" The road manager says to the troop getting ready to go on stage.

Wow! Can they do that? Yes, they can. I have read several books about happiness alone and many, many portions of books that related strategies for how to get happy. You may have too. Did they help you be happier? Did they help me get happier when I needed to? Maybe, but it seems to be an ongoing challenge.

Of course, one big impediment to happiness is fear. These self-improvement books almost always address how to combat fear. I recall reading one that said, "Fear is for suckers." That's right, after the author had sold a couple million books, she had far less to fear.

"The only thing we have to fear is fear itself." The immortal words of Franklin D. Roosevelt when he was sworn into the first of his four terms as president, the first smack dab in the middle of the Great Depression.

So, the idea is that fear itself is more harmful than the things that people have to fear. Naturally, there are some very real fearful things that people face.

Put Worry In Compartments And Put Them Away

You need to be shrewd about your focus. You can do this by ignoring anything in your life that suggests you will have a different outcome than the one you really want. If it feels like a worry, doubt, or fear, ignore it. Do not engage. Just walk on by.

If that sounds too undoable, at least decide just how much anxiety anything may be worth and refuse to give it anymore. Worrying about the past is pointless, of course. Let's not let trifles bother us. And we all need to remember that worry is bad for our health.

But maybe you have seen some of the studies that say over 50 percent of fears are unwarranted, a good portion are based on things that make no real difference, or fears are based on the past. This leaves under 10 percent that are really justifiable.

So, what do we do in those cases? Keep moving. As long as we are living, we will be facing risks and failures. It is the trials and tribulations that make us stronger people. To greatly succeed, we have to be willing to fail miserably. We have seen and heard all these sayings about how failure and fear of failure can be overcome. After changing our mindset, taking action is the strongest antidote to successfully dealing with fear.

Think The Ball Into The Basket!

Controlling your own mind, the mindfulness that we read so much about, is certainly not easy, especially if you have an active imagination. But your mindset can control not only your outlook, but also your physical performance to some degree as well.

In college, I was the captain of the tennis team, but I could not play basketball a lick, and I liked basketball. I played on an intramural team we called the Thespians. It was bad as it sounded for a sports team—we were all drama majors.

This intramural college basketball was fierce and serious. One fraternity, which I would later join, the TKEs, had at least four separate teams, Take-em, Trick-em, Took-em, and so on, each almost as good as the other. On the basketball court, I faced several disadvantages. I couldn't dribble, pass, shoot, or defend.

What's more, the concept of a team game eluded me. One day, I asked a friend who played on the college varsity team to watch me play and give me his input. Through sheer will, I got a few shots up, but none went in.

His advice: "When you shoot, convince yourself it's going to go in."

Wow. Believe in yourself and your talents. Control your mindset. Advice for life, but my basketball game was beyond help.

Proper Sleep Helps Build Our Resilience

Are you getting enough sleep? Are you worried about insomnia? The fear of insomnia could be worse than the insomnia itself. The perception becomes the reality: you lie in bed worrying about going to sleep or that you haven't had enough sleep, and that could be worse than what is really going on with you.

But on this front, there is something you can do in a less metaphysical way. That is, if you can find a doctor, tell him or her about all the challenges you face and that you are not getting the sleep you physically need. That's what they are there for among other things, to provide prescriptions.

Here is another technique that I find useful, a breathing exercise that helps you relax and, in turn, go to sleep faster and better. Take four seconds to take a deep breath through your nose, hold it for eleven seconds, and then, in a big way breath out, exhale through your mouth for eight seconds. Do this for five sets.

To make it easier, count in your mind, "one, two, three, four" in through the nose. Then hold "five, six, seven, eight, none, ten, eleven," and exhale "twelve, thirteen, fourteen, fifteen, sixteen, seventeen, eighteen and nineteen." There you have it. Don't do more than five repetitions and only a full set a couple times a day. It helps to sleep and helps to relax, which means you can do it in most places.

Three Keys To Happiness

"They" say that there are three keys to happiness:

1. Something to do
2. Someone to love
3. Something to look forward to

If you have only one or two of these, that should work.

One thing we don't want to do is compare our happiness to a couple walking hand-in-hand through the mall, to the people across the street, or to the people we know and have known. That is a losing proposition because we are getting happy!

Think back over your life so far. Have you maybe worried about the wrong things all along? So, there we have it! It's pointless because we usually worry about the wrong things.

So, we get up every day, and if we aren't already, we give ourselves a little pep talk, "Time to get happy!"

Chapter 22

How To Find Time
To Make Real Friends

"**A**re you my friend?" I was on the phone, asking a long time "friend" of mine this question. He and I had been close for over a decade, and had even gotten into business deals together, but I was starting to have my doubts about him.

There was quite a long pause, maybe a full twenty seconds. If he would have responded in a couple seconds with something like, "Hey, buddy, why are you asking me that goofball question?!" . . . if he had done that, I might have felt differently.

But after the pregnant silence, he said, "Well, of course I am your friend." And I knew in my gut that he was not my friend.

Now this approach may seem simplistic and even inane but try it sometime if you are in doubt. Life is too short to have false friends.

And they could be worse than outright enemies.

How Many Real Friends Do You Have?

How many friends do you have? Real friends? The kind if you are really in a jam, they will absolutely be there for you. If you are down and out, they will still be your friends. Do you have real friends?

Former four-term California Governor Jerry Brown (see Chapter 15 on "Reinventing Yourself") once said that James Taylor's song, "You've Got a Friend" said everything he needed to know about life.

In the song, he sings that friends can hurt us and desert us, but a real friend is just a call away.

Our real friends do not slip away, but they are few and far between. You have heard the saying that one person can probably only count real close friends with the fingers of one hand. Okay, so not counting the thumb, that's four. Who are your four?

193

Most people have different friends from different times in their lives: grade school, high school, maybe college, maybe military service, and maybe from one city to another.

Talk about different friends. By the time I was about sixteen-years-old, our family had already moved twelve times. Our dad was a restless soul. Friends came and went when we moved away. How about you? Do you have friends from way back?

It Takes Time To Make Real Friends

"Take time to make friends." My mother gave me that golden advice, and she knew a lot. Nobody in her family had gone to college. She earned a master's degree from a university—we are talking in the 1930s, when women weren't even expected to go to college.

Eva Lorraine Hampton was a Phi Beta Kappa at the University of Michigan. She transferred in from junior college as a junior and edged out everybody on the team to be the leader on the Varsity Debate Team, never losing a debate, ever. Her first year there, she gathered a group of young women together and insisted the university teach a class about auto mechanics for women. Consider that! She figured if the car broke down, she didn't have to depend on someone else. She'd be ready.

So pretty good credentials to offer advice, wouldn't you think?

I asked her once what were the most important things she had learned in life. She summed it up with two: believe in yourself and take time to make friends. Believe in yourself? Quite obvious, right? But sometimes it is a very challenging thing to do. So is to make friends.

Super Bowl "Friends"

Just before deciding to write this chapter on friends, I heard two sports commentators talking about friendships. They were talking about the Super Bowl.

One asked, "Who talks to their neighbors?" Then he proceeded to say that during the Super Bowl, his circle of friends gets together at someone's house and they "actually talk." His colleague on the show said that he guessed he got together with friends and neighbors only during block parties.

Friendship is priceless. "New friends are silver, and old friends are gold," goes the old saying. But how do you know if your friends are really your friends?

I have learned a great deal in life the hard way. I suppose it's the way most people do. Many times in my life, I found that people who I thought were friends were not my friends. I have had several "friends" who, it turned out, really resented me, perhaps because of my temporary success at the time.

Do you have "friends" who make lots of jokes at your expense? And you think they kid because they care? I have had too many in that category, who I just assumed were my friends.

Do you have would-be friends in this category? Strangely enough, it was other people, like my wife, who pointed out that they were not my friends.

I had a "friend" from college whose company I always enjoyed. He always laughed at my jokes, for one thing. We stayed in touch well after college, and looking back at it, I was the one who stayed in touch with him. Sound familiar? I used to travel great distances just to hang out with him.

I used to call him on the phone, and he would say, "You got me." Like hey, big joke, pretending like he didn't want to talk to me . . . and maybe he didn't.

A Skunk At The Top Of The Town

What took me so long? My wife and I had a gala engagement party at the Top of the Town, in Arlington, with the best view of Washington D.C. Maybe you saw *Charlie Wilson's War*, starring Tom Hanks? In the movie, he lived in the Prospect House right below this grand venue.

We really had a glittering event—a band and a disc jockey, the latter because of a heavy snow a couple days before and the fellow sponsors were not sure the band should show up. They did and so did dozens of people we knew. My fiancé actually stole the show by dancing all by herself right in the middle of a circle of admiring friends and family.

So, among the many attendees were our friends, a personal lawyer, and my banker. My "friend" made some cutting remarks right in front of me and the two of them on two separate occasions.

He had driven in from out of town, and we had put him up for the night in the spare bedroom. In the morning, when I woke up, he was gone, but he left a cheerful note. Though he tried to contact me many times in the future to get together, come to a party at his house, and so on, I had finally figured out he was the furthest thing from a friend. Have you had any of these? Do you have any now? Those are the kind of friends we do not need.

Beware Of False Flattery

After my father, Charles Francis Hampton passed away, my mother came to visit me in Arlington. I threw a small, sort of intimate party. One of my "friends," I see now, was always lavishing me with praise. Always.

After he left the party, my mother said, "What a phony."

Bingo. She had seen through him in a flash, while I never had. Have any "friends" like this?

When Blood Sweat & Tears produced the powerful, iconic "God Bless the Child" in 1968, they had a cautionary message for us all. In haunting lyrics, the song tells how having lots of money equates to lots of friends. But when the money is gone, these people do not come around anymore. They would be the fake friends.

On the flip side of this, I had a very close friend from high school, past college, and going on almost two decades. He was very successful, smart, engaging, and the president of our high school class. One day he invited me to one of those empowerment meetings, featuring, you may not remember him, Werner Erhard (the father of self-help). It was the kind of thing where your friend gives you a ride to the meeting, you find out later, because you can't leave the meeting. He is your ride! You are essentially a hostage for the evening!

So, my buddy is introduced and, with much enthusiasm, he explains an epiphany he had that he wants to share with the big audience. Talk about a butt pucker. He stands up there for fifteen minutes, telling everyone how he has always wanted to be like me. What? Now here is a good friend, one you can count on.

Okay, so we know good friends are important. How do we find the time to invest in old and new friends? What is your approach on this important aspect of life?

First, we need to stay in touch with old friends. How about you? I think about old friends with regularity, but don't call nearly enough. But when I call, or they call me, I have a more positive life. I'm not really talking about old times but more in getting caught up. Let's make those couple of calls in the next couple days.

I put off calling an older friend for a few years. I was afraid to call in the event I found out from his wife that he had gone to the great tax shelter in the sky. But I called, and he answered the phone, and we were just like old friends, like we'd seen each other yesterday. That call brightened my day and, really, my life. I will be staying in touch with him and others. I will not put it off.

Your Friends And Family

How about turning acquaintances into friends? Do you rush into the house or the apartment when you see a neighbor because you feel you don't have the time to talk? I do. But every time I stand and chat for just a couple minutes, I feel kind of refreshed.

How about those friends down the street? You know the ones where you have been telling each other, "We really should get together one of these days." Days become weeks and months and longer. Our neighbors can turn into being real friends.

All the research reports and books on the subject report that people who have more real friends have a far better chance of dealing with difficult situations successfully because they have a support system. You can't choose your relatives, but you can choose your friends.

You probably remember that haunting song, "Cat's in the Cradle."

It's about family, but it's about friends too. The guy sings about how he was too busy to hang out with his son, had to work, had bills to pay, and so forth. His son grows up, and the father wants to get together. But his son says words to the same effect and his father decides his son had grown up just like him.

Some of the best of times we will ever have is being among good friends. Let's make the effort; it's more than worth it. Take time to make good friends.

Chapter 23

Love And Marriage
On An Ocean Cruise

Are you married? If not, do you plan to get married? Do you know the keys to a happy marriage? That topic is the subject of many books, and I would not pretend to know the full answer by any means, but I have learned a thing or two that I want to share with you. Actually, I was more taught than learned. You most likely know what I mean.

Have you ever been on an ocean cruise before? My wife and I have been on one and will probably not do another. Not because it wasn't lots of fun, because it was. It's kind of like Times Square on New Year's Eve or the Mall in Washington D.C. on the Fourth of July, or maybe even going all around the world. You have done it once, you had a wonderful time, you have bragging rights, but you probably can't top it the next time.

I learned something, or a few things, most unexpectedly, which I never dreamed I would learn on a cruise. They are really important keys to love and marriage.

Are you considering a cruise? Maybe you have been on one or more. I really think a person would be hard put to beat a cruise among the islands of the Eastern Caribbean. Such as you catch a flight to Miami, then to Puerto Rico, for example, and then island hop to Barbados, St. Croix, St. Lucia, and so on.

Before the love and marriage things, we learned a few other things.

Many people say one cruise is great. Check out all the islands, and then next time, go to your favorite island and stay put. That would be St. Lucia, far and away.

Finding Love In The Buffet Line

We learned early on that they want you to go to the buffet, not make reservations for a sit-down dinner. They make that the most challenging when it should be easy.

But two main things we learned. Number one: when you dock at some island, there is really a better way to go than signing up for the guided tour, getting in a crowded bus, and being held kind of hostage by their schedule. Who wants to be on a schedule on a vacation, anyway?

So, what we did, and perhaps you have done this too, is we left the ship when we were good and ready, walked down the dock, and negotiated rather quickly with entrepreneurs with cars. "How much for a tour of the island? We want to be gone for about three hours with a lunch in the middle." Native people showed us the highlights of the island and always took us to a very neat place for lunch.

Number two: the ship had free entertainment in a big theatre every single night, ranging from comedy, to magic, to great singing groups, with no tickets required. You just go right in, and it's great entertainment, like Las Vegas or something. You may know this. Don't miss this fun freebie on your cruise.

More Buffet Means Bigger Belly Flops

One night the fare is "Love and Marriage." Big stage, hundreds of people of all ages, and there leading the show is the ship fun lover, or what I call the Cruise Director. This is the guy who says this is the most fun he has on a cruise, and that includes the Belly Flop Contest, where he persuades very fat people to jump in the pool and be graded.

So, someone has selected three couples in advance. They are up there on the stage. One newlywed couple, one couple married for like a decade or two, and the third enjoying their fiftieth wedding anniversary on the cruise. The first and third were far more memorable.

The routine is that the Cruise Director asks the couple questions, both together and separately. First up are the young couple. The new groom is already backstage. I met him later in the ship's casino. He was an Army active-duty Captain.

Parrot In The Bedroom Says What?!

The cruise director asks the young bride, "If there was a parrot in your bedroom, what would the parrot say?"

The new bride does not blink or hesitate, "You dirty, rotten, Irish floozy!"

Wow! Talk about a showstopper. A stunned Cruise Director emits nervous laughter and then out-right laughter. Later, the bride is sent to the green room and the Army Captain is ushered out and asked the same question. The parrot on the wall and so forth.

The Captain looks around, apparent immediate recognition on his face, and with a bit of hesitation, he says, "I can't tell you that. There are children in the audience."

The cruise director laughs. He is clearly visibly relieved and says, "I am glad somebody noticed that." Unrestrained laughter all around.

Secret Of A Happy Marriage Is What?

But for me, and I think everyone, the couple on their fiftieth anniversary stole the show. Actually, the husband did, with a little help from his bride. The husband and wife were sitting side by side, and the show master had the mic. The wife seemed shy, even retiring. She was wearing glasses, her hands were folded in her lap, and she was looking down. We all wondered what was going to happen next.

In contrast, the husband was a pretty big, burly guy, like a Marine type ("You can always tell a Marine, but you can never tell him much" is the joke we Army types save for Marines. They *always* like it). The husband looked fit and alert.

The director built it up. "You have been married for fifty years and are still going strong." He built it up a little more. The wife was looking very demur and still looking down. The tour director said, "So, what is the key to your success, to being married for fifty years?"

The wife was silent.

Without a pause, the husband looked up and replied with one word alone. "Surrender."

The audience erupted into howling and yelling and applauding. Talk about stealing the show, and with a message I will remember in perpetuity (see Chapter 14, "Words To Confound Your Friends And Enemies").

Now this really got my attention, especially because a couple other things had happened on the cruise. But it was not like I was a babe in the woods on what makes for a happy marriage. My wife had been coaching me up from about the honeymoon onward.

This reminds me to pass along to you: marriage is one of the things you can joke about, but not so much politics and religion, that is for sure.

A very good friend got married years ago. He had a fancy wedding at a country club outside of Cleveland. Peter Dunchin's Band, maybe Tony Bennet, someone like that, entertained. All the sorority gals and fraternity guys were there. They had all gone to the University of Michigan (the big rival of my alma mater, Michigan State).

The Best Day Of His Marriage Was . . .

Well, in due time, they got divorced. My friend made it exceedingly clear that he would brook no discussion of the matter, whatsoever.

Finally, after several years, he seemed ready to talk about it. They say maybe half of marriages are not so good, just like maybe half of people don't like their jobs. Combine those numbers and if you have a positive in one, you are doing fine. A positive on both fronts? You are in a really small percentage.

Anyway, I dared to bring up the subject: "Okay, Ken, how long were you married?"

"Five and a half years."

"When did it start to go bad?"

"Right after the bachelor party."

So, a happy marriage is priceless. Earlier on that cruise, the ship stopped in Barbados (great ring to it, right? We drank piña coladas in Barbados). We were at some city square, and my wife was off talking on the phone to relatives.

I was impatient, so I struck up a conversation with a constabulary, like a policeman, in a brown uniform, the real British influence there all those years. I was sort of complaining. He said simply, "This is her time" (see "Some People Have To Be Told" in Chapter 3).

I never forgot that guy or one other I met on the cruise. Michigan State was playing in the NCAA Basketball Tournament. I had my MSU t-shirt and wore it to this snug bar. The game was on. There was only one other person there, and both our wives were out and about, doing something on the big ship, probably shopping. He and I struck up a conversation— yet another one I will never forget.

"Brian," he said. "I own a plumbing company in North Carolina. It's not a big one, and it's not a small one, but there, I am in charge. Here on this ship, I am not in charge. My wife is, and I accept that. But it is alright because I know, when I get back to North Carolina, I will be in charge again." There was a man who knew the deal!

He didn't have to say he meant the work, not the home. The lessons I learned on the cruise have always stayed with me.

A few years ago, I had the golden opportunity to walk my youngest daughter down the aisle. I had given my oldest daughter away a couple years before, before that cruise.

I was invited to say a few words at the rehearsal dinner the night before the wedding. I actually didn't know that I would have a speaking part, but I was prepared in case I did. (See Chapter 13, "Public Speaking"). I sat with my party at a table on the outside so when I stood up, I could be seen by all, with no one behind me.

Listen Up, Son-In-Law!

I talked for only a couple minutes. Who cared to hear what I had to say? I related how I had learned more than I ever had before when my wife and I went on the ocean cruise. I related not the parrot part but the part about the happily married couple of fifty years. I built it up like the cruise director. He would have been proud of me.

"So, fifty years! What is the secret to your successful marriage?" I paused for three or four seconds, milking it, of course. "Surrender."

Then I turned to my new son-in-law-to-be and told him that he has to be sure to remember, "A happy wife means a happy life." Amen.

Chapter 24

Getting Happy With
Your Favorite Foods!

You know how you can know people for a very long time, and sometimes you remember just one or two exact things they ever said or maybe nothing at all specific?

There is one thing my high school government teacher said to the class, which I have never forgotten. "I like to eat, so I am happy three times a day."

What a cool guy, right? He had some of his priorities all squared away.

Time to get happy. What are your favorite foods? It's kind of fun to make a list with family and friends. Sometimes I have found that when I raise the subject, everyone has favorite foods, but most have never ranked them before (see Chapter 5 for what the doctor said when my sister lost her appetite).

Eat Your Favorite Foods More Often And Get Happier!

So, allow me to lead off. I have been eating for decades and have had my favorites but had never really ranked them either. What is in your top five or ten, in order? Does it change by the week or season? Okay, here are mine for now.

First, thick chocolate malts used to be my favorite in high school, now leading the list again.

How about you? Malts or shakes? To me, a great chocolate malt has to be made with vanilla ice cream, not chocolate. The chocolate taste comes from the syrup. Otherwise, it is too chocolatey. I always tell the counter person that. Then there are some folks who actually work in diners who do not know the difference between a malt and a shake. Have you had this experience? This is serious stuff here.

"You mean a black and white?" I was asked once. "If you want to call it a black and white, sure, but I want a malt with vanilla ice cream," I said.

"That's a black and white shake."

"No, I don't want a shake. I want a malt with vanilla ice cream."

"They are all the same."

"Actually, no they are not. The malts have malt in them, and a shake does not." This happened to me. The waiter turned on his heel and left.

I went to the counter to explain the little tutorial. I finally got the chocolate malt. Sometimes you don't get the "thick" because they put in one scoop rather than two. But the perfect is the enemy of the good. This all reminds me of a very famous scene in an old movie, *Five Easy Pieces*, where the waitress refused to get Jack Nicholson a couple eggs because it was too late for the breakfast menu, so he ordered an egg sandwich.

Second, lobster tail with plenty of butter on the side. Murphy's Law says if anything can go wrong, it will go wrong. You probably know that you have to ask them to pull it out of the shell, whatever that is called, otherwise you have to do it yourself. That's no fun.

Will You Irritate The Chef If You Ask For Medium-Well?

Third, New York strip. I like to say medium-well (I know the real connoisseur likes rare, but it is harder to digest. Each to his or her own). What is your experience? You want medium? You have to say medium-well. If you say medium, you invariably get rare. Then you send it back. Some people do have to be told (Chapter 3)!

I guess the chefs are in a hurry or are offended that someone wants a well-done steak. Some people like the rib eye, but to me, it seems mostly grizzle. Okay, enough of this, but that steak has to have sour cream on the side. We need to get up our cholesterol.

Fourth, cherry pie à la mode with French vanilla ice cream, thank you.

Fifth, caramel frozen yogurt with caramel syrup. These yogurt shops are around most everywhere. A real tasty treat and easy on the calories. A fun afternoon, a drive, and drop by the yogurt shop

And so on . . . cheesecake, chocolate ice cream, and lime regular yogurt all deserve special consideration.

Eating Without The Calories And Falling Asleep

What you can occasionally do when you are lying in bed and can't go to sleep? You can think about your favorite foods, one at a time, even imagine yourself having some the next day. Such a technique can help you fall asleep. I think it's even better than imagining you have ten million dollars and imagining what you would do with that!

I have to thank my high school teacher. I remember him vividly because a few years ago, my older sister sent me my high school report card from those days at Albion High School in Michigan.

It was a yellow card with red ink: Hampton, Brian. Grade 12. Hour 1 Subject: Gov't Teacher Oberlin.

There it is. Jerry had only put in one set of comments for any of the four quarters. In the third quarter, he wrote, "Rather wise sometimes, will argue at the drop of a point—still, once in a while he does something interesting or horrible or both."

What, Me? A Wiseacre!

He gave me straight, all the way through, low citizenship marks, with a two for "Average" and a three for "Unsatisfactory, readjustment necessary."

For the comments of the parent for the period, my father wrote, "Brian enjoys you and your courses very much."

I am glad Gerald Oberlin had gotten those words from my father at least, or else he may have never guessed that. But most of all, I thank Mr. Oberlin to this day because I can get happy every time I eat. You too! It's kind of comforting, isn't it?!

Chapter 25

Is It Happy Hour Yet?

We know it is always Happy Hour someplace. We are looking around, deciding to start drinking, or not, and somebody will always say, "It's five o'clock somewhere."

Some clock, somewhere, has nothing but fives for the hour marks. Likely an Irish bar that has all those keen sayings on the wall most of us have seen: "May you live to be 101 and outlive your enemies by a year." All those sayings on the wall seem so cool when one is having a Black and Tan.

Do you have a drinking problem?

Some say, "No, I have no problem finding something to drink."

Do people drink to forget? Remember? Drown their sorrows?

Some people are asked if they are an alcoholic, and they say, "No, I don't have time to go to the meetings."

If you drink at all, are you getting the most out of it? Too much? Too little? Too much and too much guilt afterward? Too little and feel like you are missing something good? The stories about famous drinkers are legendary, and we can all learn something from some of their ways.

She Drove Me To Drink And Thank You!

W. C. Fields once said, "My first wife drove me to drink; it is about the only thing I have to thank her for."

Somebody asked Frank Sinatra why some people drink so much when they sometimes feel so bad the next day. The Chairman said, "Because the night comes before the day, and it feels so good the night before."

Jack Daniels used to offer a square inch of land to its patrons in Lynchburg, Tennessee. Frank made his love of Jack so well known that they honored him with a full acre in Lynchburg.

Elizabeth Taylor also loved Jack. She is reported to have always asked, perhaps demanded, depending on the husband, for a glass of Jack with seventeen ice cubes.

Are you enjoying your drinking? You most certainly should. If you don't drink at all and don't miss it, more power to you.

The late Governor of Michigan, George Romney, the father of Mitt, once said, "Lips that touch liquor will never touch mine." One has to draw the line somewhere.

Years ago, in Washington D.C., I worked as an actual federal government worker (we actually worked hard until about seven or eight every weekday except Friday, then Happy Hour was about 5:30). I will never forget how the boss always set up the martinis on his desk and served one and all. He fixed his own and then stirred it with a finger. Why did he do that? He really liked his drinking, and so did we. We did take taxis or the metro home.

Knee Walking After Pub Crawling

Usually, the single ones hit one bar after the other all the way to Georgetown. Pub crawling can lead to knee walking on the way home if one is not careful, however.

Later, that boss said, "The heck with Washington," borrowed some money from his brother to buy a rather large boat, moved to Florida, and spent the rest of his life (that I know of) hiring out his board and being a guide for fishing tourists. I am sure he had a whale of a time, baiting the lines and mixing the drinks.

We need to get happy about our drinking if we do it because . . . why not?

But if you work hard and always show up for work, then looking forward to happy hour is a good thing.

At Kalamazoo College in Michigan, the people in the Development Office (read "fund-raising" . . . they now call it *Advancement*) put in very long hours. Eight or nine hours every weekday, except Friday. A simple formula for all of us was to work smart and hard and things will work out.

They Don't Call Them The Blue Devils For Nothing

But around 6 p.m. on Friday was Happy Hour. What a college! We had a suite of rooms, and about every room had a chandelier and fireplace. Happy Hour lasted for maybe thirty minutes or so. It was fun and good for morale.

I was a bit naive in those days. One day, I asked my boss if he minded if we had the Happy Hour every Friday.

He said, "When I was at Duke, we had Happy Hour every day!"

Depending on your perspective, there could be a downside to that many Happy Hours. A number of years ago, I was scheduled to give a speech at a social service organization in Maryland. I got there at 4:30 p.m. for the scheduled talk at 5 p.m. As I walked in, I quickly knew that my work was cut out for me. There was a sign, "Happy Hour from 1 to 7 p.m." There were a lot of sharpshooters in the crowd that day, but we all had a good time of it.

One can learn much about somebody by what they want to drink, maybe. After Richard Nixon resigned in 1974, he went back to California and almost died of phlebitis. But he did not drown himself in drink. He resurrected his reputation in some part.

After living in California a while, he moved into a condo in Manhattan and lived there for a couple years. How did he spend some of this time? By all accounts he had some fun. He hosted regular dinner parties for a dozen or so guests, all very prominent people both in and out of government. He mixed the martinis himself, Tanqueray. Later, he moved to upstate New York and continued his seemingly happy ways there.

What Never Fails? A Dry Martini!

The free enterprise system may fail. Our federal government can and often does fail, but a dry gin martini never fails. James Bond sure looks like he is having fun in all those movies. In a recent rendition, Daniel Craig as Bond has six martinis. His host asks him if he wants an Ambien to sleep. He wisely says no. But the next day, he is out and about in a crisp suit, looking dapper and Bond-ish.

This sort of thing is only for professionals and fictional characters.

But all sorts of drinking have worked for some successful people. Harry Truman reportedly had a glass of whiskey when he got up in the morning and then went for a walk most every day.

"Walk like you are going someplace," he said.

President Truman used to get away to Key West, where he would take up residence in the former Naval base superintendent's home. When I was there, the tour guide pointed out a bar in the corner with great pride. He said a bartender was put in place every morning at 10 a.m. because Trumann said, "If a man wants a drink, he should be able to have a drink." A truly great American.

Winston Churchill was a notorious drinker who lived well into his eighties. He would get up and have a brandy first off. Lunch was often several glasses of champagne. In the moving movie, *Darkest Hour*, over lunch, the King of England asks the great man how he can do that, and he says "Practice."

The Great Man Had Brandy For Breakfast

One day during World War II, a mother dressed her daughter up in her finest outfit and said, "Today, you are going to meet the greatest man in the world." Off they went to 10 Downing Street. The young girl became separated from her mother and followed a butler with a tray, brandy and all, through a door. The girl slipped in the room.

She went to the bed where the World War II Lion was, leaned in with eyes as big as saucers, and said, "Is it true that you are the greatest man in the world?"

"Yes," said the great man. "And close the door on your way out."

Are you drinking to get happy, without guilt and without missing work? Yes? Then it is a good thing for you. So here is to you, and here is to me and should we ever disagree, here is to . . . all of us.

The Best Place To Go On A "Bender"

Some, as we know, can take alcohol far to the extremes. However, your call here. Spencer Tracy was a notorious drinker. He made it into a kind of art form. When he decided to get away from it all and go on a bender, as one might call it, he took the train for several days or a week.

Think of it. He goes to the dining car and gets served all the food and drinks he wants. He does not have to worry about driving home, let alone walking more than a few steps back to his train suite. He sees the country as it goes by.

He does not have to go through an airport. He can sleep late without being bothered. And just as likely, maybe he met some woman he liked, and they did not have far to go for the night. Though, he did have a long-time affair with Katharine Hepburn, and as long as she was waiting, he was doing just fine.

Then there was Lyndon Johnson. The thirty-sixth President was known for his amazing appetite for life and living large. When he was majority leader of the Senate, he and some of his Senate pals, like Senators Long from Louisiana and Kerr of Oklahoma, would stay up all night marking up a bill or otherwise plotting and scheming.

Breakfast Of Champions

Come morning, Lyndon would often ask his cohorts, "Would you like the special Lyndon Breakfast?" Of course, they did. So LBJ rang up a minder, and in he came with four silver platters, each with a thick steak, scrambled eggs, mounds of bacon, and four tall glasses of whiskey.

On more than one occasion, after finishing the first course, Johnson would ask them if they wanted another glass, three shots each.

Some, but not all, took him up on the offer, but reportedly, he always had another. Then Johnson was ready to face his busy day.

But LBJ was a professional when it came to drinking. For the good life it is good that we get our share. But as Clint Eastwood said in one of his memorable movies, "A man has got to know his limitations."

So, without guilt, when the time is right, it is time to enjoy life—every golden drop of it. Let the good times roll. It is time to get happy with Happy Hour!

Chapter 26

The Law Of The Universe

"**M**ay the Force be with you! If you violate the Law of the Universe, the force is not likely to be with you." Say what?

I was watching the Michigan State University basketball game against Purdue. There were two outstanding announcers, Kevin Harwood (who is as good or better than Marv Alpert, with the bonus of not having to be Marv Alpert) and Clark Kellogg.

As an MSU alum, I was rooting for my team. With great fanfare, Harwood announced that Michigan State had won twenty-one conference games in a row. I didn't know that. It's pretty impressive. Then later on, he said it again.

My reaction was to think, please don't say that.

When one of the two said it a third time, I knew MSU would lose. I call that the Law of the Universe. You probably know it, but not by that name, which I coined myself without seeing it anywhere.

It's a basketball game. The announcer says, "He's made twelve in a row! Twelve in a row!" The chances of an eighty percent free-throw play, making the next basket, just went down below 50 percent. Maybe that's why many don't say such things anymore—because they have to confess on air that they jinxed the player.

We have seen similar things happening in baseball for a long time. Here, at least, the announcers will never say, "He has a no-hitter going! A no-hitter going!" (Joe Buck would never tempt fate in such a manner.) They are well aware of the jinx, so they may say it this way: no team has yet to get a hit.

You're Not Late Until You Get There

Do you observe the Law of the Universe? It's everywhere. It's everywhere! Do you say, "I'll meet you at Joe's Inn at 6 p.m.?" Careful, something might happen, and you could jinx it. It's better to say, "I plan to be there at 6 p.m." That way you don't tempt the Law of the Universe.

As an important aside, you are never late until you get there. Up until then you are just a no show.

How about you say, "I'll see you at the office tomorrow"? Better to say something like, "God willing and if the creek don't rise, I'll see you tomorrow."

Maybe there will be a flash flood tomorrow. Maybe there will be a snowstorm—unless you stock up on lots of salt for the driveway. In that case, you are doing your part to reduce the chances of snow.

Try it yourself. When someone says to you that it is supposed to snow five inches overnight, tell them you have done your part by buying five pounds of rock salt to help change the odds. They will thank you for it every time. Do you have your own Laws of the Universe (LOTU)?

Many famous people have said they try to avoid saying they will do something because they believe people may say what they are going to do, but it's God who decides.

I remember former Secretary of Defense, Casper Weinberger, learned this after his retirement. He was going to do this and that. He said he found out differently. I remember reading his statement to that effect. He said what he was going to do, but God decided otherwise.

Don't Compliment Your Car When You Are in the Car!

I first experienced the LOTU when I was quite young but didn't really get it at the time. My father and mother had decided to take the family out for a picnic. It was a hot summer day and the car windows were down. The Chrysler New Yorker was the apple of my father's eye. It was several years old but ran like a top. An old-fashioned stick shift, Dad would take the Chrysler out on a country road and drive just one mile per hour, just to show us kids the precision of the wonderful machine.

We three kids were in the back seat, fighting like cats and dogs, like young siblings in grade school—since we were. I remember this so vividly. You can see something along these lines coming. We kids finally shut up. The two-tone grey and white Chrysler came up to a traffic light.

My father turned to my mother and said, "You know, Eva, this has really been a good car for the family." The words were just through his lips when we heard these explosive noises: *BANG, BANG! BANG, BANG.* One right after the other. Four, as in four blown tires.

Perhaps the heat on that sweltering day expanded in the tires. I have no idea. I was just introduced to the Law of the Universe.

So, do you believe this? I am not a superstitious guy except for the number seventeen. Unpleasant things have seemed to happen to me on that day of the month. Many, many times in fact.

Let me ask you: why tempt fate? Or whatever it is. Don't wash your car and expect it not to rain. And for heaven's sake, *do not* say what a good car you have, at least not while you are in it!

Chapter 27

What Is The Meaning Of Life?

You can ask many people, what is the meaning of life? Some people will answer, "Forty-two." In his iconic book, *The Hitchhiker's Guide to the Galaxy*, Douglas Adams has an alien race program, a computer called Deep Thought, provide the ultimate answer to life. After seven and a half million years of calculation, back comes the answer "forty-two."

Then Cambridge astronomers found that forty-two is the value of an essential scientific constant, one which determines the age of the universe. So, the answer must be forty-two, but what does forty-two mean?

As we go about our daily lives, it certainly behooves us to occasionally consider just why we are here to begin with and just maybe how we can make the most of it.

Maybe you remember the famed astronomer Carl Sagan, who talked about the universe, saying "billions and billions and billions" of stars out there.

Wow. Let's see, our moon is only one-quarter million or so miles away. With light traveling at about 186,000 miles per second, the light we see from the moon actually left there a couple seconds beforehand.

Way beyond our moon, we have our solar system, (Ours so far. If others have claimed it, they have not told us.) with planets millions and millions of miles apart. There are billions of solar systems in "our" galaxy, the Milky Way.

Surely there is life out there. It's pretty egocentric not to think so. Isn't that the Air Force keeping all that from us?

How Big Is The Universe?

There are billions of galaxies in the universe. They say the universe is so out there that some of the light from those far-away stars actually take billions of years to even get to us to be able to see. Then wait, could there be more than one universe?

There are so many reasons to believe in God, in a spiritual being, in reincarnation. An old article from the *National Enquirer* said that if you are alive today (back then) you might live forever. We have heard of cybernetics—the freezing of a body or body parts to be saved for when there is a cure for whatever. Maybe we can get a new body added to our head!

The All-American Boston Red Sox slugger Ted Williams had one of the highest career batting averages ever. They said he could see the seam on the ball on its way to the plate. He hit a home run at his last time at bat. Ted Williams elected to have his head saved. It's someplace in Arizona in some lab somewhere. Unfortunately, relatives have been fighting over his head ever since.

Rumors were that Elizabeth Taylor had thought about saving at least her head—that would really be worth saving. Maybe she did not, I don't know, but she said she was not afraid to die. I believed her. She was not afraid of anything.

We shouldn't be afraid either. We know we shouldn't. But here on earth, there are only eight or so billion people. That's a lot. If a billion dollars were converted to one-dollar bills and placed end to end, they would go around the world (25,000 miles) about two-and-a-half times.

Don't Count The Days. Make The Days Count

Many people live just in our "neighborhood." But what is the point of it all? First off, as Mohammed Ali said, "Don't count the days. Make the days count."

How do you make your days count? Doing something that will outlast you is a good place to start. It could be children or the work you do that has lasting value.

We know "the unexamined life is not worth living." So, have you taken an examination? I have done it with my own life, but I have actually asked others as well.

We Decided The Meaning Of Life And Then Sent Emails

For years on a weekly or so basis, I conducted staff meetings. The agenda was always such a work-a-day world. Aren't they all? So, for a few times, I decided to change it up. I found a little book called *The Meaning of Life*, with these pithy little sayings in it, each one a take on the mystery of our being.

I passed around the book before staff meetings and asked everyone to pick a passage they could relate to and then when we went around the room, each one read that passage, and we all discussed what it meant. I can't say that lives were dramatically changed, but esprit in the office went up for sure. At least for a while, we focused on the bigger picture.

At one Hail and Farewell party, our office staff reflected about the meaning of life over drinks and appetizers. One kindly woman said the meaning was "forgiveness." In no more than a second, an older man piped up with, "revenge." Now that's a dichotomy.

I can only imagine that now and then a spouse or friend might ask the staffer, "So what did you do at the office today?" They could say they discussed the meaning of life. That alone would have been worth the price of admission.

Have you asked yourself what you think the meaning of life is? I have asked myself, but who can be sure? What do other people think? So, I took my search out to a broader plain.

You know how the customer service people in retail and related establishments usually ask (and most seem really sincere), "Can I help you?"

Drug stores, banks, wherever—I have heard them say that, and they usually seem so earnest, so wanting to help. So, a couple years ago, I would occasionally respond yes, maybe they could help me.

"Can I help you?"

"Yes, maybe. Can you tell me the meaning of life?" I started off saying that just occasionally, and I am never sure now when it will come out of my mouth.

Try it yourself. It is fun! Often, it establishes a real human connection and occasionally, you might find out something really insightful.

First, you can immediately determine how sharp people are—if their mind can process what you are saying—in a second or two. Most often, the customer service people kind of laugh and say they are still trying to figure it out themselves. In these cases, then I know I am not alone in trying to figure it out myself, and I actually felt better that I have company out there.

Other times, people are like, "Huh?"

And you say it again, "Well, you asked if you could help, and I thought maybe you could, so what is the meaning of life?"

No Clue On The Meaning Of Life?
Okay, Where Is The Soap

"Huh?"

"Okay, then, please tell me where the bars of soap are."

I never know when this question is going to come out of my mouth. But, never once has a person actually gotten their back up and asked me why I would ask her such a question. But one time a young man behind the counter was inquisitive and in a nice way asked me why I would ask such a question. I could tell he was bright, and he wanted to know.

I told him we go through the check-out lines of life and nobody says much of anything of any significance. We go through life doing all these mundane kinds of things and hardly ever ask the really big questions like, "What are we doing here?"

He smiled. The light went on. I converted him!

Okay, he understood, but if he knew, he was not telling me.

I have had better luck, though. At a drug store once, I was in that line where you drop off prescriptions.

"Can I help you?" So earnest, and that's when it seems to spring out of my mouth.

"Could you tell me the meaning of life?"

"Face the challenges in your life with courage and humor." Bingo! She did not miss a beat.

Wow, I will always try to remember that one!

Another time, at a bank, a teller was seemingly personable and really wanting to help. "Can I help you?"

She Was Short And Simple: Be Happy. Do Good!

"Yes, can you tell me the meaning of life?"

She did not miss a beat, either. "Be happy. Do good."

With only four words, I think she kind of nailed it. She made my day!

A fellow teller standing next to her said, "Gosh, that's great! Why didn't you ever tell me that?"

She turned, smiled, and said, "Because you never asked."

What is the meaning of life to you? We should continue to ask ourselves that and remind ourselves of what we think it is. If you go about your own public survey to ask others, how do you pick who you are going to ask? It is the earnest ones, not the ones who barely look at you and are just going through the motions, you want to find. You will know them when you hear them.

Do you have that Siri thing? A friend had it, and I asked them to ask Siri the question. Siri said, "To ask questions such as you did." Not so bad.

I worked in a dry-cleaning store throughout most of high school in Albion, Michigan. Vern Plassman was my boss at the One-Hour Martinizing. He told me a story once that I have always remembered. He was telling me the importance of good customer service. He said he knew if a customer walked out on him, he knew down to the dollar what it would cost him in a years' time.

He was just a good all-around guy. Maybe he thought he was looking at kindness in just dollars and sense (and cents), but I don't think so, especially after he related to me an extremely moving experience.

Vern told me there was this older guy who unfailingly, every other Monday, was there when he first opened the store. He told me the guy was such a curmudgeon, always in such a bad mood, that it was hard for Vern to maintain his composure, be friendly, and just not let it affect him the rest of the full day. The same thing happened whenever the guy picked up his laundry.

We Can Bring Peace In Unexpected Circumstances

Vern had not seen the guy pick up his laundry in some time. Then the man's wife came in with the guy's ticket to pick up the laundry. Vern asked the woman why the husband did not pick up the laundry as he always did.

The wife told Vern that her husband had died of cancer and the thing he looked forward to every week, as much as anything, was to go to the dry-cleaning store and talk with Vern.

I will remember this valuable lesson for the rest of my life. We may be just one person in this whole big world, but to one person, we may be their world.

Wait! That's On Aisle Seven

But, in a far more mundane sense, I remember one of my exchanges with a customer service rep when I went in one day. You know the drill.

"Can I help you?"

"Yes, can you tell me the meaning of life?"

"The what?"

"The meaning of life."

"I think that's on aisle seven."

Acknowledgments

I am forever blessed by having had two magnificent and highly accomplished parents, Charles and Eva Hampton, both university professors. At a very young age, they instilled in me the importance of discipline and the value of hard work. Later, they shared with me the keys to a good life: believing in yourself and taking time to make good friends.

There is no way I can thank my sister, Dr. Charlene Carter, PhD, enough for the invaluable love, support, and expertise she provided in reviewing, critiquing, and even rewriting portions of my entire manuscript. My niece, Dr. Laura Carter, PhD, provided psychological insights and moral support at every step along the way. Thank You, Charlene and Laura!

My children Tiffany and Ashley provided countless boosts of encouragement on my journey of being a published author. Along with their respective spouses, Taylor and Tyler, they have made my life as a writer, father, and grandfather much brighter than I ever could have imagined.

My great buddy and fellow Army Veteran, Bill Constantine, could have had his name on the cover as a co-author. He championed my ideas at every step along the way. He gave me insightful feedback on a vast myriad of tasks, including emails, proposals, and contracts, to say nothing about how he helped shape many portions of the book itself. He was never too busy to pick up the phone when I called. All the way every day, Bill!

The publishing industry is a world unto itself. The more one learns, the more you find you do not know. I like to tell my friends that writing a book as an unpublished author is about 5 percent of the effort required to get it published, to say nothing of getting appreciable sales. After I decided to go with a hybrid publisher, I conducted an exhaustive search and evaluation of publishers, so it was not by happenstance that my ultimate choice was Morgan James Publishing.

Before contacting Morgan James, I knew full well that they only published a small fraction of the manuscripts submitted to them. I also believed that my singular work of nonfiction was going to fill a very underserved market and I needed a visionary publishing house. I did have several contract options. One chat with CEO David Hancock, and I was all in. David has worn many vocational hats, including being an acclaimed author. He listens, he is a ready communicator, and I was fully convinced that he really cares about authors and taking their voices to the world. David, I cannot thank you enough, but I will try!

What a Welcome! I sincerely thank Welcome Coordinator Naomi Chellis for taking me under her wing as she welcomed me to the MJ family of authors and guided me on my way.

Anyone who deals with authors on a daily basis needs infinite patience and a good sense of humor. Author Relations Manager Emily Madison has always been there for me, guiding me, informing me of my responsibilities, and advising of all the multiple resources available for Morgan James authors. Thank you, Emily!

One reason David founded Morgan James is that he was not in accord with many changes made in his first book by a traditional publisher. He strongly believes that authors should have more control. Still, after I signed a contract, I was hopeful on that score, but still concerned. That was until I had a mastermind session with COO, Jim Howard. Going into that session I knew what I did not know, but I had a firm idea of what I wanted on some elements. I rejoiced after that call because Jim and I struck a very good response chord. You really fired me up, Jim!

I extend my heartfelt thanks to the full extraordinary family of Morgan James. They fill so many roles in the marvelous job of tirelessly publishing books out to the world that truly educate, encourage, inspire, and entertain.

Any author can edit and proof and edit and proof and still miss many typos and errors of every imaginable kind. An author must have a consummate professional for editing, proofing, and formatting. I was blessed that I found the multi-talented Sarah Rexford, who rescued me just in time! She polished the manuscript and brought it across the finish line. Sarah is a venerable wunderkind as an accomplished author, speaker, coach, and entrepreneur, all the while being personable, reliable, and author-friendly in every way. She can be found at sarahjrexford.com

I extend my profound thanks to a true Wonder Woman, Stephanie Swanson, my partner in marketing. An author herself, with a Master's Degree in Creative Writing, she is a high-tech wizard who has provided invaluable help to this low-tech, low-tolerance author. She is channeling her enormous energy, ingenuity, and social media presence to boost sales of this book. Stephanie, I cannot thank you enough, but I will try!

Do you know an author? Ask them about their book, and they will talk your ear off. Most authors want readers beyond all else. The reason I wrote the book was to share with readers what I learned the long and hard way. I am deriving great satisfaction in knowing I am helping to make a positive difference in the lives of others.

Thank you for taking some of your precious time to read this book. I hope the future we create together will fulfill our best and boldest dreams.

About The Author

B rian Hampton holds two master's degrees and has a distinguished career spanning several fields. He earned a commission as an Infantry Officer in the US Army, where he served tours at the Pentagon with top-secret clearance. Brian also taught courses in Persuasive Communications and Psychological Operations to esteemed Special Forces Majors and Colonels at the prestigious JFK Center for Special Warfare. Transitioning from the military, Brian assumed prominent roles in national non-profit organizations, such as the USO World Headquarters as well as the national Headquarters of the Federal Trade Commission. During many different occupations and jobs in advertising, communications, and politics, he gave over 150 public addresses, another fifty nationwide, and appeared on more than seventy television stations. He has written for a living in every position he has held, winning various recognitions, including the international HERMES Platinum award for excellence in writing. Brian currently resides with his wife in Marshall, Michigan.

A free ebook edition is available with the purchase of this book.

To claim your free ebook edition:

1. Visit MorganJamesBOGO.com
2. Sign your name CLEARLY in the space
3. Complete the form and submit a photo of the entire copyright page
4. You or your friend can download the ebook to your preferred device

A **FREE** ebook edition is available for you or a friend with the purchase of this print book.

CLEARLY SIGN YOUR NAME ABOVE

Instructions to claim your free ebook edition:
1. Visit MorganJamesBOGO.com
2. Sign your name CLEARLY in the space above
3. Complete the form and submit a photo of this entire page
4. You or your friend can download the ebook to your preferred device

Print & Digital Together Forever.

Snap a photo

Free ebook

Read anywhere

Printed in the USA
CPSIA information can be obtained
at www.ICGtesting.com
JSHW080732220624
65210JS00003B/23